301

Legal Forms
Letters & Agreements

LAWPACK

First edition 1995
Second edition 1996
Reprinted August 1996
Third edition 1997

Published by

Law Pack Publishing Limited
10-16 Cole Street
London SE1 4YH

Internet: www.lawpack.co.uk

Copyright © 1997 Law Pack Publishing

ISBN 1 898217 114

Designed by Lloyd Macdonald
Printed by Progressive Printing, Leigh-on-Sea, Essex

IMPORTANT FACTS
ABOUT THIS LAW PACK BOOK

Law Pack publications are designed to provide authoritative and accurate information on the subject matter covered. However, neither this nor any other publication can take the place of a solicitor on important legal matters.

This **Law Pack** publication is sold on the understanding that the publisher, author and retailer are not engaged in rendering legal services. If legal advice or other expert assistance is required, the services of a competent professional should be sought.

The forms included in this **Law Pack** publication cover many everyday matters, but we cannot cater for all circumstances. If what you want is not included, we advise you to see a solicitor.

This **Law Pack** publication is designed only for use in England and Wales. It is not suitable for Scotland or Northern Ireland.

The information this book contains has been carefully compiled from reliable sources but its accuracy is not guaranteed as laws and regulations may change or be subject to differing interpretations. The law is stated as at 1st May 1997.

As with any legal matter, common sense should determine whether you need the assistance of a solicitor rather than relying solely on the information and forms in this **Law Pack** book.

We strongly urge you to consult a solicitor whenever substantial amounts of money are involved, or where you do not understand the instructions or are uncertain how to complete and use a form correctly, or if you have any doubts about its adequacy to protect you, or if what you want to do is not precisely covered by the forms provided.

LAW PACK PUBLISHING LIMITED
10-16 COLE STREET
LONDON SE1 4YH

About 301 Legal Forms...

This book contains legal forms, letters and agreements to safeguard your legal rights and protect you... your family... your property... and your business from everyday legal problems.

With 301 essential legal documents in one book, you now have available the protection you need in simple legal matters without the inconvenience or cost of using a solicitor.

Law Pack publications are the ideal way to 'get it in writing'. What better way is there to document your important transactions, avoid costly disputes and enforce your legal rights? In a few minutes you can draw up the legal form or agreement you need to sidestep misunderstandings, comply with legal obligations and avoid liability.

Written by solicitors, *301 Legal Forms Letters & Agreements* has been approved for consumer use

How to use 301 Legal Forms, Letters & Agreements...

It is easy to use **Law Pack's** *301 Legal Forms, Letters and Agreements* by following these simple instructions.

1 To find the appropriate form, read the two tables of contents. The first lists each form alphabetically. The second groups them by subject.

2 You may find several forms for the same general purpose. To choose the form most appropriate for your specific needs, consult the Glossary, beginning on page 347, as a guide to the purpose of each form.

3 Cut out and photocopy the form you want and keep the original so it can be used again in the future. Alternatively you can use the form as a template to prepare your own documents. Letter-type documents can be personalised by being reproduced on your own letterhead.

4 Complete each form fully. Make certain all blanks (name, address, dates, amounts) are filled in. You may need to delete or add provisions in some forms to suit your requirements. If this is necessary, make sure each deletion or insertion is initialled by all parties. If there is not enough space on the document to make your insertion, it is best to type out the entire document, including the insertion, on a new sheet of paper.

5 Some forms have footnoted instructions, which should be observed if you are to use the form properly. Some forms refer to other forms in *301 Legal Forms, Letters & Agreements*, other documents or copies of documents which will need to be attached to the form before use.

6 The pronoun 'it' within a form can refer to an individual as well as a business entity. The pronoun 'he' can refer to a woman as appropriate.

About Deeds and Agreements

Under English law a contract does not have to be written down to be valid and enforceable. A verbal contract has just as much validity as a written contract. The problem associated with a verbal contract is that if there is a dispute over the contract the only evidence of the terms of the contract is the verbal evidence of each party to the contract which will be based on memory.

The reason that important contracts are written down, therefore, is so that a written record exists of what was agreed between the parties, to minimise the possibility of later disputes.

A contract exists where two or more parties make mutual promises to each other to take some sort of action or to make some payment to each other. An exchange of goods for money is the simplest form of contract. A simple promise by A to B, however, is not a contract, because B has given no 'consideration' to A's promise. In order to turn A's promise into an enforceable contract B must also make some promise or payment in return (the consideration). A contract like this involving mutual promises can be referred to as both a contract and an agreement, and both terms are used to mean the same thing in *301 Legal Forms, Letters & Agreements.*

It is sometimes the case that a simple promise by one party to another is all that two parties wish to record. The acceptance of such a promise is an agreement, but it is not enforceable because the other party has given no consideration for the promise. Such an agreement can be made enforceable if it is recorded in what is referred to as a deed. A deed is a written agreement which is given legal enforceability by the use of the word 'deed'.

An agreement recorded in a deed is enforceable in law regardless of whether mutual promises are made or not. You will find many of the agreements in *301 Legal Forms, Letters & Agreements* are set up as deeds to make them enforceable.

Signature of Agreements. The part of an agreement or deed that the parties sign is known as the attestation clause. *In simple agreements, the attestation clause is the same for both companies and individuals.* Each party should sign the agreement and also get a witness to sign and provide his or her name and address.

Signature of Deeds. *In deeds, the attestation clauses are different for companies and individuals.* On each deed there is space for two individuals to sign, or two companies, or a combination of the two, depending on who is drawing up the deed. Each party should sign the deed and get a witness to sign and provide his or her name and address.

Use caution and common sense when using *301 Legal Forms, Letters & Agreements* – or any other do-it-yourself legal product. Whilst these forms are generally considered appropriate for self-use, you must nevertheless decide when you should seek professional legal advice instead. You should consult a solicitor if:

- You need a complex or important agreement.
- Your transaction involves substantial amounts of money or expensive property.
- You don't understand how to use a document – or question its adequacy to fully protect you.

Because we cannot be certain that the forms in this book are appropriate to your circumstances – or are being properly used – we cannot assume any liability or responsibility in connection with their use.

TABLE OF CONTENTS

A

B

C

D

E

F

G

H

I

J

L

M

N

O

P

Q

R

S

T

U

V

W

TABLE OF CONTENTS
by Category

I. Basic Agreements

II. Loans & Borrowing

III. Employment

IV. Credit & Debt Collection

V. Buying/Selling

VI. Residential Tenancy

VII. Transfers & Assignments

VIII. Personal & Family

IX. Business

X. Other Legal Forms

ACCIDENT CLAIM NOTICE

Date _____

To _____

_____

_____

Dear _____

You are hereby notified of a claim against you for damages arising from the following accident or injury, to which I believe you and/or your agents are liable.

Description of Accident _____

_____

_____

_____

_____

Date _____

Time _____

Location _____

Please ask your insurance company or solicitor to contact me as soon as possible.

Yours sincerely

Name _____

Address _____

_____

Telephone _____

1

ACKNOWLEDGEMENT AND ACCEPTANCE OF ORDER

Date _____

To _____

_____

_____

Dear _____

Re Your Order No. _____

We acknowledge receipt of your order no. _____ and confirm our acceptance, which, as advised, is subject to our terms and conditions of business.

Yours sincerely

_____

ACKNOWLEDGEMENT OF ALTERATION OF TERMS TO ORDER

Date _____

To _____

_____

_____

Dear _____

I refer to your order number dated _____ 19 _____.

This letter acknowledges that the order is altered and superseded by the following agreed change in terms

_____

_____

_____

All other terms shall remain as stated.

Unless we immediately hear from you to the contrary, in writing, we shall assume that the above alteration is mutually agreed, and we shall proceed on the altered terms. Please indicate your agreement to the alteration by signing below and returning one copy for our file.

Yours sincerely

_____

The above alteration is acknowledged.

_____

ACKNOWLEDGEMENT OF TEMPORARY EMPLOYMENT

I, the undersigned, understand I am being employed by_____

_____(Company) in a temporary position only and for such time as my services are required. I hereby acknowledge that this temporary employment does not entitle me to any special consideration for permanent employment. I further understand that subject to law my temporary employment may be terminated at any time following the usual disciplinary procedures applicable to permanent employees. Furthermore, I understand that I am not eligible to participate in any retirement benefits or any other benefits available to permanent employees (unless required by law) and in the event that I am allowed to participate in any benefit, then my continued participation may be withdrawn or terminated by the Company at any time and without reason.

_____
Employee

_____
Date

_____
Witness

AFFIDAVIT

I, _____(name)

of _____ (address)

_____(occupation)

MAKE OATH and say as follows:

_____

_____

_____

_____

_____

_____

_____

_____

_____

_____

_____

_____
Signature

SWORN AT _____ (address)

this _____day of _____ 19 _____

before me,

_____
(A Solicitor or Commissioner for Oaths)

AFFIDAVIT OF POWER OF ATTORNEY

I,_____ of _____, make oath and say as follows:

1. The Power of Attorney granted to me by _____, on _____, a true copy of which is annexed hereto, is in full force and effect.

2. That at the time of the execution of _____, on _____ I had no knowledge of or actual notice of the revocation or termination of the Power of Attorney by death or otherwise.

3. I make this affidavit for the purpose of inducing _____ to accept the above described instrument as executed by me as attorney knowing that in accepting the aforesaid instrument they will rely upon this affidavit.

Sworn at _____

the ____ day of _____ 199 ___

Before me _____
A Solicitor

AFFIDAVIT OF TITLE

I, _____(name)

of _____ (address)

_____(occupation)

MAKE OATH and say as follows:

1.   I certify that I am now in possession of and am the absolute owner of the following property _____

_____

2.   I also state that its possession has been undisputed and that I know of no fact or reason that may prevent transfer of this property to the buyer.

3.   I also state that no liens, contracts, debts, or lawsuits exist regarding this property, except the following _____

_____

_____

4.   I finally state that I have full power to transfer full title to this property to the buyer.

_____

Signature

SWORN AT _____ (address)

this _____day of _____ 19 _____.

before me,

_____

(A Solicitor or Commissioner of Oaths)

AGENCY AGREEMENT WITH RETENTION OF TITLE

THIS AGREEMENT is made the _____ day of _____ 19_____

BETWEEN:

(1) _____ (the "Consignor"); and

(2) _____ (the "Agent").

NOW IT IS HEREBY AGREED that the terms of consignment are the following:

1. The Agent acknowledges receipt of goods from the Consignor as described on the attached schedule (the "Goods"). The Goods shall remain the property of the Consignor until sold.

2. The Agent, at its own cost and expense, agrees to keep and display the goods only in its place of business, and agrees to return the same on demand in good order and condition to the Consignor.

3. The Agent agrees to use its best efforts to sell the Goods for the Consignor's account on cash terms and at such prices as shall from time to time be designated by the Consignor.

4. The Agent agrees, upon sale, to maintain the sale proceeds due to the Consignor separate and apart from its own funds, and to deliver such proceeds, less commission, to the Consignor, together with an account, within _____ days of sale.

5. The Agent agrees to accept as full payment for its obligations hereunder a commission equal to _____% of the gross sales price exclusive of any VAT.

6. The Agent agrees to permit the Consignor to enter its premises during business hours to examine and inspect the Goods.

7. The Agent agrees to issue such accounts for public filing as may reasonably be required by Consignor.

IN WITNESS OF WHICH the parties have signed the agreement the day and year first above written

_____   _____
Signed for and on behalf of the Consignor   Signed for and on behalf of the Agent

_____   _____
in the presence of (witness)   in the presence of (witness)

Name _____   Name _____

Address _____   Address _____

_____   _____
Occupation   Occupation

AGREEMENT

THIS AGREEMENT is made the _____ day of _____ 19_____

BETWEEN:

(1) _____ of _____ (the "First Party");and

(2) _____ of _____ (the "Second Party").

NOW IT IS HEREBY AGREED as follows:

1.   That in consideration of the mutual covenants and agreements to be kept and performed on the part of said parties hereto, respectively as herein stated, the First Party hereby covenants and agrees that it shall:

_____

_____

_____

_____

_____

_____

2.   And the Second Party hereby covenants and agrees that it shall:

_____

_____

_____

_____

_____

_____

3.   Other terms to observed by and between the parties:

_____

_____

_____

_____

_____

4.   This agreement shall be binding upon the parties, their successors and assigns. This is the entire agreement.

IN WITNESS OF WHICH the parties have signed this agreement the day and year first above written.

_____

Signed by or on behalf of the First Party

_____

in the presence of (witness)

Name _____

Address _____

_____

Occupation _____

_____

Signed by or on behalf of the Second Party

_____

in the presence of (witness)

Name _____

Address _____

_____

Occupation _____

AGREEMENT FOR THE SALE OF GOODS

THIS AGREEMENT is made the _____ day of _____ 19_____

BETWEEN:

(1) _____ of _____ (the "Buyer"); and

(2) _____ of _____ (the "Seller").

NOW IT IS HEREBY AGREED as follows:

1.   In consideration for the sum of £ _____, receipt of which the Seller hereby acknowledges, the Seller hereby sells and transfers to the Buyer and his/her successors and assigns absolutely, the following goods (the "Goods"):

_____

_____

_____

_____

2.   The Seller warrants and represents that he/she has good title to the Goods, full authority to sell and transfer the Goods and that the Goods are sold free and clear of all liens, encumbrances, liabilities and adverse claims, of every nature and description.

3.   The Seller further warrants that he/she shall fully defend, protect, indemnify and hold harmless the Buyer and his/her lawful successors and assigns from any and all adverse claims, that may be made by any party for possession of the Goods.

IN WITNESS OF WHICH the parties have signed this agreement the day and year first above written

_____   _____
Signed by or on behalf of the Buyer   Signed by or on behalf of the Seller

_____   _____
in the presence of (witness)   in the presence of (witness)

Name _____   Name _____

Address _____   Address _____

_____   _____
Occupation   Occupation

AGREEMENT FOR THE SALE OF A VEHICLE

THIS AGREEMENT is made the _____ day of _____ 19_____

BETWEEN:

(1) _____ (the "Buyer"); and

(2) _____ (the "Seller").

NOW IT IS HEREBY AGREED as follows:

1.   In consideration for the sum of £ _____, receipt of which the Seller hereby acknowledges, the Seller hereby sells and transfers to the Buyer the following vehicle (the "Vehicle"):

Make: _____ Model: _____

Registration Number: _____ Chassis Number: _____

Year of Manufacture: _____ Mileage: _____

Colour: _____ Extras: _____

2.   The Seller warrants to the Buyer the following: (i) the Seller is the owner of the Vehicle; (ii) the Seller has the legal right to sell the Vehicle; (iii) the Vehicle is free and clear of all liens and encumbrances; and (iv) the Vehicle is not the subject of a hire purchase agreement.

3.   The Buyer has examined or has had an opportunity to examine the Vehicle. The Vehicle is sold and delivered strictly as seen and the seller expressly disclaims all warranties, express or implied, of merchantability or fitness for a particular purpose.

4.   The Seller warrants that while the Vehicle was in the Seller's possession, the odometer was not altered or disconnected and that to the best of the Seller's knowledge the odometer reading above (tick one box ONLY):

( ) reflects the actual mileage.
( ) reflects the actual mileage in excess of 99,999 miles.

IN WITNESS OF WHICH the parties have signed this agreement the day and year first above written

_____   _____

Signed by or on behalf of the Buyer   Signed by or on behalf of the Seller

_____   _____

in the presence of (witness)   in the presence of (witness)

Name _____   Name _____

Address _____   Address _____

_____   _____

Occupation   Occupation

AGREEMENT TO ACCEPT NIGHT WORK

A second shift is or may be required to meet our present or future needs. All new employees are hired on the understanding that they are able and willing to work night shifts.

Please answer the following:

	YES	NO
1. Do you have any physical disability that would prevent you from working night shifts?	_____	_____
2. Do you know of any personal reasons that would interfere with your working night shifts?	_____	_____
3. Are you willing to work night shifts?	_____	_____

I understand that any employment is conditional upon my acceptance of a night assignment if required.

_____
Signed

_____
Date

_____
Witness

In case of emergency notify:

Name _____   Tel _____

Address _____   Relationship _____

_____

Name _____   Tel _____

Address _____   Relationship _____

_____

AGREEMENT TO ASSUME DEBT

THIS AGREEMENT IS MADE the _____ day of _____ 19 ____

BETWEEN:

(1) _____ of _____ (the "Creditor");

(2) _____ of _____ (the "Debtor"); and

(3) _____ of _____ (the "Customer").

1.   The Customer acknowledges that the Customer presently owes the Creditor the sum of £_____ (the "Debt") and that the Customer is currently in the possession of certain assets or goods which are the property of the Creditor (the "Goods").

2.   The Debtor unconditionally and irrevocably agrees to assume and pay the Debt, and otherwise guarantees to the Creditor payment of the Debt and to indemnify and hold harmless the Creditor from any loss thereto in return for the transfer of the Goods from the Customer to the Debtor.

3.   The Debt shall be due and payable on the following terms:

_____

_____

4.   Nothing in this agreement shall constitute a release or discharge of the obligations of the Customer to the Creditor for the payment of the Debt, provided that so long as the Debtor shall promptly pay the Debt in the manner above described, the Creditor shall forebear in commencing any action against the Customer. In the event of any default, the Creditor shall have full rights, jointly and severally, against both the Customer and/or the Debtor for any balance then owing.

5.   This agreement shall be binding upon and inure to the benefit of the parties, their successors and assigns.

IN WITNESS OF WHICH the parties have signed this agreement the day and year first above written

_____   _____
Signed by or on behalf of the Creditor   Signed by or on behalf of the Debtor

_____   _____
in the presence of (witness)   in the presence of (witness)

Name _____   Name _____

Address _____   Address _____

_____   _____
Occupation _____   Occupation _____

_____
Signed by or on behalf of the Customer

_____
in the presence of (witness)

Name _____

Address _____

_____
Occupation _____

AGREEMENT TO COMPROMISE DEBT

THIS DEED is made the _____ day of _____ 19_____

BETWEEN:

(1) _____ of _____ (the "Customer"); and

(2) _____ of _____ (the "Creditor").

WHEREAS:

(A) The Customer and the Creditor acknowledge that the Customer is indebted to the Creditor in the sum of £ _____ (the "Debt"), which sum is now due and payable.

(B) The Creditor agrees to forgo payment of part of the Debt.

NOW THIS DEED WITNESSES as follows:

1.   The parties agree that the Creditor shall accept £ _____ (the "Sum") in full and final settlement of the Debt and in complete discharge and satisfaction of all monies due, provided the Sum is punctually paid as follows:

_____

_____

2.   Should the Customer fail to pay the Sum on the terms set out in paragraph 1, the Creditor shall have full rights to prosecute its claim for the full total of the Debt, less any payments made.

3.   Upon default, the Customer agrees to pay all reasonable solicitors' fees and costs of collection.

4.   This agreement shall be binding upon and inure to the benefit of the parties, their successors and assigns.

IN WITNESS OF WHICH the parties have executed this deed the day and year first above written

(Individual)   (Company)

_____   Signed for and on behalf of:
Signed by the Customer
                                                  _____ Ltd

_____
in the presence of (witness)   _____
                                                  Director
Name _____
                                                  _____
Address _____   Director/Secretary

_____
Occupation _____

                                                  Signed for and on behalf of:

_____   _____ Ltd
Signed by the Creditor

_____   _____
in the presence of (witness)   Director

Name _____   _____
                                                  Director/Secretary
Address _____

_____
Occupation _____

AGREEMENT TO EXTEND DEBT PAYMENT

THIS DEED is made the _____ day of _____ 19_____

BETWEEN:

(1) _____ of _____ (the "Customer"); and

(2) _____ of _____ (the "Creditor").

WHEREAS:

(A) The Customer and the Creditor acknowledge that the Customer is indebted to the Creditor in the sum of £ _____ (the "Debt"), which sum is now due and payable.

(B) The Creditor agrees to extend the term for payment of the Debt.

NOW THIS DEED WITNESSES as follows:

1. The Creditor agrees to the payment of the Debt on extended terms, together with interest on the unpaid balance at the rate of _____ % per annum, payable in the following manner:

_____

_____

2. The Customer agrees to pay the Debt to the Creditor together with interest thereon under the terms set out in paragraph 1.

3. In the event the Customer shall fail to make any payment on the due date, the Creditor shall have full rights to collect the entire balance then remaining which amount shall be immediately due and payable.

4. In the event of default, the Customer agrees to pay all reasonable solicitors' fees and costs of collection.

5. At the election of the Creditor, the Customer agrees to execute note(s) evidencing the balance then due on terms consistent with this agreement.

6. This agreement shall be binding upon and inure to the benefit of the parties, their successors and assigns.

IN WITNESS OF WHICH the parties have executed this deed the day and year first above written

(Individual)   (Company)

_____   Signed for and on behalf of:
Signed by the Customer
                                                                                    Ltd
_____   _____
in the presence of (witness)

Name _____
Address _____   Director

_____   _____
Occupation   Director/Secretary

_____   Signed for and on behalf of:
Signed by the Creditor
                                                                                    Ltd
_____   _____
in the presence of (witness)

Name _____
Address _____   Director

_____   _____
Occupation   Director/Secretary

AGREEMENT TO EXTEND PERFORMANCE DATE

THIS DEED is made the _____ day of _____ 19_____

BETWEEN:

(1) _____ of _____ (the "First Party"); and

(2) _____ of _____ (the "Second Party").

WHEREAS:

(A) The parties entered into an agreement dated _____ 19_____ (the "Agreement") which provides that full performance of the Agreement shall be completed by both parties on or before _____ 19_____, (the "Completion Date").

(B) The parties acknowledge that the Agreement cannot be performed and completed by both parties by the Completion Date and therefore wish to extend the date for mutual performance of the Agreement.

NOW THIS DEED WITNESSES as follows:

1.   The parties hereby agree that the date for performance of the Agreement be continued and extended to _____ 19_____, time being of the essence.

2.   No other variation of terms or extension of time shall be permitted.

3.   This agreement shall be binding upon and inure to the benefit of the parties, their successors and assigns.

IN WITNESS OF WHICH the parties have executed this deed the day and year first above written

(Individual)   (Company)

_____   Signed for and on behalf of:
Signed by the First Party
                                                                                          Ltd
                                                         _____
_____
in the presence of (witness)

Name _____   _____
                                                         Director
Address _____
                                                         _____
_____   Director/Secretary
Occupation _____

_____   Signed for and on behalf of:
Signed by the Second Party
                                                                                          Ltd
                                                         _____
_____
in the presence of (witness)

Name _____   _____
                                                         Director
Address _____
                                                         _____
_____   Director/Secretary
Occupation _____

AGREEMENT TO SELL PERSONAL PROPERTY

THIS AGREEMENT is made the _____ day of _____ 19_____

BETWEEN:

(1) _____ of _____ (the "Buyer"); and

(2) _____ of _____ (the "Seller").

NOW IT IS HEREBY AGREED as follows:

1.   The Seller agrees to sell, and the Buyer agrees to buy the following property (the "Property"):

_____

2.   The Buyer agrees to pay to the Seller and the Seller agrees to accept as total purchase price the sum of £ _____, payable as follows:

£ _____ deposit herewith paid; and

£ _____ the balance payable on delivery by cash, or cheque supported by bankers card.

3.   The Seller warrants it has good and legal title to the Property, full authority to sell the Property, and that the Property shall be sold free of all liens, charges, encumbrances, liabilities and adverse claims of every nature and description whatsoever.

4.   The property is sold as seen, and the Seller disclaims any warranty of working order or condition of the Property except that it shall be sold in its present condition, reasonable wear and tear excepted.

5.   The parties hereto agree to transfer title on _____ 19_____, at the address of the Seller.

6.   This agreement shall be binding upon and inure to the benefit of the parties, their successors and assigns.

IN WITNESS OF WHICH the parties have signed this agreement the day and year first above written

_____   _____
Signed by the Buyer   Signed by the Seller

_____   _____
in the presence of (witness)   in the presence of (witness)

Name _____   Name _____

Address _____   Address _____

_____   _____
Occupation   Occupation

ANTI-GAZUMPING AGREEMENT
(an Exclusivity Contract between the Buyer & Seller of Property)

THIS AGREEMENT is made the _____ day of _____ 199 ___

BETWEEN (1) _____ of _____

_____ (the "Seller");

and

(2) _____ of _____

_____ (the "Buyer").

BACKGROUND

A The parties have, subject to contract, agreed to a transaction ("the Sale") in which the Seller will sell and the Buyer will buy the property described in the First Schedule ("the Property") at the price of _____

_____ (£ _____).

B The solicitors specified in the Second Schedule ("the Seller's Solicitors") will act for the Seller on the Sale.

C The solicitors specified in the Third Schedule ("the Buyer's Solicitors") will act for the Buyer on the Sale.

NOW IT IS HEREBY AGREED as follows:

1. Exclusivity Period

1.1 The Exclusivity Period shall begin on the exchange of this Agreement and shall end (subject to Clause 5.1 below) at 5 pm on the _____ day after the Buyer's Solicitors receive the draft contract from the Seller's Solicitors pursuant to Clause 2(b) below.

1.2 If and for as long as the Buyer complies with his obligations under this Agreement, the Seller agrees that during the Exclusivity Period neither the Seller nor anyone acting on the Seller's behalf will:

(a) seek purchasers for the Property;

(b) allow any prospective purchaser or mortgagee or any surveyor, valuer or other person acting on his or their behalf to enter the Property (other than under clause 4.3 below);

(c) provide a draft contract or property information concerning the Property to anyone other than the Buyer's Solicitors;

(d) negotiate or agree with anyone other than the Buyer or the Buyer's Solicitors any terms for the sale of the Property;

(e) enter into a commitment to proceed with any other purchaser immediately after the expiry of the Exclusivity Period.

2. Seller's instructions to solicitors

The Seller will immediately:

(a) appoint the Seller's Solicitors to act for him on the Sale; and

(b) instruct them to send to the Buyer's Solicitors as soon as practicable a draft contract for the Sale and such information about the Property as accords with good conveyancing practice and to deal promptly and reasonably with any enquiries asked by the Buyer's Solicitors and with any amendments to the draft contract proposed by the Buyer's Solicitors.

3. Buyer's instructions to solicitors

The Buyer will immediately:

(a) appoint the Buyer's Solicitors to act for him on the Sale; and

(b) instruct them to make all necessary searches and enquiries as soon as practicable and to deal promptly and in accordance with good conveyancing practice with the draft contract for the Sale and such title and other information about the Property as they receive from the Seller's Solicitors and to negotiate with the Seller's Solicitors promptly and reasonably any amendments to the draft contract which the Buyer's Solicitors propose.

4. Surveys, mortgages, etc.

4.1 If the Buyer requires a mortgage loan in connection with the purchase of the Property, the Buyer shall within [one week] from the date of this Agreement apply to such building society, bank or other prospective lender ("the Mortgagee") as may reasonably be expected to lend the required amount to the Buyer and the Buyer shall complete such application forms and pay such fees as the Mortgagee shall require in order to process the Buyer's application as quickly as possible.

4.2 If the Buyer or the Mortgagee require the Property to be surveyed and/or valued, the Buyer will use all reasonable endeavours to arrange for the survey and/or valuation inspection to take place within _____ days of the date of this Agreement.

4.3 The Seller will give such access to the Property as is reasonably required by any surveyor or valuer appointed by the Buyer or the Mortgagee for the purpose of surveying and/or valuing the Property.

5. Good faith and withdrawal

5.1 During the Exclusivity Period the Seller and the Buyer will deal with each other in good faith and in particular (but without limiting the above):

(a) if during the Exclusivity Period the Buyer decides not to buy the Property or becomes unable to buy the Property, he will immediately give written notice to that effect to the Seller and the Exclusivity Period will then cease;

(b) if during the Exclusivity Period the Seller decides not to proceed with the Sale or becomes unable to sell the Property, he will immediately give written notice to that effect to the Buyer and the Buyer's obligations under this Agreement will cease but the restrictions imposed on the Seller by Clause 1.2 above shall continue until the expiry of the Exclusivity Period.

5.2 Nothing in Clause 5.1 above or elsewhere in this Agreement will impose on the Seller any greater duty to disclose matters affecting the Property than are imposed by statute or common law.

6. Miscellaneous

6.1 This Agreement does not bind the parties to the Sale.

6.2 This Agreement does not form part of any other contract.

6.3 In this Agreement the expression "property information" includes title details and any other information about the Property which a prudent prospective buyer or his solicitors would require the seller or his solicitors to provide.

6.4 The headings shall not affect the interpretation of this Agreement.

THE FIRST SCHEDULE	THE SECOND SCHEDULE	THE THIRD SCHEDULE
The Property	The Seller's Solicitors	The Buyer's Solicitors
_____	_____	_____
_____	_____	_____
_____	_____	_____

SIGNED _____   **SIGNED** _____

      by or on behalf of the Seller   by or on behalf of the Buyer

APPLICANT'S REQUEST FOR AN EMPLOYMENT REFERENCE

Date _____

From _____

_____

_____

To _____

_____

_____

I have applied for a job with _____

Address _____

_____

Contact _____

I have been asked to provide references to this potential employer to support my job application.

I would be grateful if you could write a reference on my behalf to the above Company based on your knowledge and experience of my work and character while under your employment.

Thank you in advance for your co-operation.

Yours sincerely

_____

APPLICATION TO OPEN A CREDIT ACCOUNT

with _____ Ltd

Company Name	
Address	Invoice Address (if different)
Tel No.	Fax No.

Name of Buyer		
Registration No.	Value of Initial Order £	Requested Credit Limit £
Trade Reference (1)	Trade Reference (2)	Bank Reference

Parent Company (if applicable) _____

I hereby agree to the terms and conditions of sale accompanying this application.

NAME _____

POSITION _____

SIGNED _____ DATE _____

OFFICE USE ONLY

	Date	Agency Rating	Credit Limit	Authorised	Date
Application Rec'd		Accounts Rec'd			
Refs Applied For					
Account Opened					

Account No. [_____]   Credit Limit [_____]

ASSIGNMENT OF ACCOUNTS RECEIVABLE WITH NON-RECOURSE

THIS AGREEMENT is made the _____ day of _____ 19_____

BETWEEN:

(1) _____ of _____ (the "Assignor"); and

(2) _____ of _____ (the "Assignee").

NOW IT IS HEREBY AGREED as follows:

1.   In consideration for the payment of the sum of £ _____ (receipt of which the Assignor hereby acknowledges) the Assignor hereby assigns and transfers to the Assignee all right, title and interest in and to the account(s) receivable described as follows (the "Accounts"):

_____

_____

_____

_____

2.   The Assignor warrants that the Account(s) are due and the Assignor has not received payment for same or any part thereof.

3.   The Assignor further warrants that it has full title to the Accounts, full authority to sell and transfer the Accounts and that the Accounts are sold free and clear of all liens, encumbrances and any known claims.

4.   This agreement shall be binding upon and inure to the benefit of the parties, their successor and assigns.

IN WITNESS OF WHICH the parties have signed this agreement the day and year first above written

_____   _____
Signed by or on behalf of the Assignor   Signed by or on behalf of the Assignee

_____   _____
in the presence of (witness)   in the presence of (witness)

Name _____   Name _____

Address _____   Address _____

_____   _____

Occupation _____   Occupation _____

ASSIGNMENT OF CONTRACT

THIS DEED is made the _____ day of _____ 19_____

BETWEEN:

(1) _____ of _____ (the "Assignor");

(2) _____ of _____ (the "Assignee"); and

(3) _____ of _____ (the "Third Party").

WHEREAS:

(A) The Assignor and the Third Party have entered into an agreement dated_____
_____ 19_____ (the "Agreement").

(B) With the consent of the Third Party the Assignor wishes to assign all its rights and obligations under the Agreement to the Assignee.

NOW THIS DEED WITNESSES as follows:

1.   The Assignor warrants and represents that the Agreement is in full force and effect and is fully assignable.

2.   The Assignee hereby assumes and agrees to perform all the remaining and executory obligations of the Assignor under the Agreement and agrees to indemnify and hold the Assignor harmless from any claim or demand resulting from non-performance by the Assignee.

3.   The Assignee shall be entitled to all monies remaining to be paid under the Agreement, which rights are also assigned hereunder.

4.   The Assignor warrants that the Agreement is without modification, and remains on the terms contained therein.

5.   The Assignor further warrants that it has full right and authority to transfer the Agreement and that the Agreement rights herein transferred are free of lien, encumbrance or adverse claim.

6.   The Third Party agrees to the assignment of the Agreement upon the terms stated herein.

7.   This assignment shall be binding upon and inure to the benefit of the parties, their successors and assigns.

IN WITNESS OF WHICH the parties have executed this deed the day and year first above written

(Individual)   (Company)

_____   Signed for and on behalf of
Signed by the Assignor
                                                          _____ Ltd
_____
in the presence of (witness)
Name _____   _____
Address _____   Director

_____   _____
Occupation _____   Director/Secretary

_____   Signed for and on behalf of:
Signed by the Assignee
                                                          _____ Ltd
_____
in the presence of (witness)
Name _____   _____
Address _____   Director

_____   _____
Occupation _____   Director/Secretary

24

ASSIGNMENT OF INSURANCE POLICY

THIS DEED is made the _____ day of _____ 19_____

BETWEEN:

(1) _____ of _____ (the "Assignor"); and

(2) _____ of _____ (the "Assignee").

WHEREAS:

(A) The Assignor is the holder of a Policy of Insurance number _____ issued by the _____ Insurance Company (the "Policy").

(B) The Assignor wishes to assign the benefit of the Policy to the Assignee.

NOW THIS DEED WITNESSES as follows:

1.   The Assignor warrants that the Policy is in full force and effect and all premiums thereon have been paid in full to date.

2.   The Assignor further warrants that he/she has full authority to transfer the Policy, and shall execute all further documents as may be required by the Insurance Company or broker to effect this Assignment.

3.   The Assignor hereby assigns to the Assignee and the Assignee hereby accepts the assignment of the Policy and all the obligations and benefits attaching thereto.

4.   This assignment shall by binding upon and inure to the benefit of the parties, their successors and assigns.

IN WITNESS OF WHICH the parties have executed this deed the day and year first above written

(Individual)   (Company)

_____   Signed for and on behalf of
Signed by the Assignor
                                                         _____ Ltd
_____
in the presence of (witness)
Name   _____
_____   Director
Address
_____   _____
Occupation   Director/Secretary
_____

_____   Signed for and on behalf of:
Signed by the Assignee
                                                         _____ Ltd
_____
in the presence of (witness)
Name   _____
_____   Director
Address
_____   _____
Occupation   Director/Secretary
_____

ASSIGNMENT OF MONEY DUE

THIS AGREEMENT is made the _____ day of _____ 19_____

BETWEEN:

(1) _____ of _____ (the "Assignor"); and

(2) _____ of _____ (the "Assignee").

WHEREAS:

(A) The Assignor is entitled to the payment of certain monies under a contract dated _____ 19_____ and made between the Assignor and_____ _____ (the "Contract").

(B) The Assignor wishes to assign the benefit of the Contract to the Assignee.

NOW IT IS HEREBY AGREED as follows:

1.   In consideration for the sum of £_____, receipt of which the Assignor hereby acknowledges, the Assignor assigns and transfers to the Assignee all monies now due and payable to the Assignor and to become due and payable to the Assignor under the terms of the Contract to the Assignee.

2.   The Assignor hereby warrants that there has been no breach of the Contract by any party, and that the Assignor is in full compliance with all the terms and conditions of the Contract, and has not assigned or encumbered all or any rights under said contract.

3.   The Assignor authorises and directs _____, to deliver any and all cheques, drafts, or payments to be issued pursuant to Contract to the Assignee; and further authorises the Assignee to receive such cheques, drafts, or payments from, and to collect any and all funds due or to become due pursuant thereto.

IN WITNESS OF WHICH the parties have signed this agreement the day and year first above written

_____   _____
Signed by or on behalf of the Assignor   Signed by or on behalf of the Assignee

_____   _____
in the presence of (witness)   in the presence of (witness)

Name _____   Name _____

Address _____   Address _____

_____   _____

Occupation _____   Occupation _____

ASSIGNMENT OF OPTION

THIS AGREEMENT is made the _____ day of _____ 19_____

BETWEEN:

(1) _____ of _____ (the "Assignor"); and

(2) _____ of _____ (the "Assignee").

WHEREAS:

(A) The Assignor has been granted the following option (the "Option"):

_____

_____

_____

_____

(B) The Assignor wishes to sell the Option to the Assignee.

NOW IT IS HEREBY AGREED as follows:

1.   In consideration for the payment of £ _____, receipt of which the Assignor hereby acknowledges, the Assignor hereby transfers his/her entire interest in the Option and all his/her right thereunder to the Assignee.

2.   The Assignee, by accepting the transfer of this Option, agrees to exercise the Option, if at all, according to its terms.

3.   This agreement shall be binding upon and inure to the benefit of the parties, their successors and assigns.

IN WITNESS OF WHICH the parties have signed this agreement the day and year first above written

_____   _____
Signed by or on behalf of the Assignor   Signed by or on behalf of the Assignee

_____   _____
in the presence of (witness)   in the presence of (witness)

Name _____   Name _____

Address _____   Address _____

_____   _____

Occupation _____   Occupation _____

ASSIGNMENT OF OPTION TO PURCHASE LAND

THIS AGREEMENT is made the _____ day of _____ 19_____

BETWEEN:

(1) _____ of _____ (the "Assignor"); and

(2) _____ of _____ (the "Assignee").

WHEREAS:

(A) The Assignor is the holder of an option to purchase property located at _____

_____ which expires on _____ 19_____ (the

"Option"), a copy of which is annexed.

(B) The Assignor wishes to sell the Option to the Assignee.

NOW IT IS HEREBY AGREED as follows:

1.   In consideration for the payment of £ _____, receipt of which the Assignee hereby acknowledges, the Assignor hereby transfers his/her entire interest in the Option and all his/her rights thereunder to the Assignee.

2.   The Assignor warrants that the Option is fully assignable.

3.   The Assignee, by accepting the transfer of the Option, agrees to exercise the Option, if at all, according to its terms.

4.   This agreement shall by binding upon and inure to the benefit of the parties, their successors and assigns.

IN WITNESS OF WHICH the parties have signed this agreement the day and year first above written.

_____   _____
Signed by or on behalf or the Assignor   Signed by or on behalf of the Assignee

_____   _____
in the presence of (witness)   in the presence of (witness)

Name _____   Name _____

Address _____   Address _____

_____   _____
Occupation   Occupation

28

AUTHORISATION TO RELEASE CONFIDENTIAL INFORMATION

Date _____

To _____

_____

_____

Dear _____

I hereby authorise and request you to send copies of the following documents which I believe to be in your possession and which contain confidential information concerning me to:

Name _____

Address _____

_____

_____

Documents:

_____

_____

_____

_____

I shall of course reimburse you for any reasonable costs incurred by you in providing the requested information.

Yours sincerely

Name _____

Address _____

_____

_____

AUTHORISATION TO RELEASE EMPLOYMENT INFORMATION

Date _____

To _____

_____

_____

Dear _____

I hereby authorise and request you to send the information ticked below to:

_____ the following party: _____

_____ any third party

The information to be released includes: (tick)

_____ Salary
_____ Position/department/section
_____ Date employment commenced
_____ Part-time/full-time or hours worked
_____ Garnishee orders or wage attachments, if any
_____ Reason for redundancy
_____ Medical/accident/illness reports
_____ Work performance rating
_____ Other: _____

Yours sincerely

Employee Signature _____ Print Name _____

Address _____ Position or Title _____

_____ Department _____

_____

_____

AUTHORISATION TO RELEASE MEDICAL INFORMATION

Date _____

To _____

_____

_____

Dear _____

I hereby authorise and request that you release and deliver to:

_____

_____

_____

all my medical records, files, charts, x-rays, laboratory reports, clinical records, and such other information concerning me that is in your possession. I would also request that you do not disclose any information concerning my past or present medical condition to any other person without my express written permission.

Yours sincerely

Name _____

Address _____

_____

_____

In the presence of

_____

Witness

AUTHORISATION TO RETURN GOODS

Date _____

To _____

_____

_____

Dear _____

This letter is to confirm that we shall accept the return of certain goods we have supplied to you and credit your account. The terms for return are:

1. The value of the goods returned shall not exceed £ _____.

2. We shall deduct _____ % of the invoice value as a handling charge and credit your account with the balance.

3. All return goods shall be in a re-saleable condition and must be goods we either currently stock or can return to our supplier for credit. We reserve the right to refuse the return of goods that do not correspond with this description.

4. You shall be responsible for the costs of shipment and the risk of loss or damage in transit. Goods shall not be accepted for return until we have received, inspected and approved the goods at our place of business.

5. Our agreement to accept returns for credit is expressly conditional upon your agreement to settle any remaining balance due on the following terms: _____

_____

_____

Yours sincerely

_____

BREACH OF CONTRACT NOTICE

Date _____

To _____

_____

_____

Dear _____

We refer to the agreement between us dated _____ 19 _____, which provides that:

_____

_____

_____

PLEASE TAKE NOTE that you are in breach of your obligations under the agreement as follows:

_____

_____

_____

We invite you to remedy the breach by immediately taking steps to do the following:

_____

_____

_____

If you fail to remedy the breach as requested within 14 days of the date of this letter, we shall have no alternative but to commence legal proceedings to claim damages from you as a result of the breach. We will also hold you liable for the costs of those proceedings.

Yours sincerely

Name _____

Address _____

_____

BUILDER/DECORATOR CONTRACT

THIS AGREEMENT is made the _____ day

of _____ 199 ____

BETWEEN **(1)** _____ of _____

_____ (the "Employer");

and

(2) _____ of _____

_____ (the "Contractor").

WHEREAS

A The Employer requires the following works to be carried out (the "Works") at _____

_____:

_____

_____

_____

_____

_____

_____

_____

to be carried out under the direction of _____

B The Contractor is prepared to carry out the Works in return for payment of the Sum (as hereinafter defined).

NOW IT IS HEREBY AGREED as follows:

1. In consideration for the payment of the Sum in the manner set out below the Contractor agrees to carry out the Works with due diligence and with all reasonable speed in a proper and workmanlike manner.

2. The Sum shall be a total of £ _____ (exclusive of VAT) payable as follows: _____

_____

_____

_____

3. Any plans or specifications that form part of the description of the Works are attached hereto and have been signed by or on behalf of the parties hereto and form part of this Agreement.

4. The Contractor may be required by the Employer to carry out other works in addition to the Works in which case any such works and the fee payable for such works must be agreed in writing between the parties hereto before commencement.

5. Any dispute or difference arising out of or in connection with this contract shall be determined by the arbitration of a single arbitrator who failing agreement shall be appointed by the President or a Vice-President of the Royal Institution of Chartered Surveyors.

6. No variation of this Agreement will be effective unless it is in writing and is signed by both parties. This Agreement binds and benefits both parties and any successors. Time is of the essence in this Agreement. This document, including any attachments, is the entire agreement between the parties.

IN WITNESS OF WHICH the parties hereto have signed this Agreement the day and year first above written.

SIGNED _____ _____

Signed by or on behalf of the Contractor   in the presence of (witness)

Name _____

Address _____

_____

DATED _____   Occupation _____

SIGNED _____ _____

Signed by the Employer   in the presence of (witness)

Name _____

Address _____

_____

DATED _____   Occupation _____

CANCELLATION OF AN ORDER TO STOP A CHEQUE

Date _____

To _____

_____

_____

Dear _____

On _____ 19 _____, we requested you to stop payment on the following cheque that we issued:

Cheque No: _____

Dated: _____

Amount: _____

Payable to: _____

Account No: _____

We have now advised the payee to re-present the cheque for payment, and we should be grateful if you would now honour the cheque on re-presentation.

Yours sincerely

_____

Account _____

Account No. _____

CERTIFICATE OF PRODUCT CONFORMITY

_____ Ltd

To:			Order No:		
			Ref No:		
FAO:			Date:		

Product ID	Qty	Description	Spec no.	Model no	Test reports

This certifies that all of the above goods have been inspected, tested and unless otherwise stated conform in all respects to the order requirements.

Signed _____
Customer Services Manager

CHANGE IN PAY OR GRADING FOLLOWING JOB EVALUATION

Date _____

To _____

_____

_____

Dear _____

Following our job evaluation review it has been decided to upgrade your job title to _____ with effect from _____ 19 _____.

From that date your salary will be increased to £ _____ per _____. All other terms and conditions of your employment remain unchanged.

We offer our congratulations on your promotion, and hope that you enjoy your new position.

Yours sincerely

_____

CHANGE IN SALES REPRESENTATIVE AGREEMENT

Date _____

To _____

_____

_____

Dear _____

I refer to the sales representative agreement between us dated _____ 19 ____, a copy of which is attached.

This letter acknowledges that the agreement is modified and superseded by the following agreed change in terms:

_____

_____

_____

All other terms shall remain as stated.

Please sign below to indicate your acceptance of the modified terms.

Yours sincerely

_____

Company _____

I agree to the above modification:

_____

Sales Representative

CHANGE OF ADDRESS NOTICE

Date _____

To _____

_____

_____

Dear _____

Please note that as from _____ 19 _____, our address will
change from:

_____

_____

_____

to

_____

_____

_____

Our new telephone number will be _____

and fax number _____

Please make note of the above information and direct all future correspondence to us at our
new address. Thank you.

Yours sincerely

_____

CHANGE TO EMPLOYMENT CONTRACT

Date _____

To _____

_____

_____

Dear _____

Following discussions with you and/or your trade union, it has been decided to vary the terms of your contract of employment as follows:

_____

_____

_____

_____

_____

_____

_____

_____

All other terms and conditions of your contract of employment remain unchanged.

I attach two copies of the revised contract. If satisfactory, please sign and return one copy to me.

Yours sincerely

_____

Agreed and accepted

_____

the Employee

CHILD GUARDIANSHIP CONSENT FORM

I _____, of _____

_____, hereby appoint _____,

of _____, _____, as the

legal guardian of my child(ren). The guardian shall have the following powers:

_____

_____

_____

_____

_____

_____

_____

_____

_____

_____

_____

Signed this _____ day of _____, 19 _____.

_____

_____

COHABITATION AGREEMENT
(for Unmarried Partners)

THIS DEED OF AGREEMENT is made the _____ day of _____ 199__

BETWEEN:

(1) _____ of _____ ("the First Party"); and

(2) _____ of _____ ("the Second Party").

WHEREAS:

(a) The Parties live together and wish to enter this Agreement to set out their rights and responsibilities towards each other.

(b) The Parties intend that this Agreement will be legally binding on them.

(c) Each Party enters this Agreement freely and voluntarily and without coercion or pressure from the other Party or anyone else.

1. OWNERSHIP OF THE HOME

The Parties live at the address given above ("the Home") which is a property purchased in their joint names/ in the sole name of the First/Second Party*.

(*delete as appropriate)

2. DIVISION OF PROCEEDS OF SALE OF THE HOME

Where the Home is owned in joint names:

Option 1: The rights and interests of the Parties in the Home and its net proceeds of sale are set out in a Declaration of Trust dated _____ and are not in any way varied or affected by this Deed.

Option 2: The Parties agree that they shall hold the beneficial interest in the Home as tenants in common; in equal shares.

OR

as to _____ % for the First Party and as to _____ % for the Second Party.

OR

in the proportions in which they contribute to the purchase of the Home whether by contribution to the purchase price, payment of mortgage instalments and mortgage-linked endowment premiums, or by way of improvements which add to the value of the Home (and if the Parties cannot agree the value of any such improvements the value shall be determined by a valuer appointed by the President of the Royal Institution of Chartered Surveyors).

Where the Home is owned in the sole name of one Party:

Option 3: The Parties agree that they shall hold the beneficial interest in the Home; in equal shares.

OR

as to _____ % for the First Party and as to _____ % for the Second Party.

OR

in the proportions in which they contribute to the purchase of the Home whether by contribution to the purchase price, payment of mortgage instalments and mortgage-linked endowment premiums, or by way of improvements which add to the value of the Home (and if the Parties cannot agree the value of any such improvements the value shall be determined by a valuer appointed by the President of the Royal Institution of Chartered Surveyors).

43

Option 4: The Parties agree that the First/Second* Party is the sole beneficial owner of the Home and that regardless of contributions to the purchase maintenance or improvement of the Home the other Party is not and will not acquire any beneficial interest in the Home or in its proceeds of sale.

(*delete as appropriate)

3. CONTENTS AND PERSONAL BELONGINGS

Any household and personal item shall be owned:

Option 1: By the Party who acquired it alone (whether by inheritance, gift, purchase or otherwise).

Option 2: By both Parties equally (regardless of when or by whom it was acquired) unless the Parties expressly agree otherwise in writing. Unless the Parties shall agree otherwise within one month of the date of termination of this Agreement all jointly owned items shall be sold and the net proceeds of sale divided equally between them.

4. BANK OR BUILDING SOCIETY ACCOUNTS

It is agreed that:

Option 1: The Parties do not intend to open a joint account. Each Party shall maintain separate bank or building society accounts and the money in each account will remain his or her separate property.

Option 2: The Parties shall maintain a joint bank or building society account ("The Joint Account").

The Parties shall pay into the Joint Account sums sufficient to meet their agreed share of common expenses (referred to in clause 5). The money in the Joint Account shall belong to the Parties in equal shares regardless of the actual sums which either of them may have paid into or withdrawn from the Joint Account. Any money in any bank or building society account maintained separately by either Party shall belong to that Party alone.

5. COMMON EXPENSES

Common household expenditure including mortgage repayments, mortgage-linked endowment premiums, ground rent, service charges, rental payments, buildings and household insurance premiums, council or other local taxes, charges for water rates, gas, electricity, telephone, television licence and rental, food, decoration and repairs shall be:

Option 1: paid by the First/Second* Party alone.

Option 2: shared equally by the Parties.

Option 3: paid as to _____ % by the first Party and as to _____ % by the Second Party.

6. VARIATION/TERMINATION

This Agreement shall be varied only by written agreement of the Parties. This Agreement shall terminate by written agreement of the Parties or upon the death or marriage of either one of them or upon the Parties separation for a period exceeding three months following which the Home shall be valued and either sold and the proceeds divided or the Party leaving compensated appropriately in accordance with the provisions of this Agreement.

SIGNED AS A DEED

by the said_____

Name_____

in the presence of

Signature_____

Name_____

Address_____

SIGNED AS A DEED

by the said_____

Name_____

in the presence of

Signature_____

Name_____

Address_____

NOTE: OPTION CLAUSES SHOULD BE DELETED AS APPROPRIATE AND BOTH PARTIES SHOULD INITIAL THE DELETION

COMPANY LET
(For a Furnished or Unfurnished House or Flat)

The PROPERTY _____

_____

The LANDLORD _____

_____

_____

The TENANT _____LIMITED/PLC

whose Registered Office is at _____

_____

_____

_____(Company Registration No._____)

The TERM   _____ months beginning on _____

(delete paragraph if not required)   ⌈Subject to the right for either party at any time during the Term to end this Agreement⌉ (* delete as appropriate)

earlier by giving to the other written notice of _____ week(s)/month(s)*

The RENT   £ _____ per week/month* payable in advance on the _____ of each week/month*

The DEPOSIT   £ _____

⌈**The INVENTORY** means the list of the Landlord's possessions at the Property which has been signed by the⌉ (delete if unfurnished)

Landlord and the Tenant

DATED   _____

SIGNED   _____   _____

_____   _____

(The Landlord)   (Director/Secretary for and on

behalf of The Tenant)

THIS AGREEMENT comprises the particulars detailed above and the terms and conditions printed overleaf whereby the Property is hereby let by the Landlord and taken by the Tenant for the Term at the Rent.

Terms and Conditions on next page

45

COMPANY LET

Terms and Conditions

1. The Tenant will:

1.1 pay the Rent at the times and in the manner aforesaid without any deduction abatement or set-off whatsoever

1.2 pay all charges in respect of any electric, gas, water and telephonic or televisual services used at or supplied to the Property and Council Tax or any similar tax that might be charged in addition to or replacement of it

1.3 keep the interior of the Property in a good, clean and tenantable state and condition and not damage or injure the Property or any part of it

1.4 yield up the Property at the end of the Term in the same clean state and condition it was in at the beginning of the Term

1.5 maintain at the Property and keep in a good and clean condition all of the items listed in the Inventory

1.6 not make any alteration or addition to the Property nor without the Landlord's prior written consent to do any redecoration or painting of the Property

1.7 not do or omit to do anything on or at the Property which may be or become a nuisance or annoyance to the Landlord or owners or occupiers of adjoining or nearby premises or which may in any way prejudice the insurance of the Property or cause an increase in the premium payable therefor

1.8 not without the Landlord's prior consent allow or keep any pet or any kind of animal at the Property

1.9 not use or occupy the Property in any way whatsoever other than as a private residence

1.10 not assign, sublet, charge or part with or share possession of occupation of the Property or any part thereof provided however that the Tenant may permit the residential occupation of the Property as a whole by the Tenant's officers, employees, customers and visitors so long as the Tenant continues to be responsible for the Rent and all other outgoings and does not make any charge whatsoever in respect of the same to the occupier and no relationship of landlord and tenant is created or allowed to arise between the tenant and the occupier

1.11 permit the Landlord or anyone authorised by the Landlord at reasonable hours in the daytime and upon reasonable prior notice (except in emergency) to enter and view the Property for any proper purpose (including the checking of compliance with the Tenant's obligations under this Agreement and during the last month of the Term the showing of the Property to prospective new tenants)

1.12 pay interest at the rate of 4% above the Base Lending Rate for the time being of the Landlord's bankers upon any Rent or other money due from the Tenant under this Agreement which is more than 10 days in arrear in respect of the period from when it became due to the date of payment

2. Subject to the Tenant paying the rent and performing his/her obligations under this Agreement the Tenant may peaceably hold and enjoy the Property during the term without interruption from the Landlord or any person rightfully claiming under or in trust for the Landlord

3. In the event of the Rent being unpaid for more than 10 days after it is due (whether demanded or not) or there being a breach of any other of the Tenant's obligations under this Agreement or the Tenant entering into liquidation then the Landlord may re-enter the Property and this Agreement shall thereupon determine absolutely but without prejudice to any of the Landlord's other rights and remedies in respect of any outstanding obligations on the part of the Tenant

4. The Deposit has been paid by the Tenant and is held by the Landlord to secure compliance with the Tenant's obligations under this Agreement (without prejudice to the Landlord's other rights and remedies) and if, at any time during the Term, the Landlord is obliged to draw upon it to satisfy any outstanding breaches of such obligations then the Tenant shall forthwith make such additional payment as is necessary to restore the full amount of the Deposit held by the Landlord. As soon as reasonably practicable following termination of this Agreement the Landlord shall return to the Tenant the Deposit or the balance thereof after any deductions properly made

5. The Landlord hereby notifies the Tenant under Section 48 of the Landlord & Tenant Act 1987 that any notices (including notices in proceedings) should be served upon the Landlord at the address stated with the name of the Landlord overleaf

6. In the event of damage to or destruction of the Property by any of the risks insured against by the Landlord the Tenant shall be relieved from payment of the Rent to the extent that the Tenant's use and enjoyment of the Property is thereby prevented and from performance of its obligations as to the state and condition of the Property to the extent of and so long as there prevails such damage or destruction (except to the extent that the insurance is prejudiced by any act or default of the Tenant)

7. So long as the reference to a right of early termination in the definition of the "TERM" overleaf (the "early termination right") has not been deleted then either party may at any time during the Term terminate this Agreement by giving to the other prior written notice to that effect, the length of such notice to be that stated in the early termination right, and upon the expiry of said notice this Agreement shall end with no further liability of either party save for any antecedent breach

8. Where the context so admits:

8.1 The "Landlord" includes the persons for the time being entitled to the reversion expectant upon this Tenancy

8.2 The "Tenant" includes any persons deriving title under the Tenant

8.3 The "Property" includes all of the Landlord's fixtures and fittings at or upon the Property

8.4 The "Term" shall mean the period stated in the particulars overleaf or any shorter or longer period in the event of an earlier termination or an extension or holding over respectively

9. All references to the singular shall include the plural and vice versa and any obligations or liabilities of more than one person shall be joint and several and an obligation on the part of a party shall include an obligation not to allow or permit the breach of that obligation

CONCESSION NOTE

_____Ltd

To _____ Ltd   Concession Note No _____

_____

_____   Customer Order No _____

Please indicate whether or not you accept the concession for material/product non-conformity described below by completing this form and returning is to us as soon as possible. We will only despatch goods upon receipt of your approval.

This product/material non-conformity will be investigated as part of our quality management system.

Product Code _____   Product Description _____

Details of Concession Required _____

_____

_____

Reason for Concession   _____

_____

_____

_____
Customer Service Officer

The above concession is approved/not approved within the following batch/time/other parameters

_____

_____

_____

Name _____   Position _____

Signed _____   Date _____

CONFIDENTIALITY AGREEMENT

THIS AGREEMENT is made the _____ day of _____ 19_____

BETWEEN:

(1) _____ (the "Company"); and

(2) _____ (the "Employee").

WHEREAS:

(A) The Company agrees to give the Employee access to certain confidential information relating to the affairs of the Company solely for purposes of:

_____

_____

_____

_____

_____

_____

(B) The Employee agrees to obtain, inspect and use such information only for the purposes described above, and otherwise to hold such information confidential and secret pursuant to the terms of this agreement.

NOW IT IS HEREBY AGREED as follows:

1.   The Company has or shall furnish to the Employee confidential information, described on the attached list, and may further allow suppliers, customers, employees or representatives of the Company to disclose information to the Employee.

2.   The Employee agrees to hold all confidential or proprietary information or trade secrets ("Information") in trust and confidence and agrees that the Information shall be used only for the contemplated purpose, and not for any other purpose or disclosed to any third party under any circumstances whatsoever.

3.   No copies may be made or retained of the Information.

4.   At the conclusion of our discussions, or upon demand by the Company, all Information, including written notes, photographs, or memoranda shall be promptly returned to the Company. The Employee shall retain no copies or written documentation relating thereto.

5.   This Information shall not be disclosed to any employee, consultant or third party unless that third party agrees to execute and be bound by the terms of this agreement, and disclosure by the Company is first approved.

6.   It is understood that the Employee shall have no obligation with respect to any information known by the Employee, or as may be generally known within the industry, prior to date of this agreement, or that shall become common knowledge within the industry thereafter.

7. The Employee acknowledges the Information disclosed herein contains proprietary or trade secrets and in the event of any breach, the Company shall be entitled to apply for injunctive relief and to claim for damages of breach.

8. This agreement shall be binding upon and inure to the benefit of the parties, their successors and assigns.

9. This constitutes the entire agreement.

IN WITNESS OF WHICH the parties have signed this agreement the day and year first above written

Signed for and on behalf of the Company by

_____

Director

_____

Director/Secretary

_____

Signed by or on behalf of the Employee

_____

in the presence of (witness)

Name _____

Address _____

_____

Occupation _____

CONFIRMATION OF AGREEMENT TO PAY

Date _____

To _____

_____

_____

Dear _____

We send you this letter to confirm our agreement, made on _____ 19 ___ , that you will pay your overdue balance of £ _____ according to the following terms:

_____

_____

_____

_____

If this letter does not conform to our agreement, please inform us immediately.

We understand your financial difficulties and, to accommodate you, will accept payments on these extended terms provided each payment is punctually made when due.

Whilst this balance remains outstanding we shall supply you on a cash on delivery basis.

We are pleased this matter could be resolved on terms satisfactory to us both, and we look forward to your payments and continued business.

Yours sincerely

_____

CONFIRMATION OF VERBAL ORDER

Date _____

To _____

_____

_____

Dear _____

This letter confirms our verbal order of _____ 19 _____ .

A copy of our confirmatory purchase order containing the stated terms is enclosed as order no.:_____

Unless we receive written objection within ten (10) days of your receipt of this written order, we shall consider the order confirmed on its terms and shall anticipate delivery of all ordered goods on the date indicated.

Thank you for your cooperation.

Yours sincerely

_____

CONFLICT OF INTEREST DECLARATION

Employee _____

Company _____

_____

_____

I acknowledge that I have read the Company policy statement concerning conflicts of interest and I hereby declare that neither I, nor any other business to which I may be associated, nor, to the best of my knowledge, any member of my immediate family has any conflict between our personal affairs or interests and the proper performance of my responsibilities for the Company that would constitute a violation of that Company policy. Furthermore, I declare that during my employment, I shall continue to maintain my affairs in accordance with the requirements of the Company policy.

_____

Employee's Signature

Date _____

CONSENT TO DRUG/ALCOHOL SCREENING

I _____, have been fully informed by my potential employer of the reasons for a urine test for drugs and/or alcohol. I understand what the test is for and the procedure involved, and do hereby freely give my consent. In addition I understand that the result of a test will be forwarded to my potential employer and become part of my record.

If test results proves positive and I am not offered employment, I understand that I will be given the opportunity to explain such results.

I hereby authorise test results to be released to:

_____

_____   _____
Signature   Date

_____   _____
Witness   Date

CONSENT TO RELEASE OF INFORMATION

To _____

From Personnel Office

A request for certain employment information concerning you has been received from:

_____

_____

_____

_____

Please tick below those items of information that you permit us to disclose.

_____   Salary

_____   Position

_____   Department

_____   Supervisor

_____   Health records

_____   Dates of employment

_____   Part-time/Full-time

_____   Hours worked

_____   Whether you work under a maiden name

_____   Wage attachments

_____   Reason for redundancy

_____   Other:

_____

_____

_____

_____   _____

Employee Signature   Date

Please return this form to the Personnel Office as soon as possible. Your consent on this occasion will not constitute a consent to release information on future occasions.

CONSENT TO SHORT NOTICE OF AN
ANNUAL GENERAL MEETING

_____ Limited

We, the undersigned, being all members for the time being of the company having the right to attend and vote at the Annual General Meeting of such company convened to be held at _____ _____ on the _____ day of _____ 199 ___ (the attached notice being the notice convening the meeting), hereby agree:

a) in accordance with s.369(3) of the Companies Act 1985 to the holding of such meeting notwithstanding that less than the statutory period of notice thereof has been given; and

b) to accept service of documents in accordance with s.238(4) of the Companies Act 1985 notwithstanding that the documents were sent less than 21 day before the meeting.

Dated this _____ day of _____ 199 ___.

_____
Member's signature

_____
Member's signature

_____
Member's signature

_____
Member's signature

CONSENT TO SHORT NOTICE OF AN
EXTRAORDINARY GENERAL MEETING

_____ Limited

We, the undersigned, being a majority in number of the above-named company and entitled to attend and vote at the Extraordinary General Meeting of the said company convened by a Notice of Meeting dated _____ 199 _____ and to be held on _____ _____ 199 _____ and together holding 95 per cent and upward in nominal value of the shares giving that right, hereby agree to the holding of such meeting and to the proposing and passing of the resolutions on the day and at the time and place set out in such Notice, notwithstanding that less than the statutory period of the Notice thereof has been given to us.

Dated this _____ day of _____ 199 ___.

_____
Member's signature

_____
Member's signature

_____
Member's signature

_____
Member's signature

CONSULTANT NON-DISCLOSURE AGREEMENT

THIS AGREEMENT is made the _____ day of _____ 19_____

BETWEEN:

(1) _____ of _____ (the "Client"); and

(2) _____ of _____ (the "Consultant").

NOW IT IS HEREBY AGREED as follows:

That to induce the Client to retain the Consultant as an outside consultant and to furnish the Consultant with certain information that is proprietary and confidential, the Consultant hereby warrants, represents, covenants, and agrees as follows:

1. **Engagement.** The Consultant, in the course of engagement by the Client, may or will have access to or learn certain information belonging to the Client that is proprietary and confidential (Confidential Information).

2. **Definition of Confidential Information.** Confidential Information as used throughout this agreement means any secret or proprietary information relating directly to the Client's business and that of the Client's affiliated companies and subsidiaries, including, but not limited to, products, customer lists, pricing policies, employment records and policies, operational methods, marketing plans and strategies, product development techniques or plans, business acquisition plans, new personnel acquisition plans, methods of manufacture, technical processes, designs and design projects, inventions and research programs, trade "know-how," trade secrets, specific software, algorithms, computer processing systems, object and source codes, user manuals, systems documentation, and other business affairs of the Client and its affiliated companies and subsidiaries.

3. **Non-disclosure.** The Consultant agrees to keep strictly confidential all Confidential Information and will not, without the Client's express written authorisation, signed by one of the Client's authorised officers, use, sell, market, or disclose any Confidential Information to any third person, firm, corporation, or association for any purpose. The Consultant further agrees not to make any copies of the Confidential Information except upon the Client's written authorisation, signed by one of the Client's authorised officers, and will not remove any copy or sample of Confidential Information from the premises of the Client without such authorisation.

4. **Return of Material.** Upon receipt of a written request from the Client, the Consultant will return to the Client all copies or samples of Confidential Information that, at the time of the receipt of the notice, are in the Consultant's possession.

5. **Obligations Continue Past Term.** The obligations imposed on the Consultant shall continue with respect to each unit of the Confidential Information following the termination of the business relationship between the Consultant and the Client, and such obligations shall not terminate until such unit shall cease to be secret and confidential and shall be in the public

domain, unless such event shall have occurred as a result of wrongful conduct by the Consultant or the Consultant's agents, servants, officers, or employees or a breach of the covenants set forth in this agreement.

6.   **Equitable Relief.** The Consultant acknowledges and agrees that a breach of the provisions of Paragraph 3 or 4 of this Agreement would cause the Client to suffer irreparable damage that could not be adequately remedied by an action at law. Accordingly, the Consultant agrees that the Client shall have the right to seek specific performance of the provisions of Paragraph 3 to enjoin a breach or attempted breach of the provision thereof, such right being in addition to all other rights and remedies that are available to the Client at law, in equity, or otherwise.

7.   **Invalidity.** If any provision of this agreement or its application is held to be invalid, illegal, or unenforcable in any respect, the validity, legality, or enforceability of any of the other provisions and applications therein shall not in any way be affected or impaired.

IN WITNESS OF WHICH the parties have signed this agreement the day and year first above written

_____

Signed by or on behalf of the Client

_____

in the presence of (witness)

Name _____

Address _____

_____

Occupation _____

_____

Signed by or on behalf of the Consultant

_____

in the presence of (witness)

Name _____

Address _____

_____

Occupation _____

CONTRACT FOR THE SALE OF GOODS BY DELIVERY

THIS AGREEMENT is made the _____ day of _____ 19_____

BETWEEN:

(1) _____ (the "Seller"); and

(2) _____ (the "Buyer").

NOW IT IS HEREBY AGREED as follows:

1.   In consideration for the payment of £ _____ (the "Purchase Price"), on the terms set out below, the Seller agrees to sell and the Buyer agrees to buy the following goods (the "Goods"):

_____

_____

2.   The Buyer agrees to pay the Purchase Price and the Seller agrees to accept such payment on the following terms:

_____

_____

3.   The Seller agrees that the Goods will be delivered to the Buyer's place of business by _____ 19 _____ . The shipping costs are estimated at £ _____ and will be paid by the _____.

4.   The Seller represents that it has legal title to the goods and full authority to sell the goods. The Seller also represents that the property is sold free and clear of all liens, mortgages, indebtedness, or liabilities.

5.   No variation of this Contract will be effective unless it is in writing and is signed by both parties. Time is of the essence for the purposes of this Contract. This Contract binds and benefits both the Buyer and Seller and any successors. This Contract, including any attachments, is the entire agreement between the Buyer and Seller.

IN WITNESS OF WHICH the parties have signed this agreement the day and year first above written.

_____   _____
Signed by or on behalf of the Seller   Signed by or on behalf of the Buyer

_____   _____
in the presence of (witness)   in the presence of (witness)

Name _____   Name _____

Address _____   Address _____

_____   _____
Occupation   Occupation

CONTRACTOR/SUBCONTRACTOR AGREEMENT

THIS AGREEMENT is made the _____ day of _____ 19_____

BETWEEN:

(1) _____.of _____ (the "Contractor"); and

(2) _____ of _____ (the "Subcontractor").

WHEREAS:

(A) The Contractor has entered into an agreement dated _____ 19_____,
with _____ (the "Company") for the performance of certain
works (the "Works"),

(B) The Contractor wishes to subcontract certain portions of the Works to the Subcontractor.

NOW IT IS HEREBY AGREED as follows:

1.   The Subcontractor, as an independent contractor, agrees to furnish all of the labour and
materials as may reasonably by required to complete the following portions of the Works:

_____

_____

_____

_____

_____

2.   The Subcontractor agrees that the following portions of the Works will be completed by
the dates specified:

Work	Date
_____	_____
_____	_____
_____	_____
_____	_____
_____	_____
_____	_____
_____	_____

3.   The Subcontractor agrees to perform this work in a workmanlike manner according to
standard practices. If any plans or specifications are part of this job, they are attached to and
form part of this agreement.

4.   The Contractor agrees to pay the Subcontractor £ _____ as payment for the full
performance of its obligations hereunder. This sum will be paid to the Subcontractor on
satisfactory completion of the work in the following manner and on the following dates:

_____

_____

5. The Contractor and Subcontractor may agree to extra services and work, but any such extras must be set out and agreed to in writing by both the Contractor and the Subcontractor.

6. The Subcontractor agrees to indemnify and hold the Contractor harmless from any claims or liability arising from the Subcontractor's work under this Contract.

7. No modification of this agreement will be effective unless it is in writing and is signed by both parties. This agreement binds and benefits both parties and any successors. Time is of the essence in this agreement. This document, including any attachments is the entire agreement between the parties.

IN WITNESS OF WHICH the parties have signed this agreement the day and year first above written

_____

Signed by or on behalf of the Contractor

_____

in the presence of (witness)

Name _____

Address _____

_____

Occupation _____

_____

Signed by or on behalf of the Subcontractor

_____

in the presence of (witness)

Name _____

Address _____

_____

Occupation _____

CREDIT INFORMATION

Date _____

To _____

_____

_____

Dear _____

Re _____

This letter is in reply to your request for credit information on the above account. Accordingly, we submit the following information:

1. The account was opened with us on _____ 19 _____

2. The account's present balance is:

Under 30 days	£_____
30-60 days	£_____
60-90 days	£_____
Over 90 days	£_____
Total owed	£_____

3. The credit limit is:

_____

4. Other credit information:

_____

_____

_____

We are pleased to be of service to you and trust this information will be held in strict confidence.

Yours sincerely

_____

CREDIT INFORMATION REQUEST

Date _____

To _____

_____

_____

Dear _____

Thank you for your recent order dated _____ 19 _____.

We would be pleased to offer you credit under our standard terms and conditions. In order to enable us to do so, we should be grateful if you would supply us with the following references and information regarding your financial status:

_____

_____

_____

_____

_____

_____

Pending receipt of this information we suggest C.O.D. terms or a deposit of £ _____ to enable us to deliver your order. Upon receipt of your confirmation we shall immediately deliver your order.

Of course, all credit information submitted shall be held in strict confidence.

Yours sincerely

_____

CREDIT REFERENCE

Date _____

To _____

_____

_____

Dear _____

Re _____

In response to your letter dated _____ 19 _____, the above mentioned has been known to us for _____ years. Over that period they have faithfully and honourably discharged all their obligations.

We have extended them credit and they have never abused our trust nor delayed payment of due accounts. We would, without hesitation, extend credit to them in the amount you have indicated.

We are giving this reference in an endeavour to be helpful to you. We must, however, make it clear that in doing so we accept no legal liability to you.

Yours sincerely

_____

DAMAGED GOODS ACCEPTANCE

Date _____

To _____

_____

_____

Dear _____

In fulfilment of our order dated _____ 19 _____, we have received goods from you which are defective in the following manner:

_____

_____

_____

_____

We shall accept the goods provided we are allowed a price deduction of £ _____.

If you do not accept our suggested price reduction, we request that you collect the goods immediately. We undertake to be responsible for their safekeeping for a maximum of 14 days from the date of this letter.

Yours sincerely

_____

DEBT ACKNOWLEDGEMENT

The undersigned hereby confirms and acknowledges to _____

("the Creditor") that the undersigned is indebted to the Creditor in the amount of £ _____

as of the date hereof, which amount is due and owing and includes all accrued interest and

other permitted charges to date. The undersigned further acknowledges that there are no

credits or rights of set off against the balance owing.

Signed this _____ day of _____ 19 _____.

In the presence of

_____   _____
Witness   Debtor

DEFECT REPORT MEMORANDUM

_____ Ltd

Date:	Report No:	
Product code:	Description:	Batch:

Defect:

Non-conformity details:

Non-conformity cause:

Corrective action to be taken:

Signed _____
Customer Services Officer

Result of corrective action:

Signed _____ Date: _____
Customer Services Officer

DEFECTIVE GOODS NOTICE

Date _____

To _____

_____

_____

Dear _____

This is to inform you that we have received goods delivered by you as per your invoice or order no. _____, dated _____ 19 _____.

Certain goods as listed on the attached sheet are defective or do not comply with our order for the following reasons:

_____

_____

_____

_____

_____

Accordingly, we wish to return these goods in exchange for a credit note in the amount of £_____. We also intend to return the goods to you at your cost unless you collect them.

Please confirm the credit and also issue instructions for the return of the goods.

You are advised by this notice that we reserve our legal rights.

We look forward to your prompt reply.

Yours sincerely

_____

DEMAND FOR DELIVERY

Date _____

To _____

_____

_____

Dear _____

We have made full payment to you in the sum of £ _____ for the delivery of certain goods pursuant to our accepted order dated _____ 19 _____. We demand delivery of the goods in accordance with our order, since the goods have not been received as per the terms of our order.

Unless the goods are received by us on or before _____ 19 _____, we shall consider you to be in breach of contract and we shall thereupon expect a full refund, reserving such further rights as we have under the law for any other damages sustained.

We would appreciate immediate notification of your intentions in this matter.

Yours sincerely

_____

DEMAND FOR EXPLANATION OF REJECTED GOODS

Date _____

To _____

_____

_____

Dear _____

Re _____

On _____ 19 _____, we shipped the following goods to you pursuant to your order no. _____, dated _____ 19 _____:

_____

_____

_____

_____

On _____ 19 _____, we received notice that you had rejected delivery of these goods without satisfactory explanation. We therefore request that you provide us with an adequate explanation for this rejection. Unless we are provided with such explanation within 10 days, we will have no option but to enforce payment for these goods.

Please be advised that we reserve all our rights under the law.

Thank you for your immediate attention to this matter.

Yours sincerely

_____

DEMAND FOR PAYMENT

Date _____

To _____

_____

_____

Dear _____

We have tried on several occasions to secure payment of your overdue account but it remains unpaid. Your account is overdue in the amount of £ _____.

This is your final notice. Unless we receive your cheque for _____pounds (£ _____) within ten (10) days, we shall have to consider referring your account to our solicitors for collection.

Please note that immediate payment is in your own best interests as it will save you further interest and costs, and help preserve your credit rating.

Yours sincerely

_____

DEMAND TO ACKNOWLEDGE DELIVERY DATES

Date _____

To _____

_____

_____

Dear _____

We request that you confirm and specify delivery arrangements in respect of our order dated _____ 19 ____, and further confirm that you will abide by those arrangements.

Failure to provide this confirmation shall constitute a breach of contract and we shall no longer consider ourselves bound by this contract. Further, we shall hold you responsible for all resultant damages as provided by law.

Please confirm delivery dates, in writing, no later than _____ 19 ____.

Yours sincerely

_____

DEMAND TO GUARANTOR FOR PAYMENT

Date _____

To _____

_____

_____

Dear _____

As you are aware, we hold your guarantee dated _____ 19 ____, wherein you guaranteed the debt owed to us by

_____

You are advised that this debt is now in default. Accordingly, demand is made upon you as guarantor for full payment on the outstanding debt due us in the amount of £ _____.

In the event payment is not made within _____ (_____) days, we shall be compelled to enforce our rights against you under the guarantee by referring this matter to our solicitors.

Yours sincerely

_____

DEMAND TO PAY PROMISSORY NOTE

Date _____

To _____

_____

_____

Dear _____

I refer to a promissory note dated _____ 19 ____ , in the original principal amount of £ _____ and of which I am the holder.

You are in default under the note in that the following payment(s) have not been made:

Payment Date   Amount Due

_____   _____

_____   _____

_____   _____

_____   _____

Accordingly, demand is hereby made for full payment of the entire balance of £ _____ due under the note. In the event payment is not received within _____ days, this note shall be forwarded to our solicitors for collection.

Yours sincerely

_____

DIRECTOR'S RESIGNATION WITHOUT PREJUDICE

Date _____ .

To: Board of Directors

_____ Limited

_____

_____

Dear Sirs

I resign my office of director of the company with immediate effect and without prejudice. I hereby reserve my right to take all proceedings which may be available to me to recover any fees, expenses, compensation and damages to which I am entitled.

Yours faithfully

_____

DIRECTORS' RESOLUTION TO CALL ANNUAL GENERAL MEETING

_____ Limited

We, being all the directors of _____ Limited who are entitled to receive notice of a meeting of the directors, RESOLVE that an annual general meeting of the company shall be convened on the _____ day of _____ 199___ for the following purposes:

_____

_____

_____

_____

_____

_____

_____

_____

and that the secretary be instructed to give notice of the meeting to all shareholders.

Dated this _____ day of _____ 199 ___

_____
Director's Signature

_____
Director's Signature

_____
Director's Signature

DIRECTORS' RESOLUTION TO CALL EXTRAORDINARY GENERAL MEETING

_____ Limited

We, being all the directors of _____ Limited who are entitled to receive notice of a meeting of directors, RESOLVE that an extraordinary general meeting of the company be convened forthwith for the purpose of considering and, if thought fit, passing the following resolution(s) as (a) special resolution(s) or (an) ordinary resolution(s) as appropriate:

_____

_____

_____

_____

_____

_____

Dated this _____ day of _____ 199 ___

_____
Director's Signature

_____
Director's Signature

_____
Director's Signature

DISCIPLINARY RULES AND PROCEDURE
at _____Limited

1. The Company's aim is to encourage improvement in individual performance and conduct. Employees are required to treat members of the public and other employees equally in accordance with the Equal Opportunities Policy. This procedure sets out the action which will be taken when disciplinary rules are breached.

2. Principles:

   (i) The list of rules is not to be regarded as an exhaustive list.

   (ii) The procedure is designed to establish the facts quickly and to deal consistently with disciplinary issues. No disciplinary action will be taken until the matter has been fully investigated.

   (iii) At every stage employees will have the opportunity to state their case and be accompanied by a fellow employee of their choice at the hearings.

   (iv) Only a Director has the right to suspend or dismiss. An employee may, however, be given a verbal or written warning by their immediate superior.

   (v) An employee has the right to appeal against any disciplinary decision.

3. The Rules:

   Breaches of the Company's disciplinary rules which can lead to disciplinary action are:

   - failure to observe a reasonable order or instruction;

   - failure to observe a health and safety requirement;

   - inadequate time keeping;

   - absence from work without proper cause;

   - theft or removal of the Company's property;

   - loss, damage to or misuse of the Company's property through negligence or carelessness;

   - conduct detrimental to the interests of the Company;

   - incapacity for work due to being under the influence of alcohol or illegal drugs;

   - physical assault or gross insubordination;

   - committing an act outside work or being convicted for a criminal offence which is liable adversely to affect the performance of the contract of employment and/or the relationship between the employee and the Company;

   - failure to comply with the Company's Equal Opportunities Policy.

DISHONOURED CHEQUE NOTICE

Date _____

To _____

_____

_____

Dear _____

Payment of your cheque no. _____ in the sum of £ _____ , tendered to us on _____ 19 _____, has been dishonoured by your bank.

Please therefore ensure sufficient funds are put into your account to enable us to re-present the cheque immediately, or remit your payment in cash to our address by hand.

Unless we receive payment of the outstanding sum within seven days we may take steps towards a formal recovery of the debt.

Yours sincerely

_____

DISMISSAL LETTER FOR INTOXICATION ON THE JOB

Date _____

To _____

_____

_____

Dear _____

This letter is to inform you that we are terminating your employment with effect from _____. This decision is based on an incident reported to me on _____ 19 _____ by your supervisor, _____. The report recommended your dismissal because of your repeated intoxication during working hours.

As you are aware, the first reported incident of your intoxication on the job was on _____ 19 _____. That report was placed on your personnel file, and you were informed at that time that another incident would result in a disciplinary action or possible dismissal.

This second incident of intoxication adversely affected the operational efficiency and effectiveness of your department and threatened the safety of other employees.

Your final pay cheque, including all forms of compensation due to you, can be picked up in the personnel office on your way out.

Yours sincerely

_____
Personnel Manager

DISPUTED ACCOUNT SETTLEMENT

THIS DEED IS MADE the _____ day of _____ 19_____

BETWEEN:

(1) _____ (the "Creditor"); and

(2) _____ (the "Debtor").

WHEREAS:

(A) The Creditor asserts a claim (the "Claim") against the Debtor in the amount of £ _____ arising from the following transaction:

_____

_____

_____

(B) The Debtor disputes the Claim, and denies the said debt is due.

(C) The parties desire to resolve and forever settle and adjust the Claim.

NOW IT IS HEREBY AGREED as follows:

1.   The Debtor agrees to pay the Creditor and the Creditor agrees to accept from the Debtor the sum of _____ Pounds (£ _____) in full payment, settlement, satisfaction, discharge and release of the Claim and in release of any further claims thereto.

2.   This agreement shall be binding upon and inure to the benefit of the parties, their successors and assigns.

IN WITNESS OF WHICH the parties have executed this deed the day and year first above written

(Individual)   (Company)

_____   Signed for and on behalf of
Signed by the Creditor
                                               _____ Ltd
_____
in the presence of (witness)
Name _____   _____
Address _____   Director
_____   _____
Occupation _____   Director/Secretary

_____   Signed for and on behalf of:
Signed by the Debtor
                                               _____ Ltd
_____
in the presence of (witness)
Name _____   _____
Address _____   Director
_____   _____
Occupation _____   Director/Secretary

DORMANT COMPANY ACCOUNTS

_____ LIMITED

No. _____

DORMANT COMPANY ACCOUNTS

TO

_____ 199___

Directors' Report

The company has not engaged in any activity since its incorporation on _____ 19_____.

As the company has been dormant since that date, and further to Section 250 of the Companies Act 1985, a special resolution will be proposed at a general meeting convened for that purpose to make the company exempt from the obligation to appoint auditors as otherwise required by Part VII of the Companies Act 1985, as amended by the Companies Act 1989.

_____
Director's Signature

_____
Date

Continued on next page

_____ **LIMITED**

BALANCE SHEET AS AT

_____ **199___**

Share Capital

    Additional Share Capital

    _____ ordinary shares of £ _____ each   £ _____

    Issued and fully paid

    _____ ordinary shares of £ _____ each   £ _____

Revenue Reserve Employment of Capital

    Fixed Assets   £ _____

    Current Assets   £ _____

    Less Current Liabilities   £ _____

    Net Current Assets   £ _____

The company has been dormant within the meaning of s.250 of the Companies Act 1985, as amended by s.14 of the Companies Act 1989, since its incorporation.

Approved by the Board _____ 199____

DORMANT COMPANY RESOLUTION

We being all the directors entitled to receive notice of meetings of the directors of _____
_____ Limited do resolve:

That an extraordinary general meeting of the company be convened for the purpose of considering and, if thought fit, passing as a special resolution the following:

"Further to Section 250 of the Companies Act 1985, it is hereby resolved as a special resolution that the company, having been dormant since its formation, be exempt from the obligation to appoint auditors as otherwise required by Part VII of the Companies Act 1985, as amended by the Companies Act 1989."

Dated this _____ day of _____ 199___

_____
Director's Signature

_____
Director's Signature

_____
Director's Signature

EMPLOYEE AGREEMENT OF INVENTIONS AND PATENTS

THIS AGREEMENT IS MADE the _____ day of _____ 19_____

BETWEEN:

(1) _____ (the "Employee"); and

(2) _____ (the "Company").

NOW IT IS HEREBY AGREED as follows:

In consideration of the employment of the Employee by the Company, the parties agree as follows:

1   The Employee shall or may have possession of or access to facilities, apparatus, equipment, drawings, systems, formulae, reports, manuals, invention records, customer lists, computer programmes, or other material embodying trade secrets or confidential technical or business information of the Company or its Affiliates. The Employee agrees not to use any such information or material for himself or others, and not to take any such material or reproductions thereof from the Company, at any time during or after employment by the Company, except as required in the Employee's duties to the Company. The Employee agrees immediately to return all such material and reproductions thereof in his possession to the Company upon request and in any event upon termination of employment.

2.   Except with prior written authorisation by the Company, the Employee agrees not to disclose or publish any trade secret or confidential technical or business information or material of the Company or its Affiliates or of another party to whom the Company owes an obligation of confidence, at any time during or after employment by the Company.

3.   The Employee shall promptly furnish to the Company a complete record of any and all inventions, patents and improvements, whether patentable or not, which he, solely or jointly, may conceive, make, or first disclose during the period of his employment by the Company.

4.   The Employee agrees to and hereby grants and assigns to the Company or its nominee the Employee's entire right, title, and interest in and to inventions, patents and improvements that relate in any way to the actual or anticipated business or activities of the Company or its Affiliates, or that are anticipated by or result from any task or work for or on behalf of the Company together with any and all domestic and foreign patent rights in such inventions and improvements. To aid the Company or its nominee in securing full benefit and protection thereof, the Employee agrees promptly to do all lawful acts reasonably requested, at any time during and after employment by the Company, without additional compensation but at the Company's expense.

5.   The Employee agrees that, in the event that the Employee accepts employment with any firm or engages in any type of activity on the Employee's own behalf or on behalf of any organisation following termination of his employment with the Company, the Employee shall notify the Company in writing within thirty days of the name and address of such organisation and the nature of such activity.

6.   The Employee agrees to give the Company timely written notice of any prior employment agreements or patent rights that might conflict with the interests of the Company or its Affiliates.

7.   No waiver by either party of any breach by the other party of any provision of this agreement shall be deemed or construed to be a waiver of any succeeding breach of such provision or as a waiver of the provision itself.

8.   This agreement shall be binding upon and pass to the benefit of the successors and assigns of the Company and, insofar as the same may be applied thereto, the heirs, legal representatives, and assigns of the Employee.

9.   This agreement shall supersede the terms of any prior employment agreement or understanding between the Employee and the Company. This agreement may be modified or amended only in writing signed by an executive officer of the Company and by the Employee.

10. Should any portion of this agreement be held to be invalid, unenforceable or void, such holding shall not have the effect of invalidating the remainder of this agreement or any other part thereof, the parties hereby agreeing that the portion so held to be invalid, unenforceable, or void shall, if possible, be deemed amended or reduced in scope.

11. The Employee acknowledges reading, understanding and receiving a signed copy of this agreement.

IN WITNESS OF WHICH the parties have signed this agreement the day and year first above written

_____

Signed by the Employee

_____

in the presence of (witness)

Name _____

Address _____

_____

Occupation _____

Signed for and on behalf of the Company

_____

Director

_____

Director/Secretary

EMPLOYEE DISCIPLINARY REPORT

Employee _____

Department _____

_____ Written Warning _____ Final Warning

1. Statement of the problem: _____

_____

_____

2. Prior discussion or warnings on this subject, whether oral or written: _____

_____

_____

3. Company policy on this subject: _____

_____

_____

4. Summary of corrective action to be taken by the Company and/or Employee: _____

_____

_____

5. Consequences of failure to improve performance or correct behaviour: _____

_____

_____

6. Employee statement: _____

_____

_____

Employee Signature: _____ Date _____

Management Approval: _____ Date _____

Distribution: One copy to Employee, one copy to Supervisor and original to Personnel File.

EMPLOYEE DISMISSAL FOR LATENESS

Date _____

To _____

_____

_____

Dear _____

You have ignored our verbal and written warnings and have again arrived late for work. We warned you of the consequences if you were late again. Accordingly, we hereby give you _____ weeks' notice of the termination your employment.

Yours sincerely

_____

EMPLOYEE FILE

Employee: _____

Address: _____

Phone: _____ National Insurance No.: _____

DOB: _____ Sex: _____M _____F

Marital Status:

_____ Single _____ Married _____ Separated _____ Widowed _____ Divorced

Name of Spouse: _____ No. Dependents _____

In Emergency Notify: _____

Address: _____

_____

Education

Secondary School_____ Years: _____

University/College _____ Years: _____

Other _____ Years: _____

Employment History

Date From /To	Position	Salary
_____	_____	£ _____
_____	_____	£ _____
_____	_____	£ _____
_____	_____	£ _____
_____	_____	£ _____
_____	_____	£ _____

Dismissal Information

Date dismissed: _____ Would we re-employ? ___ Yes ___ No

Reason for dismissal: _____

_____

_____

EMPLOYEE LET
(For a Furnished or Unfurnished House or Flat)

The PROPERTY _____

_____

The LANDLORD _____

_____

_____

The TENANT _____

_____

_____

_____

_____

The TERM   the period beginning on the date of this Agreement and ending on the date that the Tenant's employment with the Landlord ceases

(delete paragraph if not required) ⌈ Subject to the right for either party at any time during the Term to end this Agreement earlier by giving to the other written notice of _____ week(s)/month(s)* ⌉ (* delete as appropriate)

The RENT   £ _____ per week/month* payable in advance on the _____ of each week/month*

The DEPOSIT   £ _____

⌈**The INVENTORY**   means the list of the Landlord's possessions at the Property which has been signed by the Landlord and the Tenant ⌉ (delete if unfurnished)

DATED   _____

SIGNED   _____   _____

_____   _____

(The Landlord)   (The Tenant)

THIS AGREEMENT comprises the particulars detailed above and the terms and conditions printed overleaf whereby the Property is hereby let by the Landlord and taken by the Tenant for the Term at the Rent.

Terms and Conditions on next page

EMPLOYEE LET

Terms and Conditions

1. It is hereby agreed that the Landlord is letting the Property to the Tenant solely in consequence of and in connection with the Tenant's employment with the Landlord and on the termination of such employment this Agreement shall forthwith terminate and, further, that the Landlord may deduct the Rent and any other payments due and outstanding from the Tenant under this Agreement from any wages or salary that may from time to time due from the Landlord to the Tenant

2. The Tenant will:

2.1 pay the Rent at the times and in the manner aforesaid without any deduction abatement or set-off whatsoever

2.2 pay all charges in respect of any electric, gas, water and telephonic or televisual services used at or supplied to the Property and Council Tax or any similar tax that might be charged in addition to or replacement of it

2.3 keep the interior of the Property in a good, clean and tenantable state and condition and not damage or injure the Property or any part of it

2.4 yield up the Property at the end of the Term in the same clean state and condition it was in at the beginning of the Term

2.5 maintain at the Property and keep in a good and clean condition all of the items listed in the Inventory

2.6 not make any alteration or addition to the Property nor without the Landlord's prior written consent to do any redecoration or painting of the Property

2.7 not do or omit to do anything on or at the Property which may be or become a nuisance or annoyance to the Landlord or owners or occupiers of adjoining or nearby premises or which may in any way prejudice the insurance of the Property or cause an increase in the premium payable therefor

2.8 not without the Landlord's prior consent allow or keep any pet or any kind of animal at the Property

2.9 not use or occupy the Property in any way whatsoever other than as a private residence

2.10 not assign, sublet, charge or part with or share possession of occupation of the Property or any part thereof provided however that members of the Tenant's immediate family may reside at the Property with the Tenant so long as no relationship of Landlord and Tenant is thereby created or allowed to arise

2.11 permit the Landlord or anyone authorised by the Landlord at reasonable hours in the daytime and upon reasonable prior notice (except in emergency) to enter and view the Property for any proper purpose (including the checking of compliance with the Tenant's obligations under this Agreement and during the last month of the Term the showing of the Property to prospective new tenants)

2.12 pay interest at the rate of 4% above the Base Lending Rate for the time being of the Landlord's bankers upon any Rent or other money due from the Tenant under this Agreement which is more than 10 days in arrear in respect of the period from when it became due to the date of payment

3. Subject to the Tenant paying the rent and performing his/her obligations under this Agreement the Tenant may peaceably hold and enjoy the Property during the term without interruption from the Landlord or any person rightfully claiming under or in trust for the Landlord

4. In the event of the Rent being unpaid for more than 10 days after it is due (whether demanded or not) or there being a breach of any other of the Tenant's obligations under this Agreement then the Landlord may re-enter the Property and this Agreement shall thereupon determine absolutely but without prejudice to any of the Landlord's other rights and remedies in respect of any outstanding obligations on the part of the Tenant

5. The Deposit has been paid by the Tenant and is held by the Landlord to secure compliance with the Tenant's obligations under this Agreement (without prejudice to the Landlord's other rights and remedies) and if, at any time during the Term, the Landlord is obliged to draw upon it to satisfy any outstanding breaches of such obligations then the Tenant shall forthwith make such additional payment as is necessary to restore the full amount of the Deposit held by the Landlord. As soon as reasonably practicable following termination of this Agreement the Landlord shall return to the Tenant the Deposit or the balance thereof after any deductions properly made

6. The Landlord hereby notifies the Tenant under Section 48 of the Landlord & Tenant Act 1987 that any notices (including notices in proceedings) should be served upon the Landlord at the address stated with the name of the Landlord overleaf

7. In the event of damage to or destruction of the Property by any of the risks insured against by the Landlord the Tenant shall be relieved from payment of the Rent to the extent that the Tenant's use and enjoyment of the Property is thereby prevented and from performance of its obligations as to the state and condition of the Property to the extent of and so long as there prevails such damage or destruction (except to the extent that the insurance is prejudiced by any act or default of the Tenant)

8. So long as the reference to a right of early termination in the definition of the "TERM" overleaf (the "early termination right") has not been deleted then either party may at any time during the Term terminate this Agreement by giving to the other prior written notice to that effect, the length of such notice to be that stated in the early termination right, and upon the expiry of such notice this Agreement shall end with no further liability for either party save for any antecedent breach

9. Where the context so admits:

9.1 The "Landlord" includes the persons for the time being entitled to the reversion expectant upon this Tenancy

9.2 The "Tenant" includes any persons deriving title under the Tenant

9.3 The "Property" includes all of the Landlord's fixtures and fittings at or upon the Property

9.4 The "Term" shall mean the period stated in the particulars overleaf or any shorter or longer period in the event of an earlier termination or an extension or holding over respectively

10. All references to the singular shall include the plural and vice versa and any obligations or liabilities of more than one person shall be joint and several and an obligation on the part of a party shall include an obligation not to allow or permit the breach of that obligation

EMPLOYEE NON-COMPETITION AGREEMENT

THIS AGREEMENT IS MADE the _____ day of _____ 19_____

BETWEEN:

(1) _____ (the "Company"); and

(2) _____ (the "Employee").

NOW IT IS HEREBY AGREED as follows:

In consideration for the employment of the Employee by the Company the parties agree as follows:

1.   The Employee hereby agrees not directly or indirectly to compete with the business of the Company and its successors and assigns during the period of employment and for a period of _____ years following termination of employment and notwithstanding the cause or reason for termination or redundancy.

2.   The term "not compete" as used herein shall mean that the Employee shall not own, manage, operate, act as consultant to or be employed in a business substantially similar to or in competition with the present business of the Company or such other business activity in which the Company may substantially engage during the term of employment.

3.   The Employee acknowledges that the Company shall or may in reliance of this agreement allow the Employee access to trade secrets, customers and other confidential data and that the provisions of this agreement are reasonably necessary to protect the Company and its goodwill. The Employee agrees to retain this information as confidential and not to use the information on his or her own behalf or disclose the same to any third party.

4.   This agreement shall be binding upon and inure to the benefit of the parties, their successors and assigns.

IN WITNESS OF WHICH the parties have signed this agreement the day and year first above written

_____   Signed for and on behalf of the Company
Signed by the Employee

_____   _____
in the presence of (witness)   Director

Name

Address   _____
                                          Director/Secretary

_____
Occupation

EMPLOYEE NON-DISCLOSURE AGREEMENT

THIS AGREEMENT IS MADE the _____ day of _____ 19_____

BETWEEN:

(1) _____ (the "Company"); and

(2) _____ (the "Employee").

NOW IT IS HEREBY AGREED as follows:

In consideration for the employment of the Employee by the Company the parties agree as follows:

1.   That during the course of my employment there may be disclosed to me certain trade secrets of the Company consisting of but not necessarily limited to:

   a)   Technical information: methods, processes, formulae, compositions, systems, techniques, inventions, machines, computer programmes and research projects.

   b)   Business information: customer lists, pricing data, sources of supply, financial data and marketing, production, or merchandising systems or plans.

2.   I agree that I shall not during, or at any time after the termination of my employment with the Company, use for myself or others, or disclose or divulge to others including future employers, any trade secrets, confidential information, or any other proprietary data of the Company in violation of this agreement.

3.   That upon the termination of my employment by the Company:

a)   I shall return to the Company all documents and property of the Company, including but not necessarily limited to: drawings, blueprints, reports, manuals, correspondence, customer lists, computer programmes, and all other materials and all copies thereof relating in any way to the Company's business, or in any way obtained by me during the course of my employment. I further agree that I shall not retain any copies, notes or abstracts of the foregoing.

b)   The Company may notify any future or prospective employer or third party of the existence of this agreement, and shall be entitled to full injunctive relief for any breach.

4.   This agreement shall be binding upon me and my personal representatives and successors in interest, and shall inure to the benefit of the Company, its successors and assigns.

IN WITNESS OF WHICH the parties have signed this agreement the day and year first above written

_____   _____
Signed by the Employee   Signed for and on behalf of the Company

_____   _____
in the presence of (witness)   in the presence of (witness)

Name _____   Name _____

Address _____   Address _____

_____   _____
Occupation   Occupation

EMPLOYEE SUSPENSION NOTICE

Date _____

To _____

_____

_____

You have received informal notices that your conduct has been found to be unsatisfactory. On _____ 19 _____ a formal Warning Notice was placed on your permanent employment record. Your unacceptable conduct has continued; in particular you have:

_____

_____

_____

You are herewith suspended from work for a period of _____ commencing _____ 19 _____. Suspension shall be without pay; however, your health and pension benefits shall continue during the suspension providing you return to work immediately following the suspension period.

YOU MAY BE SUBJECT TO DISMISSAL IN THE FUTURE IF YOU CONTINUE TO VIOLATE COMPANY POLICY.

_____

Company Representative

ACKNOWLEDGED

Date _____

_____

Employee

EMPLOYEE WARNING

Date _____

To _____

_____

_____

_____

You are hereby warned that your work performance is unsatisfactory for the following reasons:

_____

_____

_____

_____

_____

_____

We expect immediate correction of the problem otherwise we shall have no alternative but to consider termination of your employment.

If there is any question about this notice or if we can help you improve your performance or correct the difficulties, then please discuss this matter with your supervisor at the earliest possible opportunity.

_____
Company Representative

EMPLOYEE'S COVENANTS

_____ (the "Employee"), of

_____ (address) and employed

by or about to be employed by _____(the "Company"),

hereby makes these covenants to the Company in consideration for the Company:

_____ hiring the Employee in the position of _____

_____ continuing to employ the Employee, with the following change in the nature of the

employment:_____

Covenant 1

Employee's Covenants

During the term of employment and for one (1) year after termination, the Employee agrees not to engage in the following:

1. Promoting or engaging in indirectly or directly, as an employee, principal, partner, contractor, associate, agent, manager or otherwise, or by means of any entity, any business in the same or similar business as the Company or its affiliates within the following geographic area:

_____

_____

_____

2. Soliciting the Company's customers, employees, staff, subcontractors, or prospects with services or products of a similar nature to those being sold by the Company or affiliates of the Company.

3. The Employee agrees that the Company and its affiliates hold certain trade, business, and financial secrets in connection with the business. The Employee covenants to not divulge to any party at any time, directly or indirectly, during the term of this Agreement or afterwards, unless directed by the Board of Directors, any information acquired by the Employee about the Company or its affiliates, including, but not limited to, customer lists, trade secrets, documents, financial statements, correspondence, patents, processes, formulas, research, intellectual property, expenses, costs or other confidential information of any kind, or any other data that could be used by third parties to the disadvantage of the Company. This paragraph shall survive the term of employment.

Covenant 2

Company Rights on Breach

If the Employee breaches this covenant, the Company shall have the right, in addition to all other rights available hereunder and by law, to prevent the Employee from continuing such breach. The Employee confirms the he/she has had the opportunity to discuss and negotiate this Covenant fully and confirm his/her understanding and acceptance of it. If any part of this Covenant is declared invalid, then the Employee agrees to be bound by a Covenant as near to the original as lawfully possible. This paragraph shall survive the term and termination of employment. The Employee shall further be liable for all costs of enforcement.

Covenant 3

Additional Governing Terms

No waiver of a right by the Company constitutes a waiver of any other right of the Company, and a temporary waiver by the Company does not constitute a permanent waiver or any additional temporary waiver. These Covenants may be modified only in writing and signed by the Employee and the Company. If any portion of these Covenants is declared invalid, these Covenants shall continue in effect as if the invalid portion had never been part hereof.

_____   _____

Signed by the Employee   Date

_____   _____

Signed for and on behalf of the Company   Date

EMPLOYER'S REQUEST FOR REFERENCE

Date _____

Ref _____

To _____

_____

_____

Dear _____

Re _____

The above-named candidate has applied for a position within our company and has given your name as a previous employee reference. The information requested below will help us evaluate the candidate. We will consider your comments in strict confidence. Please fill in the details below and return this letter in the envelope provided. Thank you for your cooperation.

Yours sincerely

_____

Personnel Department

Please indicate:

    Position within your firm:_____

    Employed from _____ to _____

    Salary £_____

Please rate the applicant on the basis of his/her employment with you (good/ fair/poor):

    Ability_____ Conduct_____ Attitude _____

    Efficiency _____ Attendance_____ Punctuality_____

    What was the reason for dismissal or redundancy?_____

    _____

    Would you re-employ him/her? _____. If not, please give reason: _____

    _____

_____

Signature and Title

EMPLOYMENT CONFIRMATION

Date _____

To _____

_____

_____

Dear _____

I would like to welcome you to our company as _____.

This position is important to our organisation and we look forward to your contribution of experience and expertise.

Your first day of employment is _____. Your salary will be £_____

per _____. After completing a 90-day probationary period, you will be eligible to participate in our medical and life insurance benefits. Long-term disability and family coverage under our medical plan is also available at your cost.

We are pleased to have you on board. Best wishes for success in your new position.

Yours sincerely

_____

Personnel Manager

EMPLOYMENT CONTRACT

THIS AGREEMENT IS MADE the _____ day

of _____ 199 ___

BETWEEN **(1)** _____ of _____

_____ (the "Employer");

and

(2) _____ of _____

_____ (the "Contractor").

This document sets out the terms and conditions of employment which are required to be given to the Employee under section 1 Employment Rights Act 1996 and which apply at the date hereof.

1. COMMENCEMENT AND JOB TITLE. The Employer agrees to employ the Employee from _____ 199___ in the capacity of at _____.

    [No employment with a previous employer will be counted as part of the Employee's period of continuous employment][The employment under this Agreement forms part of a continuous period of employment which began on _____]. The Employee's duties may from time to time be reasonably modified as necessary to meet the needs of the Employer's business.

2. SALARY. The Employer shall pay the Employee a salary of £ per year by equal [weekly] [monthly] instalments in arrears.

3. HOURS OF EMPLOYMENT. The Employee's normal hours of employment shall be _____ to _____ on Mondays to Fridays [and _____ to _____ on Saturdays] during which time the Employee may take up to one hour for lunch between the hours of 12pm and 2pm, and the Employee may from time to time be required to work such additional hours as is reasonable to meet the requirements of the Employer's business [at no additional payment] [at an overtime rate of £ _____ per hour].

4. HOLIDAYS. The Employee shall be entitled to _____ days holiday per calendar year at full pay in addition to the normal public holidays. Holidays must be taken at a time that is convenient to the Employer and no more than _____ weeks' holiday may be taken at any one time.

5. SICKNESS. The Employee shall be paid normal remuneration during sickness absence for a maximum of _____ weeks in any period of twelve months provided that the Employee provides the Employer with a medical certificate in the case of absence of more than seven consecutive days. Such remuneration will be less the amount of any Statutory Sick Pay or Social Security sickness benefits to which the Employee may be entitled.

6. COLLECTIVE AGREEMENTS. [There are no collective agreements in force directly relating to the terms of your employment] [The terms of the collective agreement dated _____ made between_____ and _____ shall deemed to be included in this Agreement].

7. PENSION. [There is no pension scheme applicable to the Employee] [The Employee shall be entitled to join the Employer's pension scheme the details of which are set out in the Employer's booklet/leaflet entitled _____ which is available on request]. A contracting-out certificate under the Social Security Pensions Act 1995 [is][is not] in force in respect of this employment.

8. TERMINATION. The Employer may terminate this Agreement by giving written notice to the Employee as follows:

   (a) with not less than one week's notice during the first two years of continuous employment;

   (b) with not less than one week's notice for each full year of continuous employment after the first two years until the twelfth year of continuous employment; and

   (c) with not less than twelve weeks' notice after twelve years of continuous employment.

   The Employer may terminate this Agreement without notice or payment in lieu of notice in the case of serious or persistent misconduct such as to cause a major breach of the Employer's disciplinary rules.

   The Employee may terminate this Agreement by one week's written notice to the Employer.

9. CONFIDENTIALITY. The Employee is aware that during his employment he may be party to confidential information concerning the Employer and the Employer's business. The Employee shall not during the term of this employment disclose or allow the disclosure of any confidential information (except in the proper course of his employment). After the termination of this Agreement the Employee shall not disclose or use any of the Employer's trade secrets or any other information which is of a sufficiently high degree of confidentiality to amount to a trade secret. The Employer shall be entitled to apply for an injunction to prevent such disclosure or use and to seek any other remedy including without limitation the recovery of damages in the case of such disclosure or use.

10. NON-COMPETITION. For a period of [_____ months] [_____year(s)] after the termination of this Agreement the Employee shall not solicit or seek business from any customers or clients of the Employer who were customers or clients of the Employer at any time during the _____ years immediately preceding the termination of this Agreement.

11. DISCIPLINE AND GRIEVANCE. The Employer's disciplinary rules and the grievance _ and appeal procedure in connection with these rules are set out in the Employer's booklet entitled _____ which is attached hereto.

12. NOTICES. All communications including notices required to be given under this Agreement shall be in writing and shall be sent either by personal service or first class post to the Parties' respective addresses.

13. SEVERABILITY. If any provision of this Agreement should be held to be invalid it shall to that extent be severed and the remaining provisions shall continue to have full force and effect.

14. ENTIRE AGREEMENT. This Agreement contains the entire Agreement between the Parties and supersedes all prior arrangements and understandings whether written or oral with respect to the subject matter hereof and may not be varied except in writing signed by both the Parties hereto.

15. GOVERNING LAW. This Agreement shall be construed in accordance with the laws of England and Wales and shall be subject to the exclusive jurisdiction of the English courts.

IN WITNESS OF WHICH the parties hereto have signed this Agreement the day and year first above written.

SIGNED _____   _____

              Signed by or on behalf of the Employer   in the presence of (witness)

                                               Name _____

                                               Address _____

                                               _____

              DATED _____   Occupation _____

SIGNED _____   _____

              Signed by the Employee   in the presence of (witness)

                                               Name _____

                                               Address _____

                                               _____

              DATED _____   Occupation _____

Enduring Power of Attorney

Part A: About using this form

1. **You may choose one attorney or more than one.** If you choose one attorney then you must delete everything between the square brackets on the first page of the form. If you choose more than one, you must decide whether they are able to act:

   - Jointly (that is, they must all act together and cannot act separately) or
   - Jointly and severally (that is, they can all act together but they can also act separately if they wish).

   On the first page of the form, show what you have decided by crossing out one of the alternatives.

2. **If you give your attorney(s) general power** in relation to all your property and affairs, it means that they will be able to deal with your money or property and may be able to sell your house.

3. **If you don't want your attorney(s) to have such wide powers,** you can include any restrictions you like. For example, you can include a restriction that your attorney(s) must not act on your behalf until they have reason to believe that you are becoming mentally incapable; or a restriction as to what your attorney(s) may do. Any restrictions you choose must be written or typed where indicated on the second page of the form.

4. **If you are a trustee** (and please remember that co-ownership of a home involves trusteeship), you should seek legal advice if you want your attorney(s) to act as a trustee on your behalf.

5. **Unless you put in a restriction preventing it** your attorney(s) will be able to use any of your money or property to make any provision which you yourself might be expected to make for their own needs or the needs of other people. Your attorney(s) will also be able to use your money to make gifts, but only for reasonable amounts in relation to the value of your money and property.

6. **Your attorney(s) can recover the out-of-pocket expenses** of acting as your attorney(s). If your attorney(s) are professional people, for example solicitors or accountants, they may be able to charge for their professional services as well. You may wish to provide expressly for remuneration of your attorney(s) (although if they are trustees they may not be allowed to accept it).

7. **If your attorney(s) have reason to believe** that you have become or are becoming mentally incapable of managing your affairs, your attorney(s) will have to apply to the Court of Protection for registration of this power.

8. **Before applying to the Court of Protection for registration** of this power, your attorney(s) must give written notice that that is what they are going to do, to you and your nearest relatives as defined in the Enduring Powers of Attorney Act 1985. You or your relatives will be able to object if you or they disagree with registration.

9. **This is a simplified explanation** of what the Enduring Powers of Attorney Act 1985 and the Rules and Regulations say. If you need more guidance, you or your advisers will need to look at the Act itself and the Rules and Regulations. The Rules are the Court of Protection (Enduring Powers of Attorney) Rules 1986 (Statutory Instrument 1986 No. 127). The Regulations are the Enduring Powers of Attorney (Prescribed Form) Regulations 1990 (Statutory Instrument 1990 No. 1376).

10. **Note to Attorney(s)**
    After the power has been registered you should notify the Court of Protection if the donor dies or recovers.

11. **Note to Donor**
    Some of these explanatory notes may not apply to the form you are using if it has already been adapted to suit your particular requirements.

YOU CAN CANCEL THIS POWER AT ANY TIME BEFORE IT HAS TO BE REGISTERED

Part B: To be completed by the 'donor' (the person appointing the attorney(s))
Don't sign this form unless you understand what it means

Please read the notes in the margin which follow and which are part of the form itself.

Donor's name and address.

I

of

Donor's date of birth.

born on

See note 1 on the front of this form. If you are appointing only one attorney you should cross out everything between the square brackets. If appointing more than two attorneys please give the additional name(s) on an attached sheet.

appoint

of

● [and

   of

Cross out the one which does not apply (see note 1 on the front of this form).

Cross out the one which does not apply (see note 2 on the front of this form). Add any additional powers.

If you don't want the attorney(s) to have general power, you must give details here of what authority you are giving the attorney(s).

● jointly
● jointly and severally]
to be my attorney(s) for the purpose of the Enduring Powers of Attorney Act 1985
● with general authority to act on my behalf
● with authority to do the following on my behalf:

in relation to

Cross out the one which does not apply.

● all my property and affairs
● the following property and affairs:

Part B: continued

Please read the notes in the margin which follow and which are part of the form itself.

If there are restrictions or conditions, insert them here; if not, cross out these words if you wish (see note 3 on the front of this form).

● subject to the following restrictions and conditions:

If this form is being signed at your direction: —
● the person signing must not be an attorney or any witness (to Parts B or C);
● you must add a statement that this form has been signed at your direction;
● a second witness is necessary (please see below).

I intend that this power shall continue even if I become mentally incapable.

I have read or have had read to me the notes in Part A which are part of, and explain, this form.

Your signature (or mark).

Signed by me as a deed and delivered

Date.

on

Someone must witness your signature.

Signature of witness.

in the presence of

Your attorney(s) cannot be your witness. It is not advisable for your husband or wife to be your witness.

Full name of witness

Address of witness

A second witness is only necessary if this form is not being signed by you personally but at your direction (for example, if a physical disability prevents you from signing).

in the presence of

Full name of witness

Address of witness

Signature of second witness.

Part C: To be completed by the attorney(s)

Note 1. This form may be adapted to provide for execution by a corporation.

2. If there is more than one attorney additional sheets in the form as shown below must be added to this Part C.

Please read the notes in the margin which follow and which are part of the form itself.

Don't sign this form before the donor has signed Part B or if, in your opinion, the donor was already mentally incapable at the time of signing Part B.

If this form is being signed at your direction: —
- the person signing must not be an attorney or any witness (to Parts B or C);
- you must add a statement that this form has been signed at your direction;
- a second witness is necessary (please see below).

Signature (or mark) of attorney.

Date.

Signature of witness.

The attorney must sign the form and his signature must be witnessed. The donor may not be the witness and one attorney may not witness the signature of the other.

I understand that I have a duty to apply to the Court for the registration of this form under the Enduring Powers of Attorney Act 1985 when the donor is becoming or has become mentally incapable.

I also understand my limited power to use the donor's property to benefit persons other than the donor.

I am not a minor

Signed by me as a deed and delivered

on

in the presence of

Full name of witness

Address of witness

A second witness is only necessary if this form is not being signed by you personally but at your direction (for example, if a physical disability prevents you from signing).

Signature of second witness.

in the presence of

Full name of witness

Address of witness

Court of Protection

No._____

Enduring Powers of Attorney Act 1985

Application for registration

Note. Give the full name(s) of the attorney(s).

The attorney(s)

Name(s)_____

_____

age_____ occupation _____

age_____ occupation _____

address(es)_____

_____

_____

Note. Give the full name and present address of the donor. If the donor's address on the enduring power of attorney is different give that one too.

The donor

Name _____

Address _____

_____

_____

I (we) the attorney(s) apply to register the enduring power of attorney

made by the donor under the above Act on

the_____ 19 _____

I (we) have reason to believe that the donor is or is becoming

mentally incapable

I (we) have given notice in the prescribed form to the following:

• the donor personally at _____

_____

on the_____ 19 _____

- The following relatives of the donor at the address(es) below on the dates given:

Name	Relationship	Address	Date

Note. Cross out this section if it does not apply

- The Co-Attorney _____

at _____

on _____

The Enduring Power of Attorney accompanies this application

Note. The application should be signed by all the attorneys who are making the application.

I (we) certify that the above information is correct and that to the best of my (our) knowledge and belief I (we) have complied with the provisions of the Enduring Powers of Attorney Act 1985 and of all the Rules and Regulations under it.

Signed _____

Signed _____

Dated _____

Address where notice should be sent _____

_____

_____

Court of Protection

No._____

Enduring Powers of Attorney Act 1985

In the matter of a power given by

_____**a donor**

to_____**attorney(s)**

General form of application

I (we)_____

of _____

_____

Note. Give details of the order that you are asking the court to make.

Apply for an order that_____

_____

_____

_____

_____

and for any directions which are necessary as a result of my/our application.

Note. Give details of the grounds on which you are asking the court to make the order.

The grounds on which I/we make this application are:

_____

_____

_____

_____

_____

Note. The application should be signed by all the applicants or their solicitors.

Signed _____

Dated _____

Address where notices should be sent _____

_____

_____

The Court of Protection, Stewart House, 24 Kingsway, London WC2B 6JX

Court of Protection
Enduring Powers of Attorney Act 1985

Notice of intention to apply for registration

TAKE NOTICE THAT

I (We) _____

_____

of _____

_____

the attorney(s) of _____

_____

of _____

_____

intend to apply to the Court of Protection for registration of the enduring

power of attorney appointing me (us) attorney(s) and made

by the donor on the _____ 19 _____

    1. You have 4 weeks from the day on which this notice is given to

you to object in writing to the proposed registration of the power of

attorney. Objections should be sent to the Court of Protection

and should contain the following details:

- your name and address;

- any relationship to the donor;

- if you are not the donor, the name and address of the donor;

- the name and address of the attorney;

- the grounds for objecting to the registration of the enduring power.

Note. The instrument means the enduring power of attorney made by the donor which it is sought to register.

2. The grounds on which you may object are:

- that the power purported to have been created by the instrument is not valid as an enduring power of attorney;

- that the power created by the instrument no longer subsists;

- that the application is premature because the donor is not yet becoming mentally incapable;

- that fraud or undue pressure was used to induce the donor to make the power;

- that the attorney is unsuitable to be the donor's attorney (having regard to all the circumstances and in particular the attorney's relationship to or connection with the donor).

Note. Cross this part out if the notice is not addressed to the donor.

3. You are informed that while the enduring power of attorney remains registered, you will not be able to revoke it until the Court of Protection confirms the revocation.

Note. The notice should be signed by all the attorneys who are applying to register the enduring power of attorney.

Signed ....

Signed ....

Dated ....

ENQUIRY ON OVERDUE ACCOUNT

Date _____

To _____

_____

_____

Dear _____

We have not received payment on your overdue account, and would appreciate it if you could offer your explanation by completing this form. Please tick the applicable reason, fill in the details and return this form to us.

_____ We need copies of unpaid invoices:_____

_____ We have credits outstanding:_____

_____ Payment was sent on _____ 19____.

_____ Payment will be sent on _____ 19____.

_____ Other: _____

Thank you for your kind attention.

Yours sincerely

_____

EQUAL OPPORTUNITIES POLICY
at _____ Limited

The Company's aim is to ensure that all of its employees and job applicants are treated equally irrespective of disability, race, colour, religion, nationality, ethnic origin, age, sex or marital status. This policy sets out instructions that all employees are required to follow in order to ensure that this is achieved.

Policy

1. There shall be no discrimination on account of disability, race, colour, religion, nationality, ethnic origin, age, sex or marital status.

2. The Company shall appoint, train, develop and promote on the basis of merit and ability.

3. Employees have personal responsibility for the practical application of the Company's Equal Opportunity Policy, which extends to the treatment of members of the public and employees.

4. Managers and supervisors who are involved in the recruitment, selection, promotion and training of employees have special responsibility for the practical application of the Company's Equal Opportunity Policy.

5. The Grievance Procedure is available to any employee who believes that he or she may have been unfairly discriminated against.

6. Disciplinary action under the Disciplinary Procedure shall be taken against any employee who is found to have committed an act of unlawful discrimination. Discriminatory conduct and sexual or racial harassment shall be regarded as gross misconduct.

7. If there is any doubt about appropriate treatment under the Company's Equal Opportunities Policy, employees should consult the Personnel Manager.

EXERCISE OF OPTION

Date _____

To _____

_____

_____

Dear _____

You are hereby notified that I have elected to and hereby exercise and accept the option dated _____ 19 _____, executed by you in my favour. I agree to all terms, conditions, and provisions of the option.

Yours sincerely

_____
Signed

Name _____

Address _____

_____

_____

EXPENSES RECORD

Name: _____ Department: _____

Trip Purpose: _____ From: _____ to _____

Please attach receipts before submitting for reimbursement.

Date: _____ Total £ _____

	Expense		Place
	£	p	
Airfare			
Trainfare			
Car Rental			
Fuel			
Taxi			
Breakfast			
Lunch			
Dinner			
Hotel			
Telephone			
Other			
Total £			
Amount Advanced £			
Net Due £			

_____   _____
Signed   Approved By

Dept _____   Title _____

Date _____   Date _____

EXTENSION OF OPTION TO PURCHASE PROPERTY

THIS AGREEMENT IS MADE the _____ day of _____ 19_____

BETWEEN:

(1) _____ (the "Grantor"); and

(2) _____ (the "Holder").

WHEREAS:

(A) The Grantor, as the owner of property located at _____
_____ (the "Property") granted an option to buy the
Property to the Holder on _____ 19_____ (the "Option"), which expires
on _____ 19_____.

(B) The Holder wished to extend the term of the Option.

NOW IT IS HEREBY AGREED as follows:

1.   In consideration for the payment to Grantor by Holder of the sum of _____
_____Pounds (£_____), the receipt of which is
hereby acknowledged, the Option will be extended and terminate and expire at _____ on
_____19____.

2.   The extension of the Option upon the payment as set forth above shall be an extension of
the expiration of the Option only and all other terms and conditions in the Option shall
remain in force and effect.

3.   If the Holder exercises the Option before the expiration of the further term herein granted
the payment for the Option and the payment for extension of the expiration of the Option
shall be applied towards the purchase price of the Property and the Holder shall receive a
credit on completion equal to the amount(s) paid for the Option and any extension.

4.   If the Holder fails to exercise the Option before the expiration of the further term herein
agreed the Grantor shall be entitled to return absolutely all payment made by the Holder to
the Grantor for the Option and the extension granted herein.

IN WITNESS OF WHICH the parties have signed this Agreement the day and year first above
written

_____   _____
Signed by or on behalf of the Grantor   Signed by or on behalf of the Holder

_____   _____
in the presence of (witness)   in the presence of (witness)

Name _____   Name _____

Address _____   Address _____

_____   _____
Occupation   Occupation

FAMILY TREE

Name: _____

Father:_____ Mother: _____

Father's _____ **Mother's** _____

Father:_____ Father: _____

Mother: _____ Mother: _____

Father's Paternal _____ **Mother's Paternal**

Grandfather: _____ Grandfather:_____

Grandmother: _____ Grandmother:_____

Father's Maternal_____ **Mother's Maternal**

Grandfather: _____ Grandfather:_____

Grandmother: _____ Grandmother:_____

Paternal Side: Father's Siblings: _____

_____

Your Paternal Cousins: _____

_____

Your Grandfather's Siblings: _____

_____

Your Grandmother's Siblings: _____

_____

Maternal Side: Mother's Siblings: _____

_____

Your Maternal Cousins:_____

_____

Your Grandfather's Siblings: _____

_____

Your Grandmother's Siblings: _____

_____

117

FINAL NOTICE BEFORE LEGAL PROCEEDINGS

Date _____

To _____

_____

_____

Dear _____

We have repeatedly requested payment of your long overdue account in the amount of £ _____.

Unless we receive payment in full of this amount within seven days of the date of this letter we shall have no alternative but to refer your account to our solicitors for recovery. This will result in you being liable for further costs.

Yours sincerely

_____

FINAL WARNING BEFORE DISMISSAL

Date _____

To _____

_____

_____

Dear _____

You have already been warned about your conduct within this Company. Incidents that have since come to our notice are:

_____

_____

_____

_____

There has not been a satisfactory improvement in your performance since your last warning. Accordingly, any continued violations of company policy or failure to conduct yourself according to the rules of the company shall result in immediate termination of your employment without further warning.

We remind you that you have the right of appeal against this warning according to the Terms and Conditions of Employment as supplied to you.

Please contact the undersigned or your supervisor if you have any questions.

Yours sincerely

_____

FINAL WARNING FOR LATENESS

Date _____

To _____

_____

_____

Dear _____

Despite our verbal and written warnings to you about your timekeeping, there has been no improvement and you have given no satisfactory explanation as to why you continue to be late for work.

Your behaviour is unacceptable. We therefore give you this final warning. If you are late again without offering a reasonable excuse, you will be dismissed.

We remind you that you have the right of appeal against this warning according to the Statement of Terms and Conditions of Employment as supplied to you.

Please contact the undersigned or your superior if you have any questions.

Yours sincerely

_____

FIRST WARNING FOR LATENESS

Date _____

To _____

_____

_____

Dear _____

You are aware that your hours of work are from _____ a.m. to _____ p.m. You have repeatedly arrived for work late.

You have been advised of your bad timekeeping and warned of the possible consequences. Despite those warnings you continue to be late for work and have offered no reasonable excuse.

Consider this a formal letter of warning. You must be at your place of work strictly in accordance with the terms of your employment and the hours set. If you are late again without reasonable excuse, disciplinary action will be taken.

This warning is being recorded on your personnel file.

Yours sincerely

_____

FORM OF LETTER TO EXECUTOR

Dear _____

I am writing to confirm that I have named you as an executor of my Will dated _____ 19 _____ .

- A copy of my Will is enclosed.*

- My signed original Will has been lodged with _____ .

- I have named _____ as a co-executor.

- My solicitor is _____ at _____ .*

Please confirm to me in writing that you are willing to act as one of my executors.

Yours sincerely

_____

* delete as necessary

WARNING: DO NOT INCLUDE ANY OTHER INSTRUCTIONS TO YOUR EXECUTORS IN THIS LETTER

FORM OF RESOLUTION FOR SUBMISSION
TO COMPANIES HOUSE

_____ Limited

Company Number _____

The Companies Act 1985

Ordinary/Special/Extraordinary/Elective resolution of

_____ Limited/Public Limited Company

At an extraordinary general meeting of the above named company, duly convened and held at

_____ on the _____ day of _____ 199 _____ the

following was duly passed as an ordinary/special/extraordinary/elective resolution:

_____

_____

_____

_____

_____

_____

_____
Signature of Chairman

Note: File this notice at Companies House

FUNERAL WISHES

OF

_____
(NAME)

**FUNERAL
(BURIAL/CREMATION)**
_____

_____

UNDERTAKER
_____

_____

**PLACE OF
SERVICE**
_____

_____

**TYPE OF
SERVICE**
_____

_____

**PERSON
OFFICIATING**
_____

_____

**MUSIC
SELECTION**
_____

_____

**READING
SELECTION**
_____

_____

FLOWERS
_____

_____

**SPECIAL
INSTRUCTIONS**
_____

_____

_____

_____

GENERAL ASSIGNMENT

THIS AGREEMENT IS MADE the _____ day of _____ 19 _____

BETWEEN

(1) _____ (the "Assignor");and

(2) _____ (the "Assignee").

NOW IT IS HEREBY AGREED as follows:

1. In consideration for the payment of £_____, receipt of which the Assignor hereby acknowledges, the Assignor hereby unconditionally and irrevocably assigns and transfers to the Assignee all right, title and interest in the following:

_____

_____

_____

2. The Assignor fully warrants that it has full rights and authority to enter into this assignment and that the rights and benefits assigned hereunder are free and clear of any lien, encumbrance, adverse claim or interest by any third party.

3. This assignment shall be binding upon and inure to the benefit of the parties, and their successors and assigns.

IN WITNESS OF WHICH the parties have signed this agreement the day and year first above written

_____   _____
Signed by or on behalf of the Employee   Signed by or on behalf of the Employer

_____   _____
in the presence of (witness)   in the presence of (witness)

Name   Name

Address   Address

_____   _____
Occupation   Occupation

GENERAL POWER OF ATTORNEY
(Pursuant to the Powers of Attorney Act 1971, section 10)

THIS GENERAL POWER OF ATTORNEY is made

this_____ day of _____ 19____

BY   _____

      OF   _____

              _____

I APPOINT

      _____

      _____

[jointly][jointly and severally] to be my attorney(s) in accordance with section 10 of the Powers of Attorney Act 1971.

IN WITNESS whereof I have hereunto set my hand the day and year first above written.

SIGNED as a Deed and Delivered by the

      said_____

      in the presence of _____

GENERAL PROXY

_____ **LIMITED**

I/We _____ of _____, a member/members
of the above company, hereby appoint _____ of _____
_____, as a proxy to vote in my/our name(s) and on my/our behalf at
the annual/extraordinary general meeting of the company to be held at _____
_____ on _____ 199__ and at any adjournment thereof.

_____
Shareholder

_____
Shareholder

Date _____

GENERAL RELEASE

THIS DEED IS MADE the _____ day of _____ 19 _____

BETWEEN

(1) _____ (the "First Party");and

(2) _____ (the "Second Party").

NOW IT IS HEREBY AGREED as follows:

1.   The First Party forever releases, discharges, acquits and forgives the Second Party from any and all claims, actions, suits, demands, agreements, liabilities, judgment, and proceedings arising from the beginning of time to the date of these presents and as more particularly related to or arising from:

_____

_____

_____

_____

2.   This release shall be binding upon and inure to the benefit of the parties, their successors and assigns.

IN WITNESS OF WHICH the parties have executed this deed the date and year first above written

(Individual)   (Company)

_____   Signed for and on behalf of
Signed by the First Party
                                                       _____ Ltd
_____
in the presence of (witness)
Name   _____
_____   Director
Address
_____   _____
Occupation   Director/Secretary

_____   Signed for and on behalf of
Signed by the Second Party
                                                       _____ Ltd
_____
in the presence of (witness)
Name   _____
_____   Director
Address
_____   _____
Occupation   Director/Secretary

GENERAL SUBORDINATION

THIS DEED IS MADE the _____ day of _____ 19 _____

BETWEEN

(1) _____ (the "First Creditor");and

(2) _____ (the "Second Creditor").

WHEREAS:

(A) The First Creditor has a claim against _____ (the "Debtor") for monies owed to the First Creditor by the Debtor.

(B) The Second Creditor also has a claim against the Debtor for monies owed to the Second Creditor by the Debtor.

(C) The Parties agree that the Second Creditor's debt be subordinated to that of the First Creditor.

NOW THIS DEED WITNESSES as follows:

1.   The Second Creditor hereby agrees to subordinate its claims for debts now or hereinafter due to the undersigned from the Debtor to any and all debts that may now or hereinafter be due to the First Creditor from the Debtor.

2.   This subordination shall be unlimited as to amount or duration and shall include the subordination of any secured or unsecured obligation.

3.   This subordination agreement shall be binding upon and inure to the benefit of the parties, their successors and assigns.

IN WITNESS OF WHICH the parties have executed this Deed the day and year first above written

(Individual)   (Company)

                                                      Signed for and on behalf of
_____
Signed by the First Creditor
                                                      _____ Ltd
_____
in the presence of (witness)
Name _____   _____
Address _____   Director

_____   _____
Occupation   Director/Secretary

                                                      Signed for and on behalf of
_____
Signed by the Second Creditor
                                                      _____ Ltd
_____
in the presence of (witness)
Name _____   _____
Address _____   Director

_____   _____
Occupation   Director/Secretary

GRIEVANCE PROCEDURE
at _____ Limited

1. The following procedure shall be applied to settle all disputes or grievances concerning an employee or employees of the Company (but excluding those relating to redundancy selection).

2. Principles:

    (i)   It is the intention of both parties that employees should be encouraged to have direct contact with management to resolve their problems.

    (ii)   The procedure for resolution of grievances and avoidance of disputes is available if the parties are unable to agree a solution to a problem.

    (iii) Should a matter be referred to this procedure for resolution, both parties should accept that it should be progressed as speedily as possible, with a joint commitment that every effort will be made to ensure that such a reference takes no longer than seven working days to complete.

    (iv)   Pending resolution of the grievance, the same conditions prior to its notification shall continue to apply, except in those circumstances where such a continuation would have damaging effects upon the Company's business.

    (v)   It is agreed between the parties that where the grievance is of a collective nature, i.e. affecting more than one employee, it shall be referred initially to (ii) of the procedure.

    (vi)   If the employee's immediate supervisor/manager is the subject of the grievance and for this reason the employee does not wish the grievance to be heard by him or her, it shall be referred initially to (ii) of the procedure.

3. The Procedure:

    (i)   Where an employee has a grievance, he shall raise the matter with his or her immediate supervisor/manager.

    (ii)   If the matter has not been resolved at (i), it shall be referred to a more senior manager or director and the shop steward, full time trade union officer, or fellow employee, if requested shall be present. A statement summarising the main details of the grievance and the reasons for the failure to agree must be prepared and signed by both parties.

    (iii) In the event of a failure to agree, the parties will consider whether conciliation or arbitration is appropriate. The Company may refer the dispute to the Advisory Conciliation and Arbitration Service, whose findings may, by mutual prior agreement, be binding on both parties.

GUARANTEE

THIS AGREEMENT IS MADE the _____ day of _____ 19 _____

BETWEEN

(1) _____ (the "Guarantor");and

(2) _____ (the "Creditor").

NOW IT IS HEREBY AGREED as follows:

1. As an inducement for the Creditor, from time to time extend credit to _____ _____ (the "Customer"), it is hereby agreed that the Guarantor does hereby guarantee to the Creditor the prompt, punctual and full payment of all monies now or hereinafter due to the Creditor from the Customer.

2. Until termination, this guarantee is unlimited as to amount or duration and shall remain in full force and effect notwithstanding any extension, compromise, adjustment, forbearance, waiver, release or discharge of any party or guarantor, or release in whole or in part of any security granted for the said indebtedness or compromise or adjustment thereto, and the Guarantor waives all notices thereto.

3. The obligations of the Guarantor shall at the election of the Creditor be primary and not necessarily secondary and the Creditor shall not be required to exhaust its remedies as against the Customer prior to enforcing its rights under this guarantee against the Guarantor.

4. The guarantee hereunder shall be unconditional and absolute and the Guarantor waives all rights of subrogation and set-off until all sums due under this guarantee are fully paid.

5 In the event payments due under this guarantee are not paid punctually upon demand, then the Guarantor shall pay all reasonable costs and solicitors fees necessary for the collection and enforcement of this guarantee.

6. This guarantee may be terminated by the Guarantor upon fourteen (14) days written notice of termination being delivered to the Creditor. Such termination shall extend only to credit extended by the Creditor after the expiry of the said fourteen (14) day period and not to prior extended credit, or goods in transit received by the Customer after the expiry of the fourteen day period.

7. The Guarantor warrants and represents it has full authority to enter into this guarantee.

8. This guarantee shall be binding upon and inure to the benefit of the parties, their successors and assigns.

IN WITNESS OF WHICH the parties have signed this agreement the day and year first above written

_____

Signed by or on behalf of the Guarantor

_____

in the presence of (witness)

Name _____

Address _____

_____

Occupation _____

_____

Signed by or on behalf of the Creditor

_____

in the presence of (witness)

Name _____

Address _____

_____

Occupation _____

HOLIDAY LETTING AGREEMENT
(for a Holiday Let of Furnished Property)

The PROPERTY _____

_____

The LANDLORD _____

_____

_____

The TENANT _____

_____

_____

_____

_____

The TERM _____ day(s)/week(s)/month(s)* beginning at 12 noon on _____

and expiring at 10 am on _____   (*delete as appropriate)

The RENT £ _____ per week/month* payable in advance on the ___ of each week/month*

or

£ _____payable in advance on the date of this Agreement

The DEPOSIT £ _____

The INVENTORY means the list of the Landlord's possessions at the Property which has been signed by the Landlord and the Tenant

DATED _____

SIGNED _____   _____

_____   _____

(The Landlord)   _____

(The Tenant)

THIS RENTAL AGREEMENT comprises the particulars detailed above and the terms and conditions printed overleaf whereby the Property is hereby let by the Landlord and taken by the Tenant for the Term at the Rent.

IMPORTANT NOTICE TO LANDLORDS:
This Form is intended for use only for a Holiday Let. If the circumstances make it clear that the letting is NOT for the purposes of the Tenant's holiday, for example because the Term is so long, the Courts may hold that it is an Assured Shorthold Tenancy (and you will not be able to obtain an order for possession of the Property for at least six months from the beginning of the tenancy).

Terms and Conditions on next page

Terms and Conditions

1. This Agreement is a Holiday Let solely for the purpose of the Tenant's holiday in the _____ area. This tenancy is accordingly not an assured shorthold tenancy

2. The Tenant will:

2.1 pay the Rent at the times and in the manner aforesaid without any deduction abatement or set-off whatsoever

2.2 keep the interior of the Property in a good, clean and tenantable state and condition and not damage or injure the Property or any part of it

2.3 yield up the Property at the end of the Term in the same clean state and condition it was in at the beginning of the Term reasonable wear and tear and damage by insured risks excepted

2.4 maintain at the Property and keep in a good and clean condition all of the contents of the Property as listed on the Inventory, if any, and to replace or cleanse any item(s) which become broken or damaged during the Term

2.5 not make any alteration or addition to the Property nor to do any redecoration or painting of the Property

2.6 not do or omit to do anything on or at the Property which may be or become a nuisance or annoyance to the Landlord or owners or occupiers of adjoining or nearby premises or which may in any way prejudice the insurance of the Property or cause an increase in the premium payable therefor

2.7 not without the Landlord's prior consent allow or keep any pet or any kind or animal at the Property

2.8 not use or occupy the Property in any way whatsoever other than as a private holiday residence for a maximum of _____ persons

2.9 not assign, sublet, charge or part with or share possession of occupation of the Property or any part thereof

2.10 permit the Landlord or anyone authorised by the Landlord at reasonable hours in the daytime and upon reasonable prior notice (except in emergency) to enter and view the Property for any proper purpose (including the checking of compliance with the Tenant's obligations under this Agreement and during the last month of the Term the showing of the Property to prospective new tenants)

2.11 pay interest at the rate of 4% above the Base Lending Rate for the time being of the Landlord's bankers upon any Rent or other money due from the Tenant under this Agreement which is more than 3 days in arrear in respect of the period from when it became due to the date of payment

2.12 pay for all telephone calls and services made at or rendered to the Property (except for the standing charge) during the Term

3. Subject to the Tenant paying the rent and performing his/her obligations under this Agreement the Tenant may peaceably hold and enjoy the Property during the term without interruption from the Landlord or any person rightfully claiming under or in trust for the Landlord

4. The Landlord will insure the Property and the contents of the Property which belong the Landlord, as listed on the Inventory, if any

5. In the event of the Rent being unpaid for more than 10 days after it is due (whether demanded or not) or there being a breach of any other of the Tenant's obligations under this Agreement then the Landlord may re-enter the Property and this Rental Agreement shall thereupon determine absolutely but without prejudice to any of the Landlord's other rights and remedies in respect of any outstanding obligations on the part of the Tenant

6. The Deposit has been paid by the Tenant and is held by the Landlord to secure compliance with the Tenant's obligations under this Agreement (without prejudice to the Landlord's other rights and remedies) and if, at any time during the Term, the Landlord is obliged to draw upon it to satisfy any outstanding breaches of such obligations then the Tenant shall forthwith make such additional payment as is necessary to restore the full amount of the Deposit held by the Landlord. As soon as reasonably practicable following termination of this Agreement the Landlord shall return to the Tenant the Deposit or the balance thereof after any deductions properly made

7. The Landlord hereby notifies the Tenant under Section 48 of the Landlord & Tenant Act 1987 that any notices (including notices in proceedings) should be served upon the Landlord at the address stated with the name of the Landlord overleaf

8. In the event of damage to or destruction of the Property by any of the risks insured against by the Landlord the Tenant shall be relieved from payment of the Rent to the extent that the Tenant's use and enjoyment of the Property is thereby prevented and from performance of its obligations as to the state and condition of the Property to the extent of and so long as there prevails such damage or destruction (except to the extent that the insurance is prejudiced by any act or default of the Tenant)

9. Where the context so admits:

9.1 The "Landlord" includes the persons for the time being entitled to the reversion expectant upon this Tenancy

9.2 The "Tenant" includes any persons deriving title under the Tenant

9.3 The "Property" includes all of the Landlord's fixtures and fittings at or upon the Property

9.4 The "Term" shall mean the period stated in the particulars overleaf or any shorter or longer period in the event of an earlier termination or an extension respectively

10. All references to the singular shall include the plural and vice versa and any obligations or liabilities of more than one person shall be joint and several and an obligation on the part of a party shall include an obligation not to allow or permit the breach of that obligation

HOUSE RULES

1. The price for the use of the room (with bed and breakfast and evening meal*) is £ _____ per week payable in advance on_____ of each week.

2. The room will be cleaned and sheets changed on _____ of each week.

3. Guests are requested to keep the room tidy and not to bring any food into it.

4. No overnight visitors are permitted. Any visitors must leave the premises at 10 p.m. when the doors will be locked.

5. The volume control on any television, radio, audio system or musical instrument must be turned low so that they are not audible from outside the room. The owner reserves the right to require these to be turned off if they cause annoyance to them or other occupiers.

6. Communal bathroom and kitchen facilities (if any) must be left clean and tidy by guests after use.

7. Guests may use the sitting room.

8. Guests have use of the bedroom assigned to them but they do not have exclusive possession of it. The owner reserves the right to require the guest to move to another room at short notice.

9. Guests must not move furniture, pictures or wall hangings without the consent of the owner, nor should they install their own furniture, pictures or wall hanging without such consent.

10. Guests returning to the house after 10 p.m. without prior arrangement with the owner are liable to be locked out.

* Delete as appropriate

HOUSE/FLAT SHARE AGREEMENT

(A Licence for Shared Occupation of a Furnished House or Flat – Non-Resident Owner)

The PROPERTY _____

_____

The Owner _____

of _____

The Sharer _____

_____

The PERIOD _____ weeks/months* beginning on _____

EARLY TERMINATION [Either party may at any time end this Licence earlier than the end of the Period] (*delete as appropriate)
(delete clause if not required) by giving to the other written notice of _____ week(s)/month(s)*

The PAYMENT £ _____ per week/month* payable in advance on the _____ of each week/month*

The Deposit £ _____

The Inventory means the list of the Owner's possessions at the Property which has been signed by the Owner and the Sharer

DATED _____

SIGNED _____   _____

_____   _____

(The Owner)   (The Sharer)

THIS HOUSE/FLAT SHARE LICENCE comprises the particulars detailed above and the terms and conditions printed overleaf whereby the Property is licensed by the Owner and taken by the Sharer for occupation with up to _____ other sharers during the Period upon making the Payment.

IMPORTANT NOTICE:

(1) This form of Licence does not require either party to give any form of notice to the other at the end of the fixed Period but if either party wishes to end this Licence early as referred to in the definition of 'the PERIOD' near the middle of this Licence then the Notice to Terminate may be used.

*(2) The law requires that the written notice should not be less than four weeks in the case of notices given by Non-Resident Owners (for whom this Licence is intended).

Terms and Conditions on next page

HOUSE/FLAT SHARE AGREEMENT
Non-Resident Owner

Terms and Conditions

1. The Sharer will:

1.1 be allowed to share with the other occupiers of the Property the use and facilities of the Property (including such bathroom, toilet, kitchen and sitting room facilities as may be at the Property)

1.2 pay the Payment at the times and in the manner aforesaid without any deduction or abatement or set-off whatsoever

1.3 make a proportionate contribution to the cost of all charges in respect of any electric, gas, water and telephonic or televisual services used at or supplied to the Property and Council Tax or any similar tax that might be charged in addition to or replacement of it during the Period

1.4 keep the interior of the Property in a good clean and tenantable state and condition and not damage or injure the Property or any part of it and if at the end of the Period any item on the Inventory requires repair, replacing, cleaning or laundering the Sharer will pay for the same (reasonable wear and tear and damage by an insured risk expected)

1.5 maintain at the Property and keep in a good and clean condition all of the items listed in the Inventory

1.6 not make any alteration or addition to the Property nor without the Owner's prior written consent to do any redecoration or painting of the Property

1.7 not do or omit to do anything on or at the Property which may be or become a nuisance or annoyance to the Owner or any other occupiers of the Property or owners or occupiers of adjoining or nearby premises or which may in any way prejudice the insurance of the Property or cause an increase in the premium payable therefor

1.8 not without the Owner's prior consent allow or keep any pet or any kind of animal at the property

1.9 not use or occupy the Property in any way whatsoever other than as a private residence

1.10 cook at the Property only in the kitchen

1.11 not part with or share possession or occupation of the Property or any part thereof

1.12 pay interest at the rate of 4% above the Base Lending Rate for the time being of the Owner's bankers upon any payment or other money due from the Sharer under this Licence which is more than 3 days in arrear in respect of the period from when it become due down to the date of payment

2. In the event of the Payment being unpaid for more than 10 days after it is due (whether demanded or not) or there being a breach of any other of the Sharer's obligations under this Licence or in the event of the Sharer ceasing to reside at the Property or in the event of the Sharer's death this Licence shall thereupon determine absolutely but without prejudice to any of the Owner's other rights and remedies in respect of any outstanding obligations on the part of the Sharer

3. The Deposit has been paid by the Sharer and is held by the Owner to secure compliance with the Sharer's obligations under this Licence (without prejudice to the Owner's other rights and remedies) and if, at any time during the Period, the Owner is obliged to draw upon it to satisfy any outstanding breaches of such obligations then the Sharer shall forthwith make such additional payment as is necessary to restore the full amount of the Deposit held by the Owner. As soon as reasonably practicable following determination of this Licence the Owner shall return to the Sharer the Deposit or the balance thereof after any deductions properly made

4. The Owner will insure the Property and the items listed on the Inventory

5. The Owner hereby notifies the Sharer that any notices (including notices in proceedings) should be served upon the Owner at the address stated with the name of the Owner overleaf

6. In the event of damage to or destruction of the Property by any of the risks insured against by the Owner the Sharer shall be relieved from making the Payment to the extent that the Sharer's use and enjoyment of the Property is thereby prevented and from performance of its obligations as to the state and condition of the Property to the extent of and whilst there prevails any such damage or destruction (except to the extent that the insurance is prejudiced by any act or default of the Sharer) the amount in case of dispute to be settled by arbitration

7. As long as the reference to a notice of early termination in the definition of the "PERIOD" overleaf (the "early termination notice") has not been deleted then either party may at any time during the Period terminate this Licence by giving to the other prior written notice to that effect, the length of such notice to be that stated in the early termination notice, and upon the expiry of said notice this Licence shall end with no further liability for either party save for liability for any antecedent breach

8. The Sharer shall not have exclusive possession of any part of the Property and the identity of the other occupiers of the Property shall be in the absolute discretion of the Owner

9. Where the context so admits:

9.1 the "Property" includes all of the Owner's fixtures and fittings at or upon the Property and all of the items listed in the Inventory and (for the avoidance of doubt) the Room

9.2 the "Period" shall mean the period stated in the particulars overleaf or any shorter or longer period in the event of an earlier termination or an extension of the Licence respectively

10. All references to the singular shall include the plural and vice versa and any obligations or liabilities of more than one person shall be joint and several and an obligation on the part of a party shall include an obligation not to allow or permit the breach of that obligation

HOUSE/FLAT SHARE AGREEMENT
(For a Room in a Furnished House or Flat – Resident Owner)

The PROPERTY _____

_____

The ROOM means the room at the Property which has been nominated by the Owner and agreed to by the Sharer

The OWNER _____

_____ whose address is the Property above

The SHARER _____

_____

The PERIOD _____ weeks/months* beginning on _____

EARLY TERMINATION (delete if not required) ⌈ Either party may at any time end this Agreement earlier than the end of the Period by giving to the other written notice of _____ week(s)/month(s)* ⌉ (* delete as appropriate)

The PAYMENT £ _____ per week/month* payable in advance on the _____ of each week/month*

The DEPOSIT £_____

The INVENTORY means the list of the Owner's possessions at the Property which has been signed by the Owner and the Sharer

DATED _____

SIGNED _____   _____

_____   _____

(The Owner)   (The Sharer)

THIS HOUSE/FLAT SHARE AGREEMENT comprises the particulars detailed above and the terms and conditions printed overleaf whereby the Property is licensed by the Owner and taken by the Sharer for occupation during the

---

IMPORTANT NOTICE:

(1) This form of Agreement is for use in those cases where the Room is part of a House or Flat which the Owner occupies as his/her only or principal home so that an assured tenancy is not created.

(2) This form of Agreement does not require either party to give any form of notice to the other at the end of the fixed Period but if either party wishes to end this Agreement early as referred to in the definition of the PERIOD near the middle of this Agreement then the Notice to Terminate may be used.

Terms and Conditions on next page

HOUSE/FLAT SHARE AGREEMENT
Resident Owner

Terms and Conditions

1. The Sharer will:

1.1 in conjunction with the occupation of the Room only be allowed to share with the other occupiers of the Property the use and facilities of the common parts of the Property (including such bathroom, toilet, kitchen and sitting room facilities as may be at the Property)

1.2 pay the Payment at the times and in the manner aforesaid without any deduction or abatement or set-off whatsoever

1.3 make a proportionate contribution to the cost of all charges in respect of any electric, gas, water and telephonic or televisual services used at or supplied to the Property and Council Tax or any similar tax that might be charged in addition to or replacement of it during the Period

1.4 keep the Room and share with the other occupiers of the Property the obligation to keep the interior of the Property in a good clean and tenantable state and condition and not damage or injure the Property or any part of it and if at the end of the Period any item on the Inventory requires repair replacing cleaning or laundering the Sharer will pay for the same (reasonable wear and tear and damage by an insured risk excepted)

1.5 yield up the Room at the end of the Period in the same clean state and condition it was in at the beginning of the Period

1.6 share with the other occupiers of the Property the obligation to maintain at the Property and keep in a good and clean condition all of the items listed in the Inventory

1.7 not make any alteration or addition to the Property nor without the Owner's prior written consent to do any redecoration or painting of the Property

1.8 not do or omit to do anything on or at the Property which may be or become a nuisance or annoyance to the Owner or any other occupiers of the Property or owners or occupiers of adjoining or nearby premises or which may in any way prejudice the insurance of the Property or cause an increase in the premium payable therefor

1.9 not without the Owner's prior consent allow or keep any pet or any kind of animal at the Property

1.10 not use or occupy the Property in any way whatsoever other than as a private residence

1.11 not assign, sublet, charge or part with or share possession or occupation of the Room or the Property or any part thereof

1.12 pay interest at the rate of 4% above the Base Lending Rate for the time being of the Owner's bankers upon any payment or other money due from the Sharer under this Agreement which is more than 3 days in arrear in respect of the period from when it become due down to the date of payment

2. In the event of the Payment being unpaid for more than 10 days after it is due (whether demanded or not) or there being a breach of any other of the Sharer's obligations under this Agreement then the Owner may re-enter the Room and this Agreement shall thereupon determine absolutely but without prejudice to any of the Owner's other rights and remedies in respect of any outstanding obligations on the part of the Sharer

3. The Deposit has been paid by the Sharer and is held by the Owner to secure compliance with the Sharer's obligations under this Agreement (without prejudice to the Owner's other rights and remedies) and if, at any time during the Period, the Owner is obliged to draw upon it to satisfy any outstanding breaches of such obligations then the Sharer shall forthwith make such additional payment as is necessary to restore the full amount of the Deposit held by the Owner. As soon as reasonably practicable following determination of this Agreement the Owner shall return to the Sharer the Deposit or the balance thereof after any deductions properly made

4. The Owner will insure the Property and the items listed on the Inventory

5. The Owner hereby notifies the Sharer that any notices (including notices in proceedings) should be served upon the Owner at the address stated with the name of the Owner overleaf

6. In the event of damage to or destruction of the Property by any of the risks insured against by the Owner the Sharer shall be relieved from making the Payment to the extent that the Sharer's use and enjoyment of the Property is thereby prevented and from performance of its obligations as to the state and condition of the Property to the extent of and whilst there prevails any such damage or destruction (except to the extent that the insurance is prejudiced by any act or default of the Sharer) the amount in case of dispute to be settled by arbitration

7. As long as the reference to a notice of early termination in the definition of the "PERIOD" overleaf (the "early termination notice") has not been deleted then either party may at any time during the Period terminate this Agreement by giving to the other prior written notice to that effect, the length of such notice to be that stated in the early termination notice, and upon the expiry of said notice this Agreement shall end with no further liability for either party save for liability for any antecedent breach

8. The Owner may at any time nominate for the Sharer another room in the Property in replacement of the Room occupied by the Sharer until that point ("the replacement Room") and all reference in this Agreement to the "Room" shall thenceforth be deemed to refer to the replacement Room and this process may be repeated by the Owner any number of times during the Period PROVIDED THAT the Sharer may after such a nomination give to the Owner an early termination notice as referred to in clause 6 above and be allowed to remain in the Room occupied prior to the said nomination until the expiry of the said early termination notice

9. The Sharer shall not have exclusive possession of the Room and the identity of the other occupiers of the Property shall be in the absolute discretion of the Owner

10. Where the context so admits:

10.1 the "Property" includes all of the Owner's fixtures and fittings at or upon the Property and all of the items listed in the Inventory and (for the avoidance of doubt) the Room

10.2 the "Period" shall mean the period stated in the particulars overleaf or any shorter or longer period in the event of an earlier termination or an extension or holding over respectively

11. All references to the singular shall include the plural and vice versa and any obligations or liabilities of more than one person shall be joint and several and an obligation on the part of a party shall include an obligation not to allow or permit the breach of that obligation

HOUSEHOLD INVENTORY

Re _____ (the Property)

No.	Living Room	No.		No.	
____	Armchair	____	Casserole dish	____	Pyrex dish
____	Ashtray	____	Cheese grater	____	Roasting dish
____	Chairs	____	Chopping board	____	Rolling pin
____	Coffee table	____	Coffee pot	____	Salt & pepper pots
____	Curtains	____	Corkscrew	____	Sauce pans
____	Cushions	____	Cups	____	Scales
____	Framed picture	____	Dessert spoons	____	Serving dishes
____	Stereo system	____	Dinner plates	____	Side plates
____	Mirror	____	Dishwasher	____	Sieve
____	Net curtains	____	Draining board	____	Soup spoons
____	Plant	____	Egg cups	____	Spatula
____	Rug	____	Forks	____	Storage jars
____	Sofa	____	Fridge/Freezer	____	Sugar jug
____	Table	____	Fruit bowl	____	Swing bin
____	Table lamp	____	Frying pans	____	Table
____	Telephone	____	Garlic crusher	____	Tablecloth
____	Television	____	Glasses	____	Table mats
____	Vase	____	Kettle	____	Teapot
____	Video	____	Knives	____	Tea spoons
____	Wall clock	____	Liquidiser	____	Tea towels
____		____	Measuring jug	____	Tin opener
____		____	Microwave	____	Toaster
		____	Milk jug	____	Tray
No.	**Kitchen/Dining Room**	____	Mugs	____	Washing machine
____	Apron	____	Mug tree	____	Washing up bowl
____	Baking tray	____	Oven & Hob	____	Wok
____	Bottle opener	____	Pie dishes	____	Wooden spoons
____	Bread bin	____	Potato peeler	____	
____	Carving knives	____	Pudding/Soup dishes	____	

No.	Bedroom One	No.		No.	
____	Blankets	____	Chair	____	Soap dish
____	Bed sheets	____	Chest of drawers	____	Towels
____	Chair	____	Curtains	____	Wall mirror
____	Chest of drawers	____	Double bed	____	Wooden chair
____	Curtains	____	Dressing table	____	
____	Double bed	____	Duvet	____	
____	Dressing table	____	Duvet cover		
____	Duvet	____	Framed picture	No.	Storage cupboard
____	Duvet cover	____	Lamp	____	Broom
____	Framed picture	____	Mattress cover	____	Bucket
____	Lamp	____	Net curtains	____	Clothes horse
____	Mattress cover	____	Pillows	____	Dustpan & brush
____	Net curtains	____	Pillow cases	____	Iron
____	Pillows	____	Side table	____	Ironing board
____	Pillow cases	____	Single bed	____	Mop
____	Side table	____	Table mirror	____	Vacuum cleaner
____	Single bed	____	Wall mirror	____	
____	Table mirror	____	Wardrobe	____	
____	Wall mirror	____			
____	Wardrobe	____		No.	Hall
____				____	Coat stand
____				____	Framed picture
		No.	Bathroom	____	
No.	Bedroom Two	____	Basket	____	
____	Blankets	____	Floor mat		
____	Bed sheets	____	Lavatory brush		
		____	Shower curtain		

Signed _____   _____

  (Landlord/Owner)   (Tenant/Sharer)

INDEMNITY AGREEMENT

THIS DEED IS MADE the _____ day of _____ 19 _____

BETWEEN

(1) _____ (the "First Party");and

(2) _____ (the "Second Party").

NOW THIS DEED WITNESSES as follows:

1.   The First Party agrees to indemnify and save harmless the Second Party and its successors and assigns, from any claim, action, liability, loss, damage or suit, arising from the following:

_____

_____

2.   In the event of any asserted claim, the Second Party shall provide the First Party immediate written notice of the same, and thereafter the First Party shall at its own expense defend, protect and save harmless the Second Party against that claim or any loss or liability thereunder.

3.   In the event the First Party shall fail to so defend and/or indemnify and save harmless, then in such instance the Second Party shall have the right to defend, pay or settle the claim on its own behalf without notice to the First Party and with full rights of recourse against the the First Party for all fees, costs, expenses and payments made or agreed to be paid to discharge the claim.

4.   Upon default, the First Party further agrees to pay all reasonable solicitor's fees necessary to enforce this Agreement.

5.   This Agreement shall be unlimited as to amount or duration.

6.   This Agreement shall be binding upon and inure to the benefit of the parties, their successors and assigns.

IN WITNESS OF WHICH the parties have executed this Deed the day and year first above written

(Individual)   (Company)

                                                         Signed for and on behalf of
_____
Signed by the First Party
                                                         _____ Ltd
_____
in the presence of (witness)
Name   _____
_____   Director
Address
_____   _____
Occupation   Director/Secretary

                                                         Signed for and on behalf of:
_____
Signed by the Second Party
                                                         _____ Ltd
_____
in the presence of (witness)
Name   _____
_____   Director
Address
_____   _____
Occupation   Director/Secretary

INDEPENDENT CONTRACTOR AGREEMENT

THIS AGREEMENT IS MADE the _____ day of _____ 19 _____

BETWEEN:

(1) _____ (the "Owner");and

(2) _____ (the "Contractor").

WHEREAS:

(A) The owner resides or operates a business at _____

_____(the "Site") and wishes to have certain services performed at the Site.

(B) The Contractor agrees to perform these services under the terms and conditions set forth in this agreement.

NOW IT IS HEREBY AGREED as follows:

1. **Description of Work**: In return for the payment agreed hereunder the Contractor will perform the following services at the Site:

_____

_____

_____

_____

_____

_____

_____

_____

2. **Payment:** The Owner will pay the Contractor the sum of _____Pounds (£_____) for the work performed under this agreement, under the following schedule:

_____

_____

_____

_____

3. **Relationship of the Parties:** This agreement creates an independent contractor-owner relationship. The Owner is interested only in the results to be achieved. The Contractor is solely responsible for the conduct and control of the work. The Contractor is not an agent or employee of the Owner for any purpose. Employees of the Contractor are not entitled to any benefits that the Owner provides to the Owner's employees. This is not an exclusive agreement. Both parties are free to contract with other parties for similar services.

4.   **Liability:** The Contractor assumes all risk connected with work to be performed. The Contractor also accepts all responsibility for the condition of tools and equipment used in the performance of this agreement and will carry for the duration of this agreement public liability insurance in an amount acceptable to the Owner. The Contractor agrees to indemnify the Owner for any and all liability or loss arising from the performance of this agreement.

5.   **Duration:** Either party may cancel this agreement with _____ days' written notice to the other party; otherwise, the contract shall remain in force for a term of _____ _____ from the date hereof.

IN WITNESS OF WHICH the parties have signed this agreement the day and year first above written

_____

Signed by or on behalf of the Owner

_____

in the presence of (witness)

Name _____

Address _____

_____

Occupation _____

_____

Signed by or on behalf of the Contractor

_____

in the presence of (witness)

Name _____

Address _____

_____

Occupation _____

INSURANCE CLAIM NOTICE

Date _____

To _____

_____

_____

Dear _____

You are hereby notified that I have incurred a loss which I believe is covered by my insurance policy detailed below. Details of the loss are as follows:

1. Type of loss or claim: _____

2. Date and time incurred: _____

3. Location: _____

4. Estimated loss: _____

Please forward a claim form to me as soon a possible.

Yours sincerely

Name _____

Address _____

_____

Telephone No. (Work) _____

Telephone No. (Home) _____

Policy Number _____

INTERNAL CUSTOMER COMPLAINT MEMORANDUM

Please complete and return this memorandum to Customer Services

Date:	Ref:	Complaint taken by:
Customer:		Telephone/Letter/Fax
		Contact:
		Tel:
		Fax:
Nature of complaint:		Product code:
		Supplier:
		Qty:
Action required: By whom: Date:		
Action completed:		Signed off:
		Date:

JOINT VENTURE AGREEMENT

THIS JOINT VENTURE AGREEMENT IS MADE the ____ day of _____ 19___

BETWEEN:

(1) _____ of _____ (the "First Joint Venturer"); and

(2) _____ of _____ (the "Second Joint Venturer")

hereinafter called the "Joint Venturers".

In consideration of the terms, conditions and covenants hereinafter set forth, the parties agree as follows:

1.   The Joint Venturers hereby form a joint venture (the "Joint Venture") for the purposes of _____ and shall conduct business under the name _____at _____
_____.

2.   The term of the Joint Venture shall be _____.

3.   The capital of the Joint Venture shall consist of £ _____. The First Joint Venturer shall contribute £ _____ and the Second Joint Venturer shall contribute £ _____, which shall be deposited in _____Bank plc and shall be disbursed only upon the signature of all the Joint Venturers.

4.   The profits and losses of the Joint Venture shall be determined in accordance with good accounting practices and shall be shared among the Joint Venturers in proportion to their respective capital contributions.

5._____ shall have the sole discretion, management and entire control of the conduct of the business of the Joint Venture as the "Venture Manager."

6.   As compensation for his services the Venture Manager shall be paid £ _____ per _____ during the duration of the Joint Venture and shall be reimbursed for all reasonable expenses incurred in the performance of his duties as Venture Manager.

7.   Each Joint Venturer shall be bound by any action taken by the Venture Manager in good faith under this agreement. In no event shall any Joint Venturer be called upon to pay any amount beyond the liability arising against him on account of his capital contribution.

8.   The Venture Manager shall not be liable for any error in judgment or any mistake of law or fact or any act done in good faith in the exercise of the power and authority as Venture Manager, but shall be liable for gross negligence or wilful default.

9.   The relationship between the Joint Venturers shall be limited to the performance of the terms and conditions of this agreement. Nothing herein shall be construed to create a general partnership between the Joint Venturers, or to authorise any Venturer to act as a general agent

for another, or to permit any Joint Venturer to bind the other except as set forth in this agreement, or to borrow money on behalf of another Joint Venturer, or to use the credit of any Joint Venturer for any purpose.

10. Neither this agreement nor any interest in the Joint Venture may be assigned without the prior written consent of the Joint Venturers hereto.

11. This agreement shall be governed by and interpreted under the law of England and Wales. Any claim arising out of or relating to this agreement, or the breach thereof, shall be settled by arbitration in accordance with the Rules of the Chartered Institute of Arbitrators and judgment upon the award rendered by the arbitrator(s) may be entered in any court having jurisdiction thereof.

12. Any and all notices to be given pursuant to or under this agreement shall be sent to the party to whom the notice is addressed at the address of the Joint Venturer maintained by the Joint Venture.

13. This agreement constitutes the entire agreement between the Joint Venturers pertaining to the subject matter contained in it, and supersedes all prior and contemporaneous agreements, representations, warranties and understandings of the parties. No supplement, variation or amendment of this agreement shall be binding unless executed in writing by all the parties hereto. No waiver of any of the provisions of this agreement shall be deemed, or shall constitute, a waiver of any other provision, whether similar or not similar, nor shall any waiver constitute a continuing waiver. No waiver shall be binding unless in writing signed by the party making the waiver.

IN WITNESS OF WHICH the parties have signed this agreement the day and year first above written

Signed by or on behalf of the First Joint Venturer	Signed by or on behalf of the Second Joint Venturer
in the presence of (witness)	in the presence of (witness)
Name	Name
Address	Address
Occupation	Occupation

LANDLORD'S REFERENCE REQUIREMENTS

EMPLOYMENT		
Work reference – stating	(a) Job Title	Yes ☐ No ☐
	(b) Length of Employment	Yes ☐ No ☐
	(c) Salary	Yes ☐ No ☐
Last three payslips		Yes ☐ No ☐
If self-employed	(a) Copy of last set of accounts	Yes ☐ No ☐
	(b) accountant's letter – stating	
	(i) length of time known to accountant	Yes ☐ No ☐
	(ii) indication of yearly income	Yes ☐ No ☐

BANK/BUILDING SOCIETY	
Last three bank statements	Yes ☐ No ☐
Building society book	Yes ☐ No ☐

OTHER	
Student identification (e.g. student card or letter of acceptance)	Yes ☐ No ☐
Personal reference (e.g. professional friend)	Yes ☐ No ☐

ℒast 𝔚ill & 𝔗estament

RESIDUE DIRECT TO CHILDREN

PRINT NAME AND ADDRESS

THIS Last Will and Testament is made by me _____

of _____

I REVOKE all previous wills and codicils.

EXECUTORS' NAMES AND ADDRESSES

I APPOINT as executors and trustees of my will

_____ and _____

of _____ of _____

_____ _____

SUBSTITUTIONAL EXECUTOR'S NAME AND ADDRESS

and should one or more of them fail to or be unable to act I APPOINT to fill any vacancy

_____

of _____

GUARDIAN'S NAME AND ADDRESS

I APPOINT _____

of _____

to be guardian of any of my children who are minors if my husband/wife dies before me.

SPECIFIC GIFTS AND LEGACIES

I GIVE _____

_____

_____

_____

_____

_____

RESIDUARY GIFT

(insert age at which you want your children to inherit capital)

I GIVE the rest of my estate to my executor and trustees to hold on trust, either to sell it or (if they think fit without being liable for any loss) to retain all or any part of it and pay my debts, taxes and testamentary expenses and pay the residue to those of my children who survive me and attain the age of _____ years if more than one in equal shares.

PROVIDED THAT if any of my children dies before me or after me but under that age, I GIVE the share that child would have taken to his or her own children who attain 18 equally. If no person shall inherit the residue of my estate under the preceding gifts, I GIVE it to

_____

TRUSTEE'S POWERS

IN ADDITION to their powers under the general law, my trustees may invest the balance of my estate in any manner in which they could invest their own funds. While a child is a minor, my trustees may at their absolute discretion use all or any part of the income from the child's share for the child's maintenance, education or benefit.

FUNERAL WISHES

I WISH my body to be ☐ buried ☐ cremated other instructions _____

_____

DATE

SIGNED by the above-named testator in our presence on the _____ day of _____ 19 _____ and then by us in the testator's presence

TESTATOR'S SIGNATURE

SIGNED _____

WITNESSES' SIGNATURES NAMES AND ADDRESSES

SIGNED _____ SIGNED _____

_____ _____

of _____ of _____

_____ _____

occupation _____ occupation _____

Last Will & Testament

RESIDUE TO ADULT

PRINT NAME AND ADDRESS

THIS Last Will and Testament is made by me _____

of _____

EXECUTORS' NAMES AND ADDRESSES

I REVOKE all previous wills and codicils.

I APPOINT as executors and trustees of my will

_____ and _____

of _____ of _____

_____ _____

SUBSTITUTIONAL EXECUTOR'S NAME AND ADDRESS

and should one or more of them fail to or be unable to act I APPOINT to fill any vacancy

_____

of _____

SPECIFIC GIFTS AND LEGACIES

I GIVE _____

_____

_____

_____

_____

_____

_____

_____

_____

_____

_____

_____

_____

RESIDUARY GIFT

I GIVE the residue of my estate to _____

_____

but if he/she or (if I have indicated more than one person) any of them fails to survive me by 28 days or if this gift or any part of it fails for any other reason, then I GIVE the residue of my estate or the part of it affected to

_____

FUNERAL WISHES

I WISH my body to be ☐ buried ☐ cremated other instructions _____

DATE

SIGNED by the above-named testator in our presence on the _____ day of _____ 19 ____
and then by us in the testator's presence

TESTATOR'S SIGNATURE

SIGNED _____

WITNESSES' SIGNATURES NAMES AND ADDRESSES

SIGNED _____ SIGNED _____

_____ _____

of _____ of _____

_____ _____

occupation _____ occupation _____

Last Will & Testament

RESIDUE TO AN ADULT BUT IF HE/SHE DIES TO CHILDREN

PRINT NAME AND ADDRESS

THIS Last Will and Testament is made by me _____

of _____

I REVOKE all previous wills and codicils.

EXECUTORS' NAMES AND ADDRESSES

I APPOINT as executors and trustees of my will

_____ and _____

of _____ of _____

_____ _____

SUBSTITUTIONAL EXECUTOR'S NAME AND ADDRESS

and should one or more of them fail to or be unable to act I APPOINT to fill any vacancy

_____

of _____

GUARDIAN'S NAME AND ADDRESS

I APPOINT _____

of _____

to be guardian of any of my children who are minors if my husband/wife dies before me.

SPECIFIC GIFTS AND LEGACIES

I GIVE _____

_____

_____

_____

_____

_____

_____

RESIDUARY GIFT

I GIVE the rest of my estate to my executors and trustees to hold on trust, either to sell it or (if they think fit and without being liable for any loss) to retain all or any part of it and pay my debts, taxes and testamentary expenses and pay the residue to

_____

but if he/she or (if I have indicated more than one person) any of them fails to survive me by 28 days or if this gift or any part of it fails for any other reason, then I GIVE the residue of my estate or the part of it affected to those of my children who survive me and attain the age of _____ years if more then one in equal shares

(insert age at which you want your children to inherit capital)

PROVIDED THAT if any of my children dies before me or after me but under that age, I GIVE the share that child would have taken to his or her own children who attain 18 equally. If no person shall inherit the residue of my estate or part of it under the preceding gifts, I GIVE it to

_____

TRUSTEE'S POWERS

IN ADDITION to their powers under the general law, my trustees may invest the balance of my estate in any manner in which they could invest their own funds. While a child is a minor, my trustees may at their absolute discretion use all or any part of the income from the child's share for the child's maintenance, education or benefit.

FUNERAL WISHES

I WISH my body to be ☐ buried ☐ cremated other instructions _____

_____

DATE

SIGNED by the above-named testator in our presence on the _____ day of _____ 19 ____ and then by us in the testator's presence

TESTATOR'S SIGNATURE

SIGNED _____

WITNESSES' SIGNATURES NAMES AND ADDRESSES

SIGNED _____ SIGNED _____

_____ _____

of _____ of _____

_____ _____

occupation _____ occupation _____

LETTER ACCEPTING LIABILITY

Date _____

To _____

_____

_____

Dear _____

We have now had an opportunity to investigate your complaint fully.

Whilst we do impose the most rigorous quality control on all our products, unfortunately, on rare occasions, human error allows a product to be despatched that does not reach the standards that we have set ourselves. We accept that this is one of those rare occasions.

We are prepared, at your choice, either to replace the product free of charge to you or to refund your purchase money in full. In either case, we would ask you please to return to us the item in question. We will, of course, reimburse you the cost of postage.

Please accept our apologies for the trouble caused you.

Yours sincerely

_____

LETTER ACCEPTING RETURN OF GOODS

Date _____

To _____

_____

_____

Re: Your order No. _____

Dear _____

We understand that you are rejecting the goods sent to you under the above order because

_____

_____

_____

_____

Whilst we do not accept your claim, we do not wish any customer to be dissatisfied and for

that reason we will accept return of the goods.

Yours sincerely

_____

LETTER ACCOMPANYING UNSOLICITED GOODS

Date _____

To _____

_____

_____

Dear _____

To introduce you to our range of products, we are sending to you a sample together with a leaflet specifying the prices and normal business terms which we offer.

I will telephone you within the next few days, after you have had an opportunity to inspect the goods, to discuss with you any questions you may have. You are, of course, under no obligation to purchase any of the samples, which, since they will belong to us until you purchase them, will be entirely at our risk whilst they remain on your premises.

I look forward to speaking to you, and the pleasure of doing business with you.

Yours sincerely

_____

LETTER ACKNOWLEDGING COMPLAINT

Date _____

To _____

_____

_____

Dear _____

I was sorry to hear of your complaint that _____

_____

I am investigating the matter fully and will contact you again as soon as possible.

Please be assured that we will do our very best to rectify any problem we discover, and if the fault is due to any error or omission on our part, we will make good, so far as it is possible to do so, any loss that you have suffered.

Yours sincerely

_____

LETTER ACKNOWLEDGING REQUEST FOR TRADE CREDIT

Date _____

To _____

_____

_____

Dear _____

To enable us to accommodate your request for trade credit, please let us have the name, address and sort code of your bank to whom we may apply for a reference together with your account number. Please also provide two trade references of companies with whom you have done business over the past three years.

We should be grateful if you would let us know the extent of the orders that you anticipate placing with us. Our normal payment terms require full payment within _____ days of invoice.

Yours sincerely

_____

LETTER AGREEING APPOINTMENT
OF AN ESTATE AGENT

Date _____

To _____

_____

_____

Dear _____

Re _____

We hereby instruct you to sell the above mentioned property at a price not less than £ _____ and agree to pay your fees and charges as set out in your letter of _____.

We reserve the right to withdraw these instructions at any time before you have introduced a purchaser.

We do not intend to appoint any other agent to sell the property for a period of _____ months. If after that time the property remains unsold we reserve the right to withdraw your instruction and appoint another agent if necessary.

Yours sincerely

_____

LETTER AGREEING TO TRADE TERMS

Date _____

To _____

_____

_____

Dear _____

We confirm that we are pleased to extend to you our normal trade terms. We enclose our terms and conditions of trade and draw your attention in particular to the requirement that accounts are due and payable _____ days from the date of invoice. Interest at the rate of _____% per month is payable on overdue accounts.

The maximum credit allowed will be £ _____. These trade terms may be altered or withdrawn by us at our discretion at any time.

Please sign and return one copy of this letter to confirm these terms. Until the signed copy is received, orders will be accepted on a cash on delivery basis.

Yours sincerely

_____

LETTER ALLEGING PASSING OFF

Date _____

To _____

_____

_____

Dear _____

We notice that you are advertising or promoting goods/services under the following "name and/or description." This will or may mislead prospective purchasers that your goods are ours.

We have long marketed goods/services under the name and description " _____

_____." Your use of the name "_____

_____" is misleading and likely to cause confusion with our product.

We demand that you cease further use of this name and make clear to those with whom you have previously dealt that you are not connected with our business and that the product that you offer has no connection with ours.

Unless you confirm this to us within the next ten days we shall have no option but to instruct our solicitors to commence proceedings against you for an injunction and damages.

Yours sincerely

_____

LETTER CONFIRMING APPOINTMENT
OF INDEPENDENT CONSULTANT

Date _____

To _____

_____

_____

Re _____

Dear _____

We are writing to confirm your engagement as a consultant for _____
_____ (the company) commencing on _____
_____. We have already discussed the duties you will be required to undertake and
the type of service we need.

The terms of your engagement will be:

1.   Your engagement shall continue (subject to Paragraph 8) until determined by either of us
giving to the other not less than _____ months' written notice.

2.   Your duties will include the following:

_____

_____

You will devote up to _____ hours per week to the performance of your duties.

Your place of work shall be _____.

We shall require regular progress reports on projects in which you are involved.

3.   The manner in which your services are performed will be entirely for you to decide but
you must comply with all reasonable requests from the board of the company. You must
ensure that your services are carried out in such manner that the company is in no way
prejudiced.

4.   In consideration of your providing these services we will pay to you a fee of
£ _____ per _____ in arrears. You will render us _____ invoices in respect of
these fees. If you are registered for VAT, you must show VAT separately on the invoices. Our
accountants shall have full access to all your records to enable them to audit the accounts
rendered.

5.   You will be responsible for all out-of-pocket expenses incurred by you in the performance of your duties.

6.   You will be responsible for all income tax liabilities and National Insurance or similar contributions in respect of your fees and will indemnify us against all claims that may be made against us in respect of income tax or similar contributions relating to your services.

8.   In addition to the right of determination declared in Paragraph 1, we shall be entitled to terminate your engagement forthwith, without any payment, compensation or damages, if you are guilty of any serious misconduct or material or persistent breach of any of the terms and conditions of your engagement, or you wilfully neglect or refuse to carry out your duties or to comply with any instructions given to you by the board, if you are unable to carry out your duties properly, if you bring the name of the company into disrepute, if you have a bankruptcy order made against you or compound with or enter into any voluntary arrangement with your creditors, or if you are convicted of any criminal offence. This will not prejudice any other rights or remedies which we may have against you.

9.   One matter upon which we are most insistent concerns confidentiality. You will, in providing your services, gain knowledge of our business, our business contacts, our procedures and many of our business secrets. It is fundamental that you will not declare to anyone or use for your own or another's benefit any confidential information that you acquire. This is both during and after your engagement. Any expenses, costs and all records or papers of any description are the property of the company and must be immediately delivered to the company on the termination of your engagement.

10. This agreement shall be governed by the laws of England and Wales to the non-exclusive jurisdiction of whose courts both we and you hereby submit.

If you agree to these terms please sign and return one copy of this letter.

We look forward to working with you.

Yours faithfully

_____

Agreed and accepted

_____

Consultant

LETTER CONFIRMING REASON FOR INSTANT DISMISSAL

Date _____

To _____

_____

_____

Dear _____

This letter is to confirm, formally, your instant dismissal today for the following reason(s):

_____

_____

_____

_____

_____

_____

You are aware of the code of discipline which makes it quite clear that this type of behaviour will result in immediate dismissal.

Yours sincerely

_____

LETTER DENYING LIABILITY ON COMPLAINT

Date _____

To _____

_____

_____

Dear _____

We have investigated the complaint contained in your letter of dated _____ 19___ .

I am satisfied that we are not at fault for the following reasons:

_____

_____

_____

_____

However, if you remain of the opinion that we were at fault, then I am willing to consider the possibility that the matter be referred to arbitration in order to reach a compromise in this dispute. If you agree we can discuss the appointment of an arbitrator.

Yours sincerely

_____

LETTER EXPELLING PARTNER FROM CONTINUING PARTNERSHIP

Date _____

Ref _____

To _____

_____

_____

Dear _____

In accordance with clause _____ of our partnership agreement, I/we wish to inform you that you are expelled from the partnership. Your rights to any share in the partnership profits and assets will be dealt with in accordance with the terms of the partnership agreement.

Yours sincerely

_____
Partner's signature

_____
Partner's signature

LETTER FROM EMPLOYEE INTENDING TO RESUME
WORK BEFORE END OF MATERNITY LEAVE

Date _____

To _____

_____

_____

Dear _____

This is to inform you that I intend to return to work before the end of my maternity leave period and I am giving your at least seven days notice as required by law.

I intend to return to work on _____ 199 ___.

Your sincerely

_____

LETTER OF CLAIM ADDRESSED TO A CARRIER

Date _____

To _____

_____

_____

Dear Sirs

Re: _____

We refer to consignment note no._____ concerning _____ collected by you from _____ for delivery to _____.

We have been notified by the recipient that goods to the value of £ _____ were received which were damaged or missing from the consignment.

We wish formally to notify you of this circumstance under the terms of Clause _____of our contract dated _____ 19_____ .

We have inspected the goods and estimate the replacement cost to be £ _____ and should be grateful if you would arrange for that sum to be forwarded to us within _____ days of the date hereof, failing which we shall be compelled to refer this matter to our solicitors.

Yours faithfully

_____

LETTER OF REDUNDANCY

Date _____

To _____

_____

_____

Dear _____

It is with deep regret that I must advise you that your employment with us will end on _____. The only reason for terminating your employment is the effect of the serious decline in business that the company has experienced.

We are following the principle "last in first out." Wherever possible, we have offered employees other employment, but unfortunately there are others who have been with the company longer than you have and so we must include you amongst those selected for redundancy. You are entitled to receive a payment based upon the scale laid down by law and a tax-free cheque for the amount due is enclosed together with a statement reflecting how this has been calculated.

We hope that you soon find other suitable employment. If you need a reference from us, please submit our name with the confidence that our reference will be a good one.

Yours sincerely

_____

LETTER OFFERING TO PURCHASE PROPERTY

Date _____

To _____

_____

_____

Dear _____

Re _____

Following my inspection of the above-named property, I am prepared to offer the sum of £ _____ for your existing lease, on the following terms:

1. Receipt of a satisfactory survey from my surveyors.

2. Receipt of my solicitor's advice on the terms of the lease, confirming that it contains no provisions adverse to my interests and that it is a lease for _____ years from_____ _____ at a ground rent of £ _____ per annum payable quarterly in advance (reviewable every three years, the next review being in _____ 19____).

3. Your giving us vacant possession by _____ 19 ___.

My company's solicitors are Messrs. _____ , to whom I have copied this letter. Please instruct your solicitors to send a draft contract to my solicitors. I hope we are able to proceed to a swift exchange of contracts.

Yours sincerely

_____

LETTER RE. AGENT'S AUTHORITY

Date _____

Ref _____

To _____ (name of Tenant(s))

_____

_____

Dear Tenant(s)

Re._____ (the Property)

Please note that _____ (name & address
                                                        of agent(s))

_____

_____

is/are now authorised to deal with the above property on my/our behalf so that you should until

further notice pay the rent and any other payments due under the tenancy to him/her and deal

with him/her/them in respect of any other matters relating to the property.

Yours faithfully

_____ (Landlord's signature &
                            printed name & address)

_____

_____

LETTER RE. BILLS

Date _____

Ref _____

To _____ (name and address
of Authority)

_____

_____

Dear Sir(s)

Re. _____ (the Property)

I am /we are the landlord(s) of the above property and write to advise you that with effect from

_____ (date of start of tenancy)

the property has been let to

_____ (name(s) of Tenant(s))

_____

who will therefore be responsible with effect from that date for the [council tax] [electricity charges] [gas charges] [telephone charges] [water rates] in respect of the property.

Yours faithfully

_____ (Landlord's signature &
printed name & address)

_____

_____

_____

LETTER RE. BREACH OF TENANT'S COVENANTS

Date _____

Ref _____

To _____ (name of Tenant(s))

_____

_____

Dear Tenant(s),

Re. _____ (the Property)

Your tenancy of the above property requires you to comply with a number of obligations such as payment of the rent, repair of the property, etc.

It has come to my/our attention that you have failed to comply as referred to in the Details of Breach(es) below and we ask that you attend to and rectify this situation within a reasonable time failing which I/we will be obliged to pursue our rights against you under the tenancy (including a claim against you for compensation in money for the breach).

Yours faithfully

_____ (Landlord's signature & printed name & address)

_____

_____

DETAILS OF BREACH(ES) _____ (write in here exactly what the Landlord is complaining about)

_____

_____

_____

_____

_____

_____

LETTER REFUSING RETURN OF GOODS

Date _____

To _____

_____

_____

Dear _____

Re: Your Order No. _____

Today your carrier attempted to return the goods identified in the above order.

We refuse to accept the return of the goods because we have given no permission to you either expressly or implicitly to return the goods without good reason. We therefore ask you to remove them immediately as we can accept no liability for them or for any damage that they may suffer whilst left on our premises.

Yours sincerely

_____

LETTER REFUSING TRADE OR FINANCIAL REFERENCES

Date _____

To _____

_____

_____

Dear _____

Re _____

We regret that we are unable to comply with your request for a reference in respect of the above named company. Apart from the fact that we have insufficient information upon which to make a reference, it is a policy in this company not to give such references.

Please do not take this letter as any indication whatsoever of the commercial or financial standing of the company. We suggest that you ask them for an alternative referee.

Yours sincerely

_____

LETTER REFUSING TRADE TERMS

Date _____

To _____

_____

_____

Dear _____

We have carefully considered your request for trade terms. Unfortunately, we regret that we are not prepared to extend trade terms to you until you first establish a satisfactory pattern of trade with us. We hope you understand our position on the matter.

Yours sincerely

_____

LETTER REJECTING CONDITIONS OF ORDER
AND REIMPOSING CONDITIONS OF SALE

Date _____

To _____

_____

_____

Dear _____

Re: Your Order No. _____

We are in receipt of your order referred to above which is expressed to be on your standard terms and conditions.

Unfortunately, your standard terms and conditions are unacceptable. We can only supply goods on our standard terms and conditions of sale, copies of which are enclosed.

We are despatching your ordered goods on our standard terms and conditions. Acceptance of delivery by you will constitute acceptance of our terms. If you are not prepared to accept our terms, please return the goods to avoid incurring liability for them.

Yours sincerely

_____

LETTER REJECTING INCORRECT GOODS

Date _____

To _____

_____

_____

Dear _____

Re: Our Order No. _____

Today your carrier attempted to deliver goods identified on the numbered order above.

On examination the goods delivered were found not to correspond with the sample we had received and we thereupon refused to accept the goods. The carrier was instructed to return them to you.

Yours sincerely

_____

LETTER REQUESTING THAT
COMPANY BE TREATED AS DEFUNCT

Date _____

Ref _____

To   The Registrar of Companies
     Companies House
     Crown Way
     Cardiff
     CF4 3UZ

Dear Sir

Re _____ Limited

Company number _____

The above-named company is not carrying on business nor is it in operation. It has neither assets nor liabilities nor outstanding liability to the Inland Revenue.

Please take the appropriate action under s.652 of the Companies Act 1985 to remove this company from the register.

Yours faithfully

_____

LETTER REQUESTING TRADE TERMS OF PAYMENT

Date _____

To _____

_____

_____

Dear Sirs

We wish to place orders with you for the following:

_____

_____

_____

Please advise us of your normal trade terms of payment.

If you wish to have references we suggest that you refer to our bankers who are:

_____

_____

You may also like to refer to _____, with whom we have had business relations.

Yours faithfully

_____

LETTER RESCINDING CONTRACT

Date _____

To _____

_____

_____

Dear _____

We have received notification that you have been put into receivership.

Accordingly, pursuant to our Terms and Conditions, we notify you that we consider our contract with you terminated, and that the full price of the goods delivered to you is immediately due and payable. We demand full payment forthwith. Please note that until they have been paid for in full title to goods supplied to you remains vested in us.

Yours sincerely

_____

LETTER SENDING A COPY OF AN AGREEMENT REGULATED UNDER THE CONSUMER CREDIT ACT 1974

Date _____

To _____

_____

_____

Dear _____

Re: Hire Purchase Agreement No. _____

As explained to you when you signed the above agreement, you have time to reconsider your decision. If you wish to do so you may still cancel the agreement by posting to us a written notice of cancellation within five days of receipt of this notice.

A copy of the agreement was left with you and a further copy is enclosed. Your cancellation rights are clearly stated in the agreement and in particular that you have five days from the day you receive this copy in which to cancel. The agreement further draws your attention to your rights under the Consumer Credit Act 1974.

Yours sincerely

_____

NOTE: To be sent within seven days of signature of the agreement

LETTER TAKING UP BANK REFERENCE

Date _____

To: The Manager

_____ Bank plc

_____

_____

_____

Dear Sir _____

Re _____ Limited

The above-named company, whose address is _____

_____, has applied to us for trade credit. They tell us that you

are their bankers and their account number is _____.

The amount involved will be in the order of £ _____ per month. We should be

grateful if you would supply us with a statement as to their creditworthiness and let us know

whether they can be considered good for the amount involved.

Yours faithfully

_____

LETTER TAKING UP TRADE REFERENCE

Date _____

To _____

_____

_____

Dear _____

Re _____ Limited

The above-named company has applied to us for trade credit. They tell us that they have a credit account with you and have given us your name as a reference. They have suggested that the amount of their trade with us would be in the order of £ _____ per month.

Could you please let us know, in confidence, whether their account with you has been maintained satisfactorily and whether all invoices have been paid on their date due.

A stamped and addressed envelope is enclosed for your reply.

Yours sincerely

_____

LETTER TO A SOLICITOR TO COLLECT A DEBT

Date _____

To _____

_____

_____

Dear _____

Re _____

Debt £ _____

Please issue proceedings to recover the amount £ _____ from the above named company.

We enclose a copy of our invoice together with our complete file relating to this debt. Please let us know if you require any further information.

No complaint has been received in respect of this debt and all our applications for payment have been ignored. We draw your attention to our last letter in which we gave warning that unless payment was received, proceedings would be commenced without further notice.

We will let you know immediately if any payment is received by us.

Yours sincerely

_____

LETTER TO CREDIT REFERENCE AGENCY FOR REPORT

Date _____

To _____

_____

_____

Dear _____

Re _____

We request a detailed credit report on the above. They have requested credit terms representing a monthly risk to us of approximately £ _____. We enclose our cheque for £ _____ and would ask you to fax or post your report to us as soon as possible.

Yours sincerely

_____

LETTER TO CREDIT REFERENCE AGENCY
REQUESTING REGISTERED PERSONAL DATA

Date _____

To _____

_____

_____

Dear _____

Re: Data Protection Act 1984 (the "Act")

Please let me know if you hold any personal data concerning me on you records. If you do, I should be grateful for a copy of any such data according to my entitlement under the Act. If you wish to make a charge for the supply of this information, please let me know.

Yours sincerely

_____

LETTER TO CUSTOMER WHO HAS EXCEEDED HIS/HER CREDIT LIMIT

Date _____

To _____

_____

_____

Dear _____

As you know, your credit limit with us is £ _____. Your account today stands in the sum of £ _____, which is in excess of the credit allowed. Until this amount has been paid we regret that we are not prepared to accept any further orders from you on trade terms.

Interest at the rate of _____ % per month is payable on outstanding accounts and this interest will be added to your statement.

Yours sincerely

_____

LETTER TO EMPLOYEE CONCERNING SALARY RISE

Date _____

To _____

_____

_____

Dear _____

It is with pleasure that I write to let you know of our decision to increase your salary. The increase is £ _____ per _____ .

This increase is only partly in recognition of the increase in the cost of living since your last rise. It is also made in reward for your loyal and conscientious work, and to let you know that your efforts have been recognised. The increase will take effect from the beginning of this month.

I hope that we shall be able to continue our happy working relationship for many years to come.

Yours sincerely

_____

LETTER TO EMPLOYEE ON MATERNITY LEAVE INTENDING TO TAKE MATERNITY ABSENCE

Date _____

To _____

_____

_____

Dear _____

It is now _____ weeks since the birth of your baby, and I hope all is going well. The purpose of this letter is to find out whether you will be returning to work after your maternity absence as planned.

Please write and let me know of your intentions regarding returning to work and the date on which you expect to return, if that is the case.

As a reminder, to preserve your right to return to your old job, you must write to me within 14 days of receipt of this letter and not less than 21 days before you expect to return, confirming your intention and the expected date of return.

Yours sincerely

_____

LETTER TO EMPLOYEE, ABSENT BELIEVED SICK

Date _____

To _____

_____

_____

Dear _____

You have not been to work since _____ , and have failed to contact me to let me know why.

Please let me know at once the reason for your absence from work and, if you are unwell, provide me with a certificate from your doctor. Without this certificate, you are not entitled to any sick pay.

In case you do not know about the sickness regulations, you are only entitled to statutory sick pay for the first 28 weeks of your absence through sickness. After that you must claim state benefit.

Yours sincerely

_____

LETTER TO EMPLOYER BY MOTHER TAKING MATERNITY ABSENCE

Date _____

To _____

_____

_____

Dear _____

As required, I am writing to you at least 21 days before I exercise my right to return to work.

I intend to return to work on _____ 199___

Yours sincerely

_____

LETTER TO FORMER EMPLOYEE WHO IS USING CONFIDENTIAL INFORMATION

Date _____

To _____

_____

_____

Dear _____

It has come to our attention that you are informing our customers that you can supply them at prices below our current price list. You are clearly using the information about our customers and prices that you gained whilst working for us.

Unless you return to us within seven days all customer and price lists that you have in your possession and give us your written promise not to make use of your knowledge of our customers and business, our solicitors will be instructed to make an immediate application to the courts for an injunction to prevent you approaching our customers, and they will be instructed also to bring proceedings to claim damages from you.

Yours sincerely

_____

LETTER TO RECEIVER OR LIQUIDATOR RECLAIMING GOODS

Date _____

To _____

_____

_____

Dear _____

Re: Our Invoice No. _____

The goods referred to in the above invoice were delivered to _____

_____ which is now in receivership. The goods were sold on the condition that legal title remains with us until such time as they are paid for in full. If they are not paid for in full within _____ days, we reserve the right to enter their premises to recover our goods. We have not received payment for the goods within the specified period, and therefore we intend to enter upon their premises on _____ to reclaim our goods. Please may we have your undertaking by return not to sell, deal with or otherwise dispose of the goods until such time as they have been paid for in full or collected by us.

Yours sincerely

_____

LETTER TO SHAREHOLDERS AND AUDITORS
WITH RESOLUTION TO BE PASSED

Date _____

Ref _____

To _____

_____

_____

Dear _____

The company directors propose:

_____

_____

_____

_____

To give effect to this proposal it is necessary for the shareholders to pass a formal resolution to be recorded in the company's minute book. As I understand that all shareholders have been approached and agree to the proposal, I enclose a formal written resolution.

If you confirm that you are in agreement, please sign the form where indicated and return it to me.

An identical form of resolution has been sent to all other shareholders and to the auditors.

Yours sincerely

_____
Company Secretary

Continued on next page

WRITTEN RESOLUTION

_____LIMITED

COMPANY NUMBER:_____

The following ordinary/extraordinary/special/elective resolution is signed as a written resolution pursuant to Section 381A of the Companies Act 1985 by the holders of all issued shares in the capital of the company conferring a right to vote thereon as if the resolution had been proposed at a general meeting of the company at the date hereof:

_____

_____

_____

_____

_____

_____

_____

Dated this _____ day of _____ 199___

_____
Shareholder's signature

Continued on next page

LETTER TO AUDITOR

Date _____

Ref _____

To Messrs. _____ Chartered Accountants

_____

_____

_____

Dear _____

I enclose a copy of a letter sent to all the shareholders and also a copy of the resolution that we wish to pass. As you can see, we are hoping to pass the motion by written resolution rather than by voting at a general meeting.

Could you please give the notification required by the Companies Act 1985 that the resolution does not concern you as auditors, or if you consider that it does concern you, whether, in your opinion, the resolution should be considered by the company in general meeting.

Yours sincerely

_____
Company Secretary

LETTER TO UNSUCCESSFUL CANDIDATE

Date _____

To _____

_____

_____

Dear _____

I regret to inform you that, after considering your application and meeting to interview you, I am unable to offer you the position you have applied for. Whilst you were adequately qualified for the position, another applicant was more suited to our particular field of activity.

I am grateful to you for giving your time and wish you every success in the future.

Yours sincerely

_____

LETTER TREATING BREACH OF CONTRACT
AS REPUDIATION AND CLAIMING DAMAGES

Date _____

To _____

_____

_____

Dear _____

We refer to the contract between us, under the term of which you agreed to perform the following:

_____

_____

_____

_____

We regard you to have failed to perform your obligation under the contract in the following respects:

_____

_____

_____

_____

Despite our previous protests you have not made good your failure.

We have considered the matter fully and conclude that your failure is a repudiation by you of your obligations under the contract. We consider the contract terminated because of your conduct. We are taking advice from our solicitors as to the remedies available to us and you will hear from them shortly.

Yours sincerely

_____

LICENCE FOR USE OF A CAR PARKING SPACE

Date _____

To _____

_____

_____

Dear _____

Premises _____

This is to confirm that we are giving you a licence to park _____ motor car(s) in the car parking area adjacent to the above premises (the "Licence") subject to the following conditions:

(a) Only _____ motor car(s) may be parked under the Licence and those motor cars shall only be parked in the spaces that we indicate. No special place is reserved for you and we can at any time change the area in which you may park. We accept no liability for any loss or damage to the car(s) or their contents.

(b) You will provide us with the registration number of the car(s) that will be using this permission.

(c) No vehicle may obstruct the access to the parking area and any vehicle that is parked so as to obstruct the parking or movement of any of our vehicles will be removed immediately. It is a fundamental condition of this Licence that you agree that we may at any time move any car that we consider is in breach of this term and that, unless it is caused negligently, we shall not be liable for any damage caused by our taking this action.

(d) You will pay us £_____ per _____ for this Licence, the payment to be made in advance. The first payment shall be made today and subsequent payments shall be made on the _____ day of each _____.

(e) This Licence may be terminated by either of us giving to the other seven clear days' notice.

Yours sincerely

_____

LICENCE TO USE COPYRIGHT MATERIAL

THIS LICENCE IS MADE the _____ day of _____ 19 _____

BETWEEN:

(1) _____ of _____ (the "Licensor"); and

(2) _____ of _____ (the "Licensee").

NOW IT IS HEREBY AGREED as follows:

1.   In consideration for the sum of £ _____, receipt of which the Licensor hereby acknowledges, the Licensor grants to the Licensee a licence to use, reprint and publish the following material (the "Copyright Material"):

_____

_____

2.   The Copyright Material shall be used by the Licensee only in the following manner or publication and for the following period:

_____

_____

3.   The Copyright Material shall be used by the Licensee only in the following territory of the world:

_____

_____

4.   The Licensee agrees that the Licensor shall retain the worldwide copyright in the Copyright Material, and the moral rights of the author of the Copyright Material are hereby asserted.

5.   This agreement shall be binding upon and inure to the benefit of the parties, their successor and assigns.

IN WITNESS OF WHICH the parties have agreed this licence the day and year first above written

_____   _____
Signed by or on behalf of the Licensor   Signed by or on behalf of the Licensee

_____   _____
in the presence of (witness)   in the presence of (witness)

Name _____   Name _____

Address _____   Address _____

_____   _____

Occupation _____   Occupation _____

LIMITED GUARANTEE

THIS AGREEMENT IS MADE the _____ day of _____ 19 _____

BETWEEN:

(1) _____ (the "Guarantor"); and

(2) _____ (the "Creditor").

NOW IT IS HEREBY AGREED as follows:

1. As an inducement to the Creditor to extend credit from time to time to _____ _____ (the "Customer") the Guarantor unconditionally guarantees to the Creditor the prompt and punctual payment of certain sums now or hereinafter due to the Creditor from the Customer, provided that the liability of the Guarantor hereunder shall be limited to the amount of £ _____ as a maximum liability and the Guarantor shall not be liable under this Guarantee for any greater or further amount.

2. The Guarantor agrees to remain fully bound on this Guarantee, notwithstanding any extension, forbearance, indulgence or waiver, or release or discharge or substitution of any party or collateral or security for the debt. In the event of default, the Creditor may seek payment directly from the Guarantor without need to proceed first against the Customer.

3. This Guarantee shall be binding upon and inure to the benefit of the parties, their successors and assigns.

IN WITNESS OF WHICH the parties have signed this agreement the day and year first above written

_____

Signed by or on behalf of the Guarantor

_____

in the presence of (witness)

Name _____

Address _____

_____

Occupation _____

_____

Signed by or on behalf of the Creditor

_____

in the presence of (witness)

Name _____

Address _____

_____

Occupation _____

LIMITED PROXY

_____LIMITED

I/We _____ of _____

_____, a member/members of the above company, hereby

appoint _____ of_____

_____, or failing him,_____

_____ of _____, as

my/our proxy to vote in my/our name(s) and on my/our behalf at the annual/extraordinary

general meeting of the company to be held at _____

on _____ 199 ____ and at any adjournment thereof.

This form is to be used in respect of the resolutions mentioned below as follows:

Resolution No. 1. *for *against

Resolution No. 2. *for *against

(*delete as applicable.)

Except as instructed above, the proxy may vote as he thinks fit or abstain from voting.

Signed this _____ day of _____ 199 ____.

_____
Shareholder's signature

_____
Shareholder's signature

LIVING WILL

Name _____

Address _____

Date of birth _____

Doctor's details _____

National Health Number _____

I, _____, am of sound mind and make this Advance Directive now on my future medical care to my family, my doctors, other medical personnel and anyone else to whom it is relevant, for a time when, for reasons of physical or mental incapacity, I am unable to make my views known.

INSTRUCTIONS

MEDICAL TREATMENT I DO NOT WANT:

I REFUSE medical procedures to prolong my life or keep me alive by artificial means if:

(1) I have a severe physical illness from which, in the opinion of _____ independent medical practitioners, it is unlikely that I will ever recover; ☐

or

(2) I have a severe mental illness which, in the opinion of _____ independent medical practitioners, has no likelihood of improvement and in addition I have a severe physical illness from which, in the opinion of _____ independent medical practitioners, it is unlikely that I will ever recover; ☐

or

(3) I am permanently unconscious and have been so for a period of at least ___ months and in the opinion of ___ independent medical practitioners there is no likelihood that I will ever recover. ☐

Medical treatment I DO want:

I DO wish to receive any medical treatment which will alleviate pain or distressing symptoms or will make me more comfortable. I accept that this may have the effect of shortening my life. ☐

If I am suffering from any of the conditions above and I am pregnant, I wish to RECEIVE medical procedures which will prolong my life or keep me alive by artificial means only until such time as my child has been safely delivered. ☐

203

HEALTH CARE PROXY

I wish to appoint _____of_____
_____ as my Health Care Proxy. S/he should be involved in any decisions about my health care options if I am physically or mentally unable to make my views known. I wish to make it clear that s/he is fully aware of my wishes and I request that his/her decisions be respected.

ADDITIONAL DIRECTIONS ON FUTURE HEALTH CARE

_____
_____
_____
_____
_____
_____
_____
_____

SIGNATURES

Signature _____ Date_____

Witness' signature _____ Date_____

I confirm that my views are still as stated above.

	Date	Signature	Witness' signature
1)	_____	_____	_____
2)	_____	_____	_____
3)	_____	_____	_____
4)	_____	_____	_____

LOAN AGREEMENT

THIS AGREEMENT IS MADE the _____ day of _____ 19 _____

BETWEEN:

(1) _____ (the "Borrower"); and

(2) _____ (the "Lender").

NOW IT IS HEREBY AGREED as follows:

1. **Loan**: Subject to and in accordance with this agreement, its terms, conditions and covenants the Lender agrees to lend to the Borrower on _____ 19_____ (the "Loan Date") the principal sum of _____ Pounds (£_____) (the "Loan").

2. **Note**: The Loan shall be evidenced by a Note in the form attached hereto as Exhibit A (the "Note") executed by the Borrower and delivered to the Lender on the Loan Date.

3. **Interest**: The Loan shall bear interest on the unpaid principal at an annual rate of _____ _____ percent (_____%). In the event of a default in payment the aforesaid interest rate shall apply to the total of principal and interest due at the time of default.

4. **Payment**: Payment shall be in accordance with the terms contained in the Note. The Note may, at any time and from time to time, be paid or prepaid in whole or in part without premium or penalty, except that any partial prepayment shall be (a) in multiples of £_____, (b) a minimum of £_____, applied to any instalments due under the Note in the inverse order of their maturity. Upon the payment of the outstanding principal in full or all of the instalments, if any, the interest on the Loan shall be computed and a final adjustment and payment of interest shall be made within five (5) days of the receipt of notice. Interest shall be calculated on the basis of a year of _____ days and the actual number of days elapsed.

5. **Security**: The Borrower agrees to secure the repayment of the Loan by executing those security documents attached hereto as Exhibit B (the "Security Documents") and shall deliver the Security Documents on the Loan Date. From time to time the Lender may demand, and the Borrower shall execute, additional loan documents which are reasonably necessary to perfect the Lender's security interests.

6. **Representations and Warranties**: The Borrower represents and warrants: (i) that the execution, delivery and performance of this agreement, and the Note and Security Documents have been duly authorised and are proper; (ii) that the financial statement submitted to the Lender fairly presents the financial condition of the Borrower as of the date of this agreement knowing that the Lender has relied thereon in granting the Loan; (iii) that the Borrower has no contingent obligations not disclosed or reserved against in said financial statement, and at the present time there are no material, unrealised or anticipated losses from any present commitment of the Borrower; (iv) that there will be no material adverse changes in the financial condition of the Borrower at the time of the Loan Date; (v) that the Borrower will advise the Lender of material adverse changes which occur at any time prior to the Loan Date and thereafter to the date of final payment; and (vi) that the Borrower has good and valid title to all of the property given as security hereunder. The Borrower represents and warrants that such representations and warranties shall be deemed to be continuing representations and warranties during the entire life of this agreement.

7. **Default**: The Borrower shall be in default: (i) if any payment due hereunder is not made within _____ (___) days of the date due; (ii) in the event of assignment by the Borrower for the benefit of creditors; (iii) upon the filing of any voluntary or involuntary petition for

bankruptcy by or against the Borrower; or (iv) if the Borrower has breached any representation or warranty specified in this agreement.

8. **Governing Law:** This agreement, the Note(s) and the Security Documents shall be governed by, construed and enforced in accordance with the law of England and Wales to the jurisdiction of which the parties hereto submit.

IN WITNESS OF WHICH the parties have signed this agreement the day and year first above written

---

Signed by or on behalf of the Borrower

Signed by or on behalf of the Lender

---

in the presence of (witness)

in the presence of (witness)

Name

Name

Address

Address

Occupation

Occupation

LOAN NOTE (LONG FORM)

THIS DEED IS MADE the _____ day of _____ 19 _____

BETWEEN:

(1) _____ of _____ (the "Borrower"); and

(2) _____ of _____ (the "Lender").

NOW THIS DEED WITNESSES as follows:

1.   The Borrower hereby promises to pay to the order of the Lender the sum of _____ _____ Pounds (£_____), together with interest thereon at the rate of _____% per annum on the unpaid balance. The said amount shall be paid in the following manner:

_____

_____

2.   All payments shall be first applied to interest and the balance to principal. This note may be prepaid, at any time, in whole or in part, without penalty.

3. This note shall at the option of any holder thereof be immediately due and payable upon the occurrence of any of the following:

(a) Failure of the Borrower to make any payment due hereunder within _____ days of its due date.

(b) Breach of any condition of any mortgage, loan agreement, or guarantee granted as collateral security for this note.

(c) Breach of any condition of any loan agreement or mortgage, if any, having a priority over any loan agreement or mortgage on security granted, in whole or in part, as collateral security for this note.

(d) Upon the death, incapacity, dissolution, receivership, insolvency or liquidation of either of the parties hereto, or any endorser or guarantor of this note.

4.   In the event this note shall be in default and placed for collection, then the Borrower agrees to pay all reasonable solicitors fees and costs of collection. Payments not made within five (5) days of the due date shall be subject to a charge of _____ % per annum of the sum due. All payments hereunder shall be made to such address as may from time to time be designated by any party.

5. The undersigned and all other parties to this note, whether as endorsers, guarantors or sureties, agree to remain fully bound until this note shall be fully paid and further agree to remain bound, notwithstanding any extension, modification, waiver, or other indulgence or discharge or release of the Borrower hereunder or exchange, substitution, or release of any collateral security granted as security for this note. No variation or waiver by any holder hereof shall be binding unless in writing; and any waiver on any one occasion shall not be a waiver for any other or future occasion. Any variation or change in terms hereunder granted by any holder hereof, shall be valid and binding upon each of the undersigned, notwithstanding the acknowledgement of any of the undersigned.

IN WITNESS OF WHICH the parties have signed this deed the day and year first above written

---------------------------------------   ---------------------------------------

Signed by or on behalf of the First Party   Signed by or on behalf of the Second Party

---------------------------------------   ---------------------------------------

in the presence of (witness)   in the presence of (witness)

Name   Name

Address   Address

---------------------------------------   ---------------------------------------

Occupation   Occupation

LOAN NOTE (SHORT FORM)

THIS DEED is made the _____ day of _____ 19_____

BY:

_____ of _____ (the "Borrower").

WHEREAS:

The Borrower is indebted to _____ (the "Lender") in the sum of £ _____.

NOW THIS DEED WITNESSES as follows:

1.   The Borrower promises to pay to the order of the Lender the sum of _____ _____ Pounds (£ _____), with annual interest of _____ % on any unpaid balance.

2.   This note shall be paid in _____ consecutive and equal instalments of £ _____ each with the first payment one _____ from date hereof, and the same amount on the same day of each _____ thereafter, provided the entire principal balance and any accrued but unpaid interest shall be fully paid on or before _____ 19_____.

3.   This note may be prepaid without penalty. All payments shall be first applied to interest and the balance to principal.

4.   This note shall be due and payable upon demand by any holder hereof should the Borrower default in any payment beyond _____ days of its due date.

IN WITNESS OF WHICH the Borrower has executed this deed the day and year first above written

_____

Signed by or on behalf of the Debtor

_____

in the presence of (witness)

Name _____

Address _____

_____

Occupation _____

LOAN PAYMENT RECORD

Borrower: _____ Creditor: _____

Terms: _____

Date Due	Date Paid	Amount	Balance
_____	_____	£ _____	£ _____
_____	_____	£ _____	£ _____
_____	_____	£ _____	£ _____
_____	_____	£ _____	£ _____
_____	_____	£ _____	£ _____
_____	_____	£ _____	£ _____
_____	_____	£ _____	£ _____
_____	_____	£ _____	£ _____
_____	_____	£ _____	£ _____
_____	_____	£ _____	£ _____
_____	_____	£ _____	£ _____
_____	_____	£ _____	£ _____
_____	_____	£ _____	£ _____
_____	_____	£ _____	£ _____
_____	_____	£ _____	£ _____
_____	_____	£ _____	£ _____
_____	_____	£ _____	£ _____
_____	_____	£ _____	£ _____
_____	_____	£ _____	£ _____
_____	_____	£ _____	£ _____
_____	_____	£ _____	£ _____

LOCATION OF IMPORTANT DOCUMENTS
AND SUMMARY OF PERSONAL INFORMATION

OF

Name _____

Will   _____

Birth
Certificate   _____

Marriage
Certificate   _____

Divorce Decree   _____

Title Deeds   _____

Mortgage
Documents   _____

Life Insurance
Policies   _____

Pension Details   _____

Share
Certificates   _____

Other Investment
Certificates   _____

Loan and H.P.
Agreements   _____

Bank Account
Details   _____

Building Society
Passbooks   _____

Donor Cards   _____

Passport   _____

LODGER/BED & BREAKFAST LICENCE
(For a Room in a Furnished House)

The PROPERTY _____

_____

The ROOM   means the room at the Property which has been agreed between the Licensor and Licensee to

be taken by the Licensee

The LICENSOR _____

_____ whose address is the Property above

The LICENSEE _____

_____

The PERIOD   _____ weeks/months* beginning on _____

(delete paragraph
if not required)   [Subject to the right for either party at any time during the Period to end this Agreement   (* delete as
appropriate)

earlier by giving to the other written notice of _____ week(s)/month(s)*

The SERVICES   means the services that the Licensor hereby agrees to provide to the Licensor being to

[clean the Room and Property] [provide clean sheets] [provide breakfast] [provide dinner]*

The PAYMENT   £ _____ per week/month* payable in advance on the _____ of each week/month*

being payment for the Room and Services

The DEPOSIT   £_____

The INVENTORY means the list of the Licensor's possessions at the Property which has been signed by the

Licensor and the Licensee

DATED   _____

SIGNED   _____   _____

_____   _____

(The Licensor)   (The Licensee)

THIS AGREEMENT comprises the particulars detailed above and the terms and conditions printed overleaf whereby the Room is licensed by the Licensor and taken by the Licensee for occupation during the Period upon making the Payment.

Terms and Conditions on next page

LODGER/BED & BREAKFAST LICENCE

Terms and Conditions

1. The Licensee will:

1.1 only in conjunction with the occupation of the Room be allowed to share with the other occupiers of the Property the use and facilities of the common parts of the Property (including such bathroom, toilet, kitchen and sitting room facilities as may be at the Property)

1.2 pay the Payment at the times and in the manner aforesaid without any deduction or abatement of set-off whatsoever

1.3 keep the interior of the Room in a good clean and tenantable state and condition and not damage or injure the Property or any part of it

1.4 yield up the Room at the end of the Period in the same clean state and condition it was in at the beginning of the Period

1.5 maintain in the Room and keep in a good and clean condition all of the items listed in the Inventory

1.6 not make any alteration or addition to the Room nor without the Licensor's prior written consent to do any redecoration or painting of the Room

1.7 not do or omit to do anything on or at the Property which may be or become a nuisance or annoyance to the Licensor or any other occupiers of the Property or owners or occupiers of adjoining or nearby premises or which may in any way prejudice the insurance of the Property or cause an increase in the premium payable therefor

1.8 not without the Licensor's prior consent allow or keep any pet or any kind of animal at the Property

1.9 not use or occupy the Room in any way whatsoever other than as a private residence

1.10 not assign, sublet, charge or part with or share possession or occupation of the Room or any part thereof

1.11 pay interest at the rate of 4% above the Base Lending Rate for the time being of the Licensor's bankers upon any payment or other money due from the Licensee under this Agreement which is more than 10 days in arrear in respect of the period from when it become due down to the date of payment

2. In the event of the Payment being unpaid for more than 10 days after it is due (whether demanded or not) or there being a breach of any other of the Licensee's obligations under this Agreement then the Licensor may re-enter the Room and this Agreement shall thereupon determine absolutely but without prejudice to any of the Licensor's other rights and remedies in respect of any outstanding obligations on the part of the Licensee

3. The Deposit has been paid by the Licensee and is held by the Licensor to secure compliance with the Licensee's obligations under this Agreement (without prejudice to the Licensor's other rights and remedies) and if, at any time during the Period, the Licensor is obliged to draw upon it to satisfy any outstanding breaches of such obligations then the Licensee shall forthwith make such additional payment as is necessary to restore the full amount of the Deposit held by the Licensor. As soon as reasonably practicable following determination of this Agreement the Licensor shall return to the Licensee the Deposit or the balance thereof after any deductions properly made

4. The Licensor hereby notifies the Licensee that any notices (including notices in proceedings) should be served upon the Licensor at the address stated with the name of the Licensor overleaf

5. In the event of damage to or destruction of the Property by any of the risks insured against by the Licensor the Licensee shall be relieved from making the Payment to the extent that the Licensee's use and enjoyment of the Property is thereby prevented and from performance of its obligations as to the state and condition of the Property to the extent of and whilst there prevails any such damage or destruction (except to the extent that the insurance is prejudiced by any act or default of the Licensee)

6. So long as the reference to a right of early termination in the definition of "the PERIOD" overleaf (the "early termination right) has not been deleted then either party may at an time during the period terminate this Agreement by giving to the other prior written notice to that effect, the length of such notice to be that stated in the early termination right, and upon the expiry of said notice this Agreement shall end with no further liability for either party save for any antecedent breach

7. The Licensee shall not have exclusive possession of the Room and the identity of the other occupiers of the Property shall be in the absolute discretion of the Licensor

8. Where the context so admits:

8.1 the "Licensor" includes the successors in title to the Licensor's interest in the Property

8.2 the "Property" includes all of the Licensor's fixtures and fittings at or upon the Property and all of the items listed in the Inventory and (for the avoidance of doubt) the Room

8.3 the "Period" shall mean the period stated in the particulars overleaf or any shorter or longer period in the event of an earlier termination or an extension or holding over respectively

9. All references to the singular shall include the plural and vice versa and any obligations or liabilities of more than one person shall be joint and several and an obligation on the part of a party shall include an obligation not to allow or permit the breach of that obligation

LOST CREDIT CARD NOTICE

Date _____

To _____

_____

_____

Dear _____

This is to confirm that the credit card described below has been lost or stolen. Please put a stop on all credit in respect of the card. I last remember using the card myself on _____ 19.___ at _____. I shall destroy the card if subsequently found, and I would be grateful if you could issue me with a replacement card.

Yours faithfully

_____
Cardholder

Address _____

_____

_____

_____
Credit Card Number

MAGAZINE ARTICLE ROYALTY CONTRACT

THIS AGREEMENT IS MADE the _____ day of _____ 19____

BETWEEN:

(1) _____ (the "Author"); and

(2) _____ (the "Publisher").

NOW IT IS HEREBY AGREED as follows:

1.   The Author agrees to deliver an original and one copy of the manuscript which is tentatively titled _____ (the "Work"), to the Publisher on or before _____ 19 _____. The Work is described as:

_____

_____

If the Author fails to deliver the Work within _____ days of the Work due date, the Publisher may terminate this contract.

2.   Within _____ days of receipt of the Work, the Publisher agrees to notify the Author if the Publisher finds the work unsatisfactory in form or content. The Publisher also agrees to provide the Author with a list of necessary changes. The Author agrees to make the changes within _____ days. If the Publisher still reasonably rejects the Work as unsatisfactory, the Publisher may terminate this contract.

3.   The Author grants the Publisher the first _____ Serial Rights in the Work. Any rights not specifically granted to the Publisher shall remain with the Author. The Author agrees not to exercise any retained rights in such a manner as to adversely affect the value of the rights granted to the Publisher.

4.   The Publisher shall pay to the Author upon acceptance of the Work the amount of £_____.

5.   The style, format, design, layout, and any required editorial changes of the published work shall be in the sole discretion of the Publisher.

6.   The Author warrants that:

(a)   the Work is the sole creation of the Author;

(b)   the Author is the sole owner of the rights granted under this contract;

(c)   the Work does not infringe the copyright of any other work;

(d)   the Work is original and has not been published before;

(e)   the Work is not in the public domain;

(f)   the Work is not obscene, libellous, and does not invade the privacy of any person;

(g)   all statements of fact in the Work are true and based upon reasonable research.

7.   The Publisher acknowledges that the Author retains worldwide copyright in the Work.

8.   The Publisher agrees that, within one year from the receipt of a satisfactory manuscript of the Work, the Work will be published at Publisher's sole expense. If the Publisher fails to do so, unless prevented by conditions beyond the Publisher's control, the Author may terminate this Contract.

9.   This contract is the complete agreement between the Author and Publisher. No modification or waiver of any terms will be valid unless in writing and signed by both parties.

IN WITNESS OF WHICH the parties have signed this agreement the day and year first above written

_____

Signed by the Author

_____

in the presence of (witness)

Name _____

Address _____

_____

Occupation _____

_____

Signed for and on behalf of the Publisher

_____

in the presence of (witness)

Name _____

Address _____

_____

Occupation _____

MAILING LIST NAME REMOVAL REQUEST

Date _____

To _____

_____

_____

Dear _____

Please note that I have received unsolicited mail from your firm. I request that you remove my name from your mailing list, and that you do not send me unsolicited material in the future.

My name and address appears as below (or as per mailing label attached).

Name _____

Address _____

_____

_____

_____

Thank you for your attention to this request.

Yours faithfully

_____

MILEAGE REIMBURSEMENT REPORT

Employee Name: _____

Driving Licence No. _____ Car Reg No. _____

Make/Model of Vehicle _____

Department _____ Month _____

Date	Beginning Reading	Ending Reading	Total Mileage	Reason for Travel

Total mileage this month: _____ @£_____ Per Mile = £ _____

Approved by _____ Date _____

Title _____

MINUTES OF ANNUAL GENERAL MEETING

Minutes of the annual general meeting of _____ Limited

held at _____ on the _____ day

of _____ 199 _____ .

Present: _____ (Chairman)

_____ (Managing Director)

_____ (Director)

_____ (Members)

In attendance: _____ (Company Secretary)

_____ (Auditor)

1. The chairman announced that he had received proxies from _____ members and that _____ members were present in person. He declared that a quorum was present.

2. The directors' report and the accounts for the period to _____ were presented and approved.

3. It was resolved that Messrs. _____ Chartered Accountants, having agreed to remain as auditors to the company, be reappointed auditors of the company until the conclusion of the next meeting at which the accounts of the company are laid and that the chairman be empowered to agree to their fee.

4. It was resolved that the final dividend/the dividend recommended by the directors on _____ 19____ of £_____ per share for the year ended _____ be and is paid/declared payable on the ordinary shares of the company to all members whose names appear in the Register of Members on _____ 19____ and that such dividend be paid on _____ _____ 19____ .

5. There being no further business the meeting was closed.

_____
Chairman

MINUTES OF DIRECTORS' MEETING
CHANGING OBJECTS OF COMPANY

Minutes of a meeting of the directors held on the _____ day of _____ 199 __

Present: _____ (Chairman)

               _____ (Managing Director)

               _____ (Director)

               _____ (Members)

In attendance: _____ (Company Secretary)

1.   The board considered the future activities of the company. Having determined that the objects of the company were too restrictive and should be altered, it was decided that the memorandum of association of the company should be altered by deleting subclause (__) of clause ___ of the memorandum of association and substituting therefor: "To carry on business as a general commercial company."

2.   It was resolved that an extraordinary general meeting of the company be held on _____ the ____ day of _____ 199 ___ at _____ o'clock for the purpose of considering and, if thought fit, passing as a special resolution the following:

"That the memorandum of association of the company should be altered by deleting subclause (__) of clause ___ of the memorandum of association and substituting therefor:

'To carry on business as a general commercial company.' "

Furthermore, the secretary was instructed to give notice to all shareholders of the extraordinary general meeting.

3.   There being no further business the meeting was closed.

_____
Chairman

MINUTES OF EXTRAORDINARY GENERAL MEETING

Minutes of an extraordinary general meeting of the members of _____

_____ Limited held at _____ at

___o'clock on _____ the _____day of _____ 199 _____

Present: _____ (Chairman)

_____ (Managing Director)

_____ (Director)

_____ (Members)

In attendance: _____ (Company Secretary)

1.   The chairman announced that he had received proxies from _____

_____ in favour of himself. He declared that all members of the company

were present in person or by proxy and that a quorum was present.

2.   The notice convening the meeting was read.

3.   It was proposed as a special resolution:

"That _____

_____

_____ "

_____ .

The resolution was carried unanimously.

4.   There being no further business the meeting was closed.

Dated this _____ day of _____ 199___.

_____
Chairman

MINUTES OF EXTRAORDINARY GENERAL MEETING CHANGING OBJECTS OF COMPANY

Minutes of an extraordinary general meeting of the members of _____

_____ Limited held at _____ at

___o'clock on _____ the _____day of _____ 199 _____

Present: _____ (Chairman)

                   _____ (Managing Director)

                   _____ (Director)

                   _____ (Members)

In attendance: _____ (Company Secretary)

1. The chairman declared that a quorum was present.

2. The notice convening the meeting was read.

3. It was proposed as a special resolution:

"That the memorandum of association of the company be altered by deleting subclause (___) of clause ___ and substituting therefor the following subclause:

'(___)   To carry on business as a general commercial company.' "

The resolution was carried unanimously.

4. There being no further business the meeting was closed.

Dated this _____ day of _____ 199____.

_____
Chairman

MODEL RELEASE

In consideration for the sum of £ _____, receipt of which I hereby acknowledge, I grant to: _____

the exclusive world rights, including copyright, to use any photographs containing my image for publication in _____ and for subsidiary use, promotional use, future revisions and future editions of the same.

I waive any right to inspect or approve the final use of such photographs and I waive any right to file any legal actions, including libel or invasion of privacy, based on any use of the photographs under this release.

I am of legal age and understand the content of this document.

Permission is granted on _____ 19____.

_____
Signature of Model

MUTUAL CANCELLATION OF CONTRACT

THIS AGREEMENT IS MADE the _____ day of _____ 19 ____

BETWEEN:

(1) _____ of _____ (the "First Party"); and

(2) _____ of _____ (the "Second Party").

WHEREAS:

(A) The parties entered into a Contract dated _____ 19 ____ (the "Contract").

(B) The parties wish mutually to terminate the Contract and all their obligations and rights thereunder.

NOW IT IS HEREBY AGREED as follows:

1.   The parties hereby agree to terminate the Contract.

2.   The parties further agree that the termination shall be without further recourse by either party against the other and this document shall constitute mutual releases of any further obligations under the Contract, all to the same extent as if the Contract had not been entered into in the first instance, provided the parties shall herewith undertake to perform the act, if any, described below to terminate the Contract, which obligations, shall remain binding, notwithstanding this agreement to cancel.

_____

_____

IN WITNESS OF WHICH the parties have signed this agreement the day and year first above written

_____   _____
Signed by or on behalf of the First Party   Signed by or on behalf of the Second Party

_____   _____
in the presence of (witness)   in the presence of (witness)

Name _____   Name _____

Address _____   Address _____

_____   _____
Occupation   Occupation

MUTUAL RELEASES

THIS AGREEMENT IS MADE the _____ day of _____ 19 _____

BETWEEN:

(1) _____ of _____ (the "First Party"); and

(2) _____ of _____ (the "Second Party").

NOW IT IS HEREBY AGREED as follows:

1.   The First Party and the Second Party do hereby completely, mutually and reciprocally release, discharge, acquit and forgive each other from all claims, contracts, actions, demands, agreements, liabilities, and proceedings of every nature and description that either party has or may have against the other, arising from the beginning of time to the date of these presents, including but not necessarily limited to an incident or claim described as:

_____

_____

_____

2.   This release shall be binding upon and inure to the benefit of the parties, their successors and assigns.

IN WITNESS OF WHICH the parties have signed this agreement the day and year first above written

_____   _____
Signed by or on behalf of the First Party   Signed by or on behalf of the Second Party

_____   _____
in the presence of (witness)   in the presence of (witness)

Name _____   Name _____

Address _____   Address _____

_____   _____
Occupation   Occupation

NATIONAL LOTTERY SYNDICATE AGREEMENT

SYNDICATE NAME: _____

MANAGER	DATE OF APPOINTMENT	SIGNATURE

MEMBER	INDIVIDUAL STAKE (to be paid IN ADVANCE of each Draw by the agreed deadline)	DATE JOINED SYNDICATE	MANAGER'S SIGNATURE	MEMBER'S SIGNATURE	DATE LEFT SYNDICATE	MANAGER'S SIGNATURE

The Syndicate will participate in Draws on: Wednesdays only*   (*delete as appropriate)

Saturdays only*

Wednesdays and Saturdays*

Agreed deadline for payment of Individual Stakes: Day (each week):_____

Time: _____

(Syndicate Rules on next page)

NATIONAL LOTTERY SYNDICATE RULES

1. Definitions

'**Draw**' means a draw of the Camelot National Lottery in which the Syndicate has agreed to participate;

'**Individual Stake**' means the stake payable by each Member as set out in this Agreement and received by the Manager in advance of each Draw by the agreed deadline;

'**Manager**' means the Manager of the Syndicate, who shall be appointed and may be replaced at any time without notice by a majority of the Members;

'**Members**' means all those persons who have joined and not left the Syndicate;

'**Syndicate Stake**' means the total of the Members' Individual Stakes in respect of any Draw.

2. Manager's Responsibilities

    2.1 The Manager will:

        (a) establish a procedure for agreeing the combinations of numbers to be entered by the Syndicate for each Draw;

        (b) buy tickets bearing the agreed numbers for the amount of the Syndicate Stake for each Draw. However, if the Syndicate Stake is not sufficient to buy tickets bearing all agreed combinations of numbers in any Draw, the Manager shall have absolute discretion as to which of the agreed combinations to enter;

        (c) collect any prize money and account to the Members for it in proportion to their Individual Stakes, holding it in trust for the Members in the meantime.

    2.2 If any Member fails to pay his Individual Stake to the Manager in advance of any Draw by the agreed deadline, the Manager may (but shall not be obliged to) pay that Individual Stake on the Member's behalf and, if the Manager does so, the Member will reimburse the Manager forthwith upon demand.

    2.3 The Manager shall not be liable to any Member for any loss or damage arising out of any failing of the Manager under this Agreement, provided that the Manager has acted honestly.

3. Members' Responsibilities

The Members will each pay their Individual Stake to the Manager in advance of each Draw by the agreed deadline.

4. Ceasing to be a Member

A Member shall be removed from the Group:

    4.1 if the Member wishes to leave; or

    4.2 at the discretion of the Manager, if the Member fails to pay his Individual Stake in accordance with Rule 3 in respect of any 3 weeks (whether consecutive or non-consecutive); or

    4.3 at the discretion of the Manager, if the Member fails to reimburse the Manager in accordance with Rule 2.2.

5. This Agreement

    5.1 It shall be the responsibility of the Manager to update and amend this Agreement. Any such amendment, other than the removal of a Member in accordance with Rule 4, must have been authorised by majority vote of the Members.

    5.2 The list of Members in this Agreement shall be conclusive as to the membership of the Syndicate at any point in time, provided that a person whose application for membership has been accepted by the Manager and who has duly paid an agreed Individual Stake shall not be excluded from a share of prize money under Rule 2.1(c) merely because the Agreement has not been updated to record that person as a Member.

    5.3 The appointment or replacement of the Manager shall take effect whether or not this Agreement has been amended to that effect.

NOMINATION OF A REPLACEMENT ROOM
(House/Flat Share Agreement)

Date _____

Ref _____

To _____ (name of Tenant(s))

_____

_____

Dear Sharer(s)

Re. _____ (the Property)

Our Agreement in respect of your Room at the above Property states that you may be required to move to another room in the Property if required by me/us. Please note that I/we do now wish to move you from the Room you currently occupy to another room in the Property and which is located at

_____ (the room in the Property this Sharer
and would ask that you make the move into this new Room straightaway. is now to move to)

Thanking you in anticipation of your co-operation in this.

Yours faithfully

_____ (Landlord's signature &
printed name & address)

_____

_____

_____

NOMINEE SHAREHOLDER'S DECLARATION OF TRUST

I, _____, of _____,

hereby acknowledge and declare that I hold _____ fully paid ordinary shares in _____

_____ Ltd ("the Share") registered in my name as nominee

of and Trustee for _____ ("the Owner") and I undertake and agree

not to transfer, deal with or dispose of the Share save as the Owner may from time to time

direct and further to give full effect to the trust hereby declared I hereby deposit with the

Owner the Certificate for the Share together with a transfer thereof executed by me in blank

and I hereby expressly authorise and empower the Owner at any time to complete such

transfer by inserting therein the name or names of any transferee or transferees and the date

of the transfer and to complete the same in any other necessary particular and I expressly

declare that this authority is irrevocable by me. Furthermore I irrevocably assign to the Owner

the right to receive any dividends which may be declared on the Share together with all

profits and other monies which may be paid or payable to me from time to time upon the

Share or in respect thereof, and I further agree and undertake to exercise my voting power as

Holder of the Share in such manner and for such purpose as the Owner may from time to time

direct or determine.

Dated this _____ day of _____ 199 _____.

_____
Signature

_____
Signature of Witness

Address _____

_____

_____
Occupation _____

NOTICE FOR REGULATED HIRE PURCHASE
OR CREDIT SALE AGREEMENTS

NOTE: This form is prescribed by the Consumer Credit (Cancellation Notices and Copies of Documents) Regulations 1983 (S.I. 1983 No. 1557).

YOUR RIGHT TO CANCEL. You have a right to cancel this agreement. You can do this by sending or taking a **WRITTEN** notice of cancellation to _____ _____.

You have **FIVE** days starting with the day after you receive this copy. You can use the form provided. If you cancel this agreement, any money you have paid, goods given in part-exchange (or their value) and property given as security must be returned to you. You will not have to make any further payment. If you already have goods under the agreement, you should keep them safe (legal action may be taken against you if you do not take proper care of them). You can wait for them to be collected from you and you need not hand them over unless you receive a written request. If you wish, however, you may return the goods yourself.

NOTE: COMPLETE AND RETURN THIS FORM ONLY IF YOU WISH TO CANCEL THE AGREEMENT

Date _____

To _____

_____

_____

_____

(Name and address of seller)

I/We hereby give notice that I/we wish to cancel agreement number _____.

_____

Signature

_____

Signature

NOTICE OF ACCEPTANCE OF ORDER

Date _____

Ref _____

To _____

_____

_____

Dear _____

Re: Acceptance of Order

Please note that we have received the following goods, with thanks, as per our order no. _____ dated _____ 19 _____:

_____

_____

_____

The goods are further identified by invoice no. _____ and consignment note/ packing slip no. _____

Please be advised that we have inspected the goods and they have been received in good condition, and in conformity with our order.

Yours sincerely

_____

NOTICE OF ANNUAL GENERAL MEETING

_____ LIMITED

Company number:_____

NOTICE is hereby given that the annual general meeting of _____
Limited will be held at _____ on the
_____ day of_____199 _____ at _____ o'clock.

AGENDA

1. _____

   _____

2. _____

   _____

3. _____

   _____

4. _____

   _____

5.   To transact any other lawful business.

Dated this _____ day of _____ 199 _____.

BY ORDER OF THE BOARD

_____
Company Secretary

Registered Office:

_____

_____

_____

Note:

Any member entitled to attend and vote at the meeting is entitled to appoint a proxy to attend and vote in his place. A proxy need not be a member of the company.

NOTICE OF ASSIGNMENT

Date _____

To _____

_____

_____

Dear _____

I attach a copy of an assignment dated _____ 19 _____ by which I assigned my interest in the contract referred to therein to _____ of _____ (the "Assignee") Please hold all sums of money affected by such assignment, now or hereafter in your possession, that otherwise are payable to me under the terms of our original agreement, for the benefit of the Assignee, in accordance with the provisions of the assignment.

Yours sincerely

_____

NOTICE OF CANCELLATION OF PURCHASE ORDER

Date _____

To _____

_____

_____

Dear _____

Re: Cancellation of Purchase Order

On _____ 19 _____, as per our order no. _____, a copy of which is enclosed, we ordered the following goods from you:

_____

_____

_____

We paid for these goods by our cheque no. _____, dated _____ 19 _____, in the amount of £ _____.

On _____ 19 _____, we demanded immediate delivery of the goods. To date, the goods have not been delivered to us.

By this notice we therefore cancel this order, because of late delivery, and demand immediate reimbursement. Unless we receive a refund within 10 days of the date of this letter, we will take immediate legal action. Please be advised that we reserve all our legal rights.

Thank you for your immediate attention to this matter.

Yours sincerely

_____

NOTICE OF CLAIM FOR INDEMNITY FROM JOINT-VENTURER

Date _____

To _____

_____

_____

Dear _____

Re _____

A claim has been made by _____ to
the effect that_____.

Under the terms of our joint venture agreement this is part of your responsibility. We have
denied that _____ has a valid claim
and have denied liability generally, so your position is, so far as possible at this stage,
protected.

We are advised that, in law, we have joint liability to the claim but that we are entitled to ask
you to indemnify us.

Please confirm that you accept liability for this matter (if there is any valid claim) and that
you will hold us fully indemnified against the claim and the costs of defending it.

I should be pleased to hear from you as a matter of urgency.

Yours sincerely

_____

NOTICE OF CONDITIONAL ACCEPTANCE OF FAULTY GOODS

Date _____

To _____

_____

_____

Dear _____

Re: Conditional Acceptance of Faulty Goods.

On _____ 19 _____, we received a delivery from you as per our order no. _____, dated _____ 19 _____. The goods delivered at that time were faulty for the following reasons:

_____

_____

_____

Although these goods are defective and we are not obliged to accept them, we are prepared to do so on the condition that you credit our account with you for £ _____.

This credit will make the total amount payable under this order £ _____.

If you do not accept this proposal within 10 days from the date of this letter, we will reject these goods as faulty and they will be returned to you. Please be advised that we reserve all our legal rights.

Thank you for your immediate attention to this matter.

Yours sincerely

_____

NOTICE OF CONDITIONAL ACCEPTANCE OF NON-CONFORMING GOODS

Date _____

Ref _____

To _____

_____

_____

Dear _____

Re: Conditional Acceptance of Non-Conforming Goods.

On _____ 19 _____, we received delivery from you as per our order no. _____, dated _____ 19 _____. The goods delivered at that time do not conform to the specifications that were provided with our order for the following reasons:

_____

_____

Although these goods are non-conforming and we are not obliged to accept them, we are prepared to accept these goods on the condition that you credit our account with you for £ _____. This credit will make the total amount payable under this order £ _____.

If you do not accept this proposal within 10 days from the date of this letter, we will reject these goods as non-conforming and they will be returned to you. Please be advised that we reserve all our legal rights.

Thank you for your immediate attention to this matter.

Yours sincerely

_____

NOTICE OF DEFAULT IN PAYMENT

Date _____

To _____

_____

_____

Dear _____

You are hereby notified that your payment of _____

Pounds (£ _____) due on or before _____ 19 _____, has not been

received by us. If payment is not made by _____, we shall invoke the

remedies under the agreement between us dated _____, together with

such other remedies as we may have, and this matter shall be referred to our solicitors.

Yours sincerely

_____

NOTICE OF DEMAND FOR DELIVERY OF GOODS

Date _____

Ref _____

To _____

_____

_____

Dear _____

Re: Demand for Delivery of Goods

On _____ 19 _____, as per our order no. _____, a copy of which is enclosed, we ordered the following goods from you:

_____

_____

_____

We paid for these goods by cheque no. _____, dated _____ 19 ____, in the amount of £ _____.

To date, the goods have not been delivered to us. We therefore demand the immediate delivery of these goods. Unless the goods are delivered to us within 10 days of the date of this letter, we will take action to cancel this purchase order and have our money returned. Please be advised that we reserve all our legal rights.

Thank you for your immediate attention to this matter.

Yours sincerely

_____

NOTICE OF DISMISSAL LETTER (CAPABILITY)

Date _____

To _____

_____

_____

Dear _____

I refer to our meeting on _____.

As I explained at the meeting, you have been unable to carry out your duties to the standards required by the Company. Therefore, we have no alternative but to terminate your employment with the Company with effect from _____.

As you are aware, we have provided you with training and assistance to enable you to improve your performance but without success. In addition, we have attempted to find suitable alternative employment within the Company, but regret that nothing is available.

You are entitled to be paid in full, including any accrued holiday pay, during your notice period.

I take this opportunity of reminding you that you are entitled to appeal against this decision through the Company's disciplinary procedure. If you wish to exercise this right you must let me know within two working days of receipt of this letter.

It is with regret that we have had to take this action. We should like to thank you for your past efforts for the Company and wish you every success for the future.

Yours sincerely

_____

Personnel Manager

NOTICE OF DISMISSAL LETTER (SICKNESS)

Date _____

To _____

_____

_____

Dear _____

I refer to our meeting on _____.

As I explained at the meeting, you have been unable to carry out your duties to the standards required by the Company. Therefore, we have no alternative but to terminate your employment with the Company with effect from _____.

As you are aware, we have provided you with training and assistance to enable you to improve your performance but without success. In addition, we have attempted to find suitable alternative employment within the Company, but regret that nothing is available.

You are entitled to be paid in full, including any accrued holiday pay, during your notice period.

I take this opportunity of reminding you that you are entitled to appeal against this decision through the Company's disciplinary procedure. If you wish to exercise this right you must let me know within two working days of receipt of this letter.

It is with regret that we have had to take this action. We should like to thank you for your past efforts for the Company and wish you every success for the future.

Yours sincerely

_____

Personnel Manager

NOTICE OF DISPUTED ACCOUNT

Date _____

Ref _____

To _____

_____

_____

Dear _____

We refer to your invoice/order/statement no. _____, dated _____ 19 ____, in the amount of £_____.

We dispute the balance you claim to be owed for the following reason(s):

_____ Items invoiced for have not been received.

_____ Prices are in excess of the agreed amount. A credit of £ _____ is claimed.

_____ Our payment of £ _____ made on _____ 19____, has not been credited.

_____ Goods delivered to us were not ordered and are available for return on delivery instructions.

_____ Goods were defective as per prior letter.

_____ Goods are available for return and credit as per your sales terms.

_____ Other: _____

Please credit our account promptly in the amount of £_____ so it may be satisfactorily cleared.

Yours sincerely

_____

NOTICE OF DORMANT COMPANY

THE COMPANIES ACTS 1985 AND 1989

SPECIAL RESOLUTION OF

_____LIMITED

At a general meeting of the above-named company held on the ____ day of _____
199 _____ the following special resolution was passed:

"It is resolved that the company, having been dormant since its formation, be exempt from the obligation to appoint auditors as otherwise required by Part VII of the Companies Act 1985, as amended by the Companies Act 1989".

Dated this _____ day of _____ 199 ____.

_____
Company Secretary

NOTICE OF ELECTION UNDER S.113 OF THE INCOME AND CORPORATION TAXES ACT 1988

Date _____

Ref _____

To: HM Inspector of Taxes

_____

_____

_____

Dear Sir/Madam

Re: _____ and Partners

We give you notice pursuant to s.113(2) of the Income and Corporation Taxes Act 1988, that following the admission into/departure from this partnership on the _____ day of _____ _____ 199 ____ of _____, we elect that s.113(1) of the Act shall not apply and that the business shall be treated as a continuing concern and not as though a new business has been set up.

Signed by us being all the partners engaged in the business before and after the change.

Yours faithfully

_____

Partner's signature

_____

Partner's signature

_____

Partner's signature

NOTICE OF EXTRAORDINARY GENERAL MEETING

_____ **LIMITED**

NOTICE is hereby given that an extraordinary general meeting of the above-named company will be held at _____ on _____ the _____ day of _____ 199 ____ at _____ o'clock for the purpose of considering and, if thought fit, passing the following ordinary/special/elective/extraordinary resolutions:

_____

_____

_____

_____

_____

Dated this _____ day of _____ 199 ____.

BY ORDER OF THE BOARD

_____
Company Secretary

Registered office:

_____

_____

_____

Note: Any member entitled to attend and vote at the meeting is entitled to appoint a proxy to attend and vote in his place. A proxy need not be a member of the company.

NOTICE OF EXTRAORDINARY GENERAL MEETING TO CHANGE OBJECTS OF COMPANY

_____ LIMITED

NOTICE is hereby given that an extraordinary general meeting of the above named company will be held at _____ on _____ the _____ day of _____ 199 _____ at _____ o'clock for the purpose of considering and, if thought fit, passing the following special resolution:

"That the memorandum of association of the company be altered by deleting subclause (__) of clause ___ and substituting therefor the following subclause:

(__) To carry on business as a general commercial company."

Dated this _____ day of _____ 199 _____.

BY ORDER OF THE BOARD

_____
Company Secretary

Registered office.

_____

_____

_____

Note: Any member entitled to attend and vote at the meeting is entitled to appoint a proxy to attend and vote in his place. A proxy need not be a member of the company.

NOTICE OF GOODS SOLD ON APPROVAL

Date _____

Ref _____

To _____

_____

_____

Dear _____

Re: Goods Sold on Approval

Please be advised that the following goods are being delivered to you on approval:

_____

_____

_____

If these goods do not meet your requirements, you may return all or a part of them at our expense within _____ days of your receipt of them.

Any goods sold on approval that are not returned to us by that time will be considered accepted by you and you will be invoiced for accordingly.

We trust that you will find our goods satisfactory and thank you for your custom.

Yours sincerely

_____

NOTICE OF INTENTION TO RECOVER PAYMENT IN DEFAULT

Date _____

To _____

_____

_____

Dear _____

Re: Agreement Reference:_____

We refer to the default notice which we issued on _____ in connection with the above agreement and note that the period during which you could have remedied the default has expired and we still have not received the full arrears.

In the circumstances, this letter is our formal demand for payment of the outstanding balance, as detailed below:

Outstanding Balance: £ _____

Less Rebate Allowable *:   £ _____

Amount to be paid: £ _____

* This rebate has been calculated on the assumption that payment of the amount demanded reaches us by _____. If it does not, we shall bring proceedings against you for the outstanding balance claimed and, if this results in our obtaining payment before the sum would have become due under the agreement, we shall allow any appropriate rebate of change once we have received the payment in full.

Your sincerely

_____

Signature of Authorised Signatory on behalf of the Finance Company

NOTICE OF REJECTION OF NON-CONFORMING GOODS

Date _____

Ref _____

To _____

_____

_____

Dear _____

Re: Rejection of Non-Conforming Goods

On _____ 19 _____, we received delivery from you as per our order no. _____, dated _____ 19 _____. The goods delivered at that time do not conform to the specifications that were provided with our order for the following reasons:

_____

_____

_____

We paid for these goods by our cheque no. _____, dated _____ 19 ____, in the amount of £ _____. This cheque has been cashed by you.

By this notice, we reject the delivery of these goods and request reimbursement. Unless we receive a refund of our money within 10 days of the date of this letter, we will take immediate legal action for its recovery.

Please further advise us as to your wishes for the return of the rejected goods at your expense. Unless we receive instructions within 10 days of this letter, we accept no responsibility for their safe storage. Please be advised that we reserve all our legal rights.

Thank you for your immediate attention to this matter.

Yours sincerely

_____

NOTICE OF REJECTION OF ORDER

Date _____

Ref _____

To _____

_____

_____

Dear _____

Re: Rejection of Order

On _____ 19 _____, we received delivery from you as per our order no. _____, dated _____ 19 _____. We reject these goods for the following reasons:

_____

_____

We paid for these goods by our cheque no. _____, dated _____ 19 _____, in the amount of £_____.

By this notice, we reject the delivery of these goods and request reimbursement. Unless we receive a refund of our money within 10 days of the date of this letter, we will take immediate legal action for its recovery.

Please further advise us as to your wishes for the return of the rejected goods at your expense. Unless we receive instructions for their return within 10 days of this letter, we accept no responsibility for their safe storage. Please be advised that we reserve all our legal rights.

Thank you for your immediate attention to this matter.

Yours sincerely

_____

NOTICE OF REPLACEMENT OF REJECTED GOODS

Date _____

Ref _____

To _____

_____

_____

Dear _____

Re: Notice of Replacement of Rejected Goods

On _____ 19 _____ , we delivered the following goods to you as per your order no._____ , dated_____ 19 _____:

_____

_____

_____

_____

On _____ 19 _____, we received notice that you had rejected delivery of these goods.

Please return the rejected goods to us at our expense using the same carrier that delivered the goods.

In addition, please be advised that we are shipping replacement goods to you at our expense.

If this replacement of the rejected goods is not satisfactory, please contact us immediately. We apologise for any inconvenience this may have caused you.

Yours sincerely

_____

NOTICE OF RESULT OF GRIEVANCE INVESTIGATION

Date _____

Ref _____

To _____

_____

_____

Dear _____

I am writing to let you know that your grievance relating to _____

_____ has been fully investigated in accordance with the

company's grievance procedures.

Having considered your complaint and having heard all that has been said by you, or on your

behalf, and having taken full account of all that has been said by your trade union

representative, it has been decided

_____

_____

_____

This matter has now been fully investigated and whilst I can understand that you may still feel

aggrieved, I am sorry that the matter must now be considered closed.

Yours sincerely

_____

NOTICE OF RETURN OF GOODS SOLD ON APPROVAL

Date _____

Ref _____

To _____

_____

_____

Dear _____

Re: Return of Goods Sold on Approval

On _____ 19 _____, as per our order no. _____, a copy of which is enclosed, we received the following goods from you on approval:

_____

_____

_____

_____

_____

Please be advised that we have decided to return these goods to you.

Thank you very much for the opportunity to examine the goods.

Yours sincerely

_____

NOTICE OF TRADE TERM VIOLATIONS

Date _____

Ref _____

To _____

_____

_____

Dear _____

We routinely review all our accounts. We have found a record of irregular payments on your account, which frequently leaves balances unpaid beyond our credit terms.

Whilst we value your continued custom, we would also appreciate payment within our agreed credit terms.

We look forward to your future co-operation in this matter.

Yours sincerely

_____

NOTICE OF WITHHELD DELIVERY

Date _____

Ref _____

To _____

_____

_____

Dear _____

Thank you for your order dated _____ 19 _____. It is now ready for delivery.

However, we find that the following invoices remain unpaid beyond our agreed credit terms:

Invoice no.	Amount	Due date
_____	£_____	_____
_____	£_____	_____
_____	£_____	_____
_____	£_____	_____

Please send us your cheque promptly in the amount of £_____ to clear these invoices. We shall then deliver your order immediately.

Yours sincerely

_____

NOTICE OF WRONGFUL REFUSAL TO ACCEPT DELIVERY

Date _____

Ref _____

To _____

_____

_____

Dear _____

Reference is made to your order dated _____ 19 ____, a copy of which is enclosed.

We delivered the goods in accordance with the agreed terms but you have refused to accept them. We now consider the purchase contract to have been wrongfully breached by you.

Accordingly, we shall not attempt further delivery and shall hold you liable for all damages arising from your failure to fulfil your obligations under the order.

Should you wish to rectify the situation by now accepting shipment you must call us immediately and we shall arrange re-shipment at your expense.

Please contact us immediately should you have any questions on this matter.

Yours sincerely

_____

NOTICE TO CANCEL DELAYED GOODS

Date _____

Ref _____

To _____

_____

_____

Dear _____

Reference is made to our purchase order or contract dated _____ 19 ____, a copy of which is enclosed.

Under the terms of the order, the goods were to be delivered by _____ 19 ____. Due to your failure to deliver the goods within the required time, we hereby cancel this order, reserving such further rights as we may have.

If the above goods are in transit, they shall be refused or returned at your expense and we shall await delivery instructions.

Yours sincerely

_____

NOTICE TO DISSOLVE A TWO-PARTY PARTNERSHIP

Date _____

Ref _____

To _____

_____

_____

Dear _____

I hereby give you notice to dissolve the partnership between us on _____ 19 ____. I request that final accounts of the partnership be drawn up to enable its assets to be distributed in accordance with the partnership agreement.

Yours sincerely

_____

NOTICE TO EMPLOYEE BEING LAID OFF
AND GIVING GUARANTEE PAYMENTS

Date _____

To _____

_____

_____

Dear _____

I refer to our meeting on _____.

As I explained at that meeting, we regret that because of economic pressure we have no option but to lay you off from work.

The period of lay off shall take effect from _____ and shall continue until _____. You shall receive guarantee payments of £14.50 per day for the first five days of this period.

I very much regret that we have been forced to take this action, but I should like to assure you that we are working hard to ensure that the period of lay off is kept to a minimum.

Yours sincerely

_____

Personnel Manager

NOTICE TO EMPLOYER OF INTENTION
TO TAKE MATERNITY LEAVE

Date _____

To _____

_____

_____

Dear _____

This is to inform you that I am pregnant and wish to take maternity leave. I enclose a medical/ maternity certificate dated _____ 199 ___ from Dr _____.

The expected week of childbirth is _____ and I intend to start taking my maternity leave on _____ 199 ___. I understand that I am entitled to 14 weeks' leave in total by law.

Please also let me know if I am entitled to receive Statutory Maternity Pay during my maternity leave.

Your sincerely

_____

NOTICE TO EMPLOYER OF INTENTION TO TAKE MATERNITY LEAVE AND MATERNITY ABSENCE

Date _____

To _____

_____

_____

Dear _____

This is to inform you that I am pregnant and wish to take both maternity leave and maternity absence. I understand that I have completed a sufficient period of continuous employment with you to be entitled to maternity absence. I enclose a medical/maternity certificate date _____ 199 ___ from Dr _____.

The expected week of childbirth is _____ and I intend to start taking my maternity leave on _____ 199 ___. I understand that I am entitled to 14 weeks' maternity leave, and thereafter maternity absence until the end of the 28th week after the week in which I give birth. I intend to exercise the right to return to work after that date.

I wish also to receive the Statutory Maternity Pay to which I am entitled during my maternity leave.

Yours sincerely

_____

NOTICE TO END EMPLOYMENT

Date _____

Ref _____

To _____

_____

_____

Dear _____

In accordance with your contract of employment with us we give you notice of the termination of your employment with us on the _____ day of _____ 19 _____. The reasons for this decision are:

_____

_____

_____

_____

I regret that this must be written in such formal terms and I want you to know that I deeply regret having to ask that you leave. You understand the circumstances which have brought this about, and I hope that you will soon find other employment to your satisfaction.

Yours sincerely

_____

NOTICE TO REVOKE AN ELECTION UNDER S.113
OF THE INCOME AND CORPORATION TAXES ACT 1988

Date _____

Ref _____

To: HM Inspector of Taxes

_____

_____

_____

Dear Sir/Madam

Re: _____ and Partners

We hereby revoke the election made by us pursuant to s.113(2) of the Income and Corporation Taxes Act 1988 on the _____ day of _____ 199 _____.

Yours faithfully

_____
Partner's signature

_____
Partner's signature

_____
Partner's signature

NOTICE TO STOP GOODS IN TRANSIT

Date _____

Ref _____

To _____ (Carrier)

_____

_____

Dear _____

You currently have goods of ours in transit under consignment note no. _____
for delivery to:

_____

_____

_____

This is to confirm our previous instruction by telephone to stop delivery of these goods and return them to us; we shall pay return freight charges.

No negotiable bill of lading or document of title has been delivered to our customer (the consignee).

A copy of our delivery documents for these goods is enclosed for your reference.

Yours sincerely

_____

Copy to:

Customer _____

NOTICE TO TERMINATE

(Rental Agreement or
House/Flat Share Agreement)

TO _____ (name(s) of
Tenant/Sharer)

_____

**YOUR
LANDLORD/
OWNER** _____ (name(s) and
address of
Landlord/Owner)

_____

_____

**REQUIRES
POSSESSION OF
THE PROPERTY
KNOWN AS** _____ (address of the
Property)

_____

ON THE _____ (Date for
Possession)

SIGNED BY _____ (the Landlord/
Owner **or** his/her
agent)

(if signed by the agent then the agent's name and address must

also be written here) _____

_____

_____

DATE OF NOTICE _____

IMPORTANT NOTICE TO LANDLORDS/OWNERS:

In the case of an Assured Shorthold Tenancy Rental Agreement the Date for Possession must be at least **TWO MONTHS** after the Tenant receives this Notice and in the case of a House/Flat Share Agreement (Non-Resident Owner) it must be at least **FOUR WEEKS** after the Sharer receives this Notice; in the case of a House/Flat Share Agreement (Resident Owner) ANY REASONABLE PERIOD of notice can be given.

IMPORTANT NOTICE :

(1) If the Tenant/Sharer does not leave the dwelling, the Landlord/Owner must get an order for possession from the court before the Tenant/Sharer can lawfully be evicted. The Landlord/Owner cannot apply for such an order before the Notice to Terminate has run out, i.e. the Date for Possession.

(2) A Tenant/Sharer who does not know if he has any right to remain in possession after the Notice to Terminate runs out can obtain advice from a solicitor. Help with all or part of the cost of legal advice and assistance may be available under the Legal Aid Scheme. The Tenant/Sharer should also be able to obtain information from a Citizens Advice Bureau, a Housing Aid Centre or a rent officer.

NOTICE TO TERMINATE
(House/Flat Share Agreement)

TO _____ (name(s) and
address of
_____ Owner)

_____

I/WE _____ (name(s) of
Sharer)

_____

**GIVE YOU
NOTICE THAT
OUR AGREEMENT
IN RESPECT OF** _____ (address of the
Property)

_____

**IS HEREBY
TERMINATED
WITH EFFECT
FROM THE** _____ (Date for
Possession)

SIGNED BY _____ (the Sharer(s))

DATE OF NOTICE _____

IMPORTANT NOTICE TO SHARERS:

In the case of a House/Flat Share Agreement (Non-Resident Owner) the Date For Possession must be at least FOUR WEEKS after the Owner receives this Notice and in the case of a House/Flat Share Agreement (Resident Owner) ANY REASONABLE PERIOD of notice can be given.

* An Assured Shorthold Tenancy Rental Agreement needs NO NOTICE from the Tenant at the end of the Agreement.

IMPORTANT NOTICE :

(1) If the Tenant/Sharer does not leave the dwelling, the Landlord/Owner must get an order for possession from the court before the Tenant/Sharer can lawfully be evicted. The Landlord/Owner cannot apply for such an order before the Notice to Terminate has run out, i.e. the Date for Possession.

(2) A Tenant/Sharer who does not know if he has any right to remain in possession after the Notice to Terminate runs out can obtain advice from a solicitor. Help with all or part of the cost of legal advice and assistance may be available under the Legal Aid Scheme. The Tenant/Sharer should also be able to obtain information from a Citizens Advice Bureau, a Housing Aid Centre or a rent officer.

NOTIFICATION OF BUSINESS TRANSFER — NO REDUNDANCY

Date _____

Ref _____

To _____

_____

_____

Dear _____

Our business has been acquired by _____ with effect from _____ 19 ____.

In accordance with the Transfer of Undertakings (Protection of Employment) Regulations 1981, your employment continues at your current salary and on the terms of your existing contract of employment. This change will not affect the continuity of your employment.

It is likely that you will be required to transfer to the new company's pension scheme. Another letter will be sent to you with full details of the scheme as it affects you.

Yours sincerely

_____

OFFER OF EMPLOYMENT TO AVOID REDUNDANCY

Date _____

Ref _____

To _____

_____

_____

Dear _____

After discussions with our employees and representatives of _____

_____ Union, we regretfully conclude that we must

close the _____ section of the company. This will mean

redundancy for some employees.

However, I am pleased to advise you that _____ can offer

you alternative employment as a _____. The salary and

terms of employment will approximate to what you are currently receiving from us.

Please confirm to me that you accept this employment offer.

Yours sincerely

_____

OFFER TO SETTLE BY ARBITRATION

Date _____

To _____

_____

_____

Dear _____

I am sorry that we seem to be unable to reconcile our differing points of view. I am sure that neither of us wishes to resort to the courts and I therefore suggest that we refer the dispute between us to arbitration. I propose:

1. The dispute be referred to arbitration.

2. The arbitrator shall be Mr. _____, who is an expert in these matters. If you cannot agree to him, the arbitrator shall be appointed by the President or Vice-President of the Chartered Institute of Arbitrators.

3. The Rules of the Chartered Institute of Arbitrators in a domestic arbitration shall apply.

4. The costs of the arbitration shall be left to the discretion of the arbitrator.

5. Only one expert witness shall be allowed for each side.

6. The arbitration shall take place at _____and the dispute shall be decided in accordance with English law.

7. The making of an award by the arbitrator shall be a condition precedent to any right of action by either of us against the other in respect of the matter in dispute.

If you agree to this suggestion, please sign and return the enclosed copy of this letter.

Yours sincerely

_____

OPTION TO BUY LAND AGREEMENT

THIS AGREEMENT IS MADE the _____ day of _____ 19 ____

BETWEEN:

(1) _____ of _____ (the "Buyer"); and

(2) _____ of _____ (the "Seller").

WHEREAS:

The Seller now owns the following land and/or property (the "Property"):

_____

_____

NOW IT IS HEREBY AGREED as follows:

1. In consideration of the sum of £ _____ , receipt of which is hereby acknowledged by the Seller, the Seller grants to the Buyer an exclusive option to buy the Property for the following price and on the following terms (the "Option"):

_____

_____

_____

_____ .

2. The amount received by the Seller from the Buyer referred to in paragraph 1. above will be credited against the purchase price of the Property if the Option is exercised by the Buyer. If the Option is not exercised, the Seller will retain this payment.

3. The option period will be from the date of this Agreement until _____ 19 ___, at which time the Option will expire unless exercised.

4. During this period, the Buyer has the option and exclusive right to buy the Property on the terms set out herein. The Buyer must notify the Seller in writing of the decision to exercise the Option.

5. No modification of this agreement will be effective unless it is in writing and is signed by both the Buyer and Seller. This agreement binds and benefits both the Buyer and Seller and any successors. Time is of the essence of this agreement. This document, including any attachments, is the entire agreement between the Buyer and Seller.

IN WITNESS OF WHICH the parties have signed this agreement the day and year first above written

_____

Signed by or on behalf of the Buyer

_____

in the presence of (witness)

Name _____

Address _____

_____

Occupation _____

_____

Signed by or on behalf of the Seller

_____

in the presence of (witness)

Name _____

Address _____

_____

Occupation _____

OPTION TO PURCHASE GOODS

THIS AGREEMENT IS MADE the _____ day of _____ 19 _____

BETWEEN:

(1) _____ of _____ (the "Buyer"); and

(2) _____ of _____ (the "Seller").

NOW IT IS HEREBY AGREED as follows:

1. In consideration for the sum of £ _____, receipt of which is hereby acknowledged by the Seller, the Seller grants to the Buyer an option to buy the following property (the "Property") on the terms set out herein.

_____

_____

_____

_____

_____

_____

_____

2. The Buyer has the option and right to buy the Property within the option period for the full price of £ _____.

3. This option period shall be from the date of this agreement until _____ 19 _____, at which time the option will expire unless exercised.

4. To exercise this option, the Buyer must notify the Seller in writing within the option period. All notices shall be sent to the Seller at the following address:

_____

_____

_____

5. Should the Buyer exercise the option, the Seller and the Buyer agree immediately to enter into a contract for the sale of the Property.

6. This agreement shall be binding upon and inure to the benefit of the parties, their successors and assigns.

IN WITNESS OF WHICH the parties have signed this agreement the day and year first above written

_____

Signed by or on behalf of the Buyer

_____

in the presence of (witness)

Name _____

Address _____

_____

Occupation _____

_____

Signed by or on behalf of the Seller

_____

in the presence of (witness)

Name _____

Address _____

_____

Occupation _____

ORDER TO STOP A CHEQUE

Date _____

To _____

_____

_____

Dear _____

Please stop the payment of the following cheque:

      Name of Payee: _____

      Date of Cheque: _____

      Cheque No.:   _____

      Amount: _____

If this cheque has already been honoured, please advise me of the date of payment.

Thank you for your co-operation.

Yours sincerely

_____

Name of Account _____

Account No. _____

ORGAN DONATION

of

_____ (Full name)

In the hope that I may help others, I hereby make this gift, if medically acceptable, to take effect upon my death.

The words and marks below indicate my wishes:

I give: a)_____any needed organs.

b)_____only the following organs for purposes of transplantation, education or medical research: _____

_____

_____

c)_____my entire body, for anatomical or medical study, if needed.

Limitations or special wishes:

_____

_____

Signed by the donor and following two witnesses, in the presence of each other.

_____

Signature of Donor

Date Signed _____

Date of Birth _____

Address _____

_____

_____

_____

Witness

_____

Witness

OVERDUE ACCOUNT REMINDER

Date _____

Ref _____

To _____

_____

_____

Dear _____

We sent you a statement a recently. Please note that your account is overdue in the amount of £_____.

Please remit payment to us as soon as possible.

Yours sincerely

_____

PARTIAL DELIVERY REQUEST

Date _____

Ref _____

To _____

_____

_____

Dear _____

Thank you for your order dated _____ 19 _____. The value of the order is approximately £ _____, we regret, however, that we cannot extend to credit you for the entire amount at the present time.

Accordingly we suggest that we deliver to you a partial order on our standard credit terms reducing the quantities ordered by _____ per cent. Upon payment we shall release the balance of the order. If you request a different order configuration we would, of course, be pleased to accommodate you.

Unless we hear from you to the contrary within the next 10 days, we shall assume you accept our recommendation and we shall deliver accordingly.

Hopefully, we shall soon be in a position to increase your credit limit.

Yours sincerely

_____

PARTNERSHIP AGREEMENT

THIS PARTNERSHIP AGREEMENT is made the _____ day

of _____ 199 ____

BETWEEN **(1)** _____ of _____

_____ (the "First Partner");

and

(2) _____ of _____

_____ (the "Second Partner");

hereinafter together called the "Partners".

NOW IT IS HEREBY AGREED as follows:

1. THE BUSINESS

The Partners shall carry on business in Partnership as _____ under the name of

_____ at _____

_____ as from _____ 199 ____ .

2. DURATION OF THE PARTNERSHIP

The Partnership shall continue until terminated under the terms of this Agreement or until the death or bankruptcy of either Partner.

3. CAPITAL

The Capital of the Partnership shall consist of the sum of £_____which is made up as follows:

_____

_____

Unless otherwise agreed, the capital of the Partnership shall belong to the Partners equally and any increase in capital shall be made in equal shares.

4. PROFITS AND LOSSES

Unless otherwise agreed, the Partners will share all profits and losses (including capital losses) equally.

5. BANK

The Partners shall open an account in the name of the Partnership at _____ Bank

of _____

and any money belonging to the Partnership shall be paid into the account and the signatures of both Partners shall be required on all cheques drawn and on all other instruments and instructions made in connection with the account.

6. ACCOUNTANTS

The accountants to the Partnership shall be _____

of _____

The Partners shall keep such accounting records as the accountants shall recommend. The accountants shall be instructed to prepare accounts in respect of each accounting period of the Partnership, such period to end on ____ each year, and the Partners shall agree and sign the accounts.

7. WORKING PRACTICE

Each Partner shall devote his best efforts and his whole time and attention to the business of the Partnership in good faith. Each Partner shall be entitled to take____ weeks holiday in each   calendar

year at such times as the Partners shall agree. All decisions relating to the Partnership shall be made by unanimous agreement between the Partners unless otherwise agreed[, except that neither Partner shall without the consent of the other _____

_____

_____

_____].

8. TERMINATION

Either Partner may terminate the Partnership by giving to the other not less than _ months' notice in writing, in which case the other Partner shall have the right excercisable by counternotice before the expiry of such notice to purchase the share of the outgoing Partner at the net value of such share. If such counternotice is not served before the expiry of the notice the Partnership shall be dissolved. The net value of the share shall be determined by the Partners and in default of agreement shall be decided by the accountants acting as experts not arbitrators. If any Partner commits a serious breach or consistent breaches of this Agreement or is guilty of any conduct which may have a serious and detrimental effect on the Partnership the other Partner may by notice in writing expel such Partner from the Partnership.

IN WITNESS OF WHICH the parties hereto have signed this Agreement the day and year first above written.

SIGNED   _____   **DATED** _____

Signed by the First Partner

SIGNED   _____   **DATED** _____

Signed by the Second Partner

PAY ADVICE

_____ **Ltd**

Name: _____   Date: _____

Works/Dept No.: _____   Tax Code: _____

National Insurance: _____   Tax Week: _____

Payments	Hours	Rate		Total	
		£	p	£	p
Basic	_____				
Overtime	_____				
Bonus, Holiday, Sick Pay	_____				
		Gross Payable			

Gross wages to date
£   .   p

Deductions	£	p
Company Pension		
Income Tax		
National Insurance		
Standard rate at ____%		
Reduced rate at ____%		
Other deductions		
Total deductions		
Net Payable		

Tax deducted to date
£   .   p

Keep this record of your earnings

PERMISSION TO USE PHOTOGRAPH

The copyright owner hereby grants to: _____

non-exclusive worldwide rights to the following photograph(s) for the following purposes:

_____

_____

_____

_____

The photographer hereby asserts his/her moral rights as author of the photograph(s), and the following credit should appear against every usage of the photograph(s) in acknowledgement of those rights:

_____

_____

_____

_____

In return for the grant of this permission, the copyright owner acknowledges receipt of the sum of £ _____ from the grantee.

Permission is granted on _____ 19_____.

_____

Signature of owner of copyright

PERMISSION TO USE QUOTATION OR PERSONAL STATEMENT

THIS LICENCE IS MADE the _____ day of _____ 19 _____

BETWEEN:

(1) _____ of _____ (the "Licensor"); and

(2) _____ of _____ (the "Licensee").

NOW IT IS HEREBY AGREED as follows:

1. In consideration for the sum of £ _____, receipt of which the Licensor hereby acknowledges, the Licensor hereby grants a non-exclusive worldwide licence to the Licensee (the "Licence") to use, publish or reprint in whole or in part, the following statement, picture, endorsement, quotation or other material:

_____

_____

_____

2. This Licence shall extend only to a publication known as _____ _____, including all new editions, reprints, excerpts, advertisements, publicity and promotions of the publication, and further including such publications as hold subsidiary rights thereto.

3. This agreement shall be binding upon and inure to the benefit of the parties, their successors and assigns.

IN WITNESS OF WHICH the parties have signed this licence the day and year first above written

_____   _____
Signed by or on behalf of the Licensor   Signed by or on behalf of the Licensee

_____   _____
in the presence of (witness)   in the presence of (witness)

Name _____   Name _____

Address _____   Address _____

_____   _____
Occupation   Occupation

PERSONAL PROPERTY RENTAL AGREEMENT

THIS AGREEMENT IS MADE the _____ day of _____ 19 _____

BETWEEN:

(1) _____ of _____ (the "Owner"); and

(2) _____ of _____ (the "Renter").

NOW IT IS HEREBY AGREED as follows:

1.   The Owner hereby rents to the Renter the following personal property (the "Property"):

_____

_____

2.   The Renter shall pay to the Owner the sum of £ _____ as payment for the rental herein, payable as follows:

_____

_____

_____

3.   The Renter shall during the rental term keep and maintain the Property in good condition and repair and shall be responsible for any loss, damage or destruction to the Property notwithstanding how caused and the Renter agrees to return the Property in its present condition, reasonable wear and tear excepted.

4.   The Renter shall not during the rental period allow others use of the Property.

5.   The rental period shall commence on _____ 19 _____, and terminate on _____ 19 _____, at which date the Property shall be promptly returned.

IN WITNESS OF WHICH the parties have signed this agreement the day and year first above written

_____   _____
Signed by or on behalf of the Owner   Signed by or on behalf of the Renter

_____   _____
in the presence of (witness)   in the presence of (witness)

Name _____   Name _____

Address _____   Address _____

_____   _____
Occupation   Occupation

POOLS SYNDICATE AGREEMENT

For the Football Pools competition run by:

and called: _____

SYNDICATE NAME: _____

MANAGER	DATE OF APPOINTMENT	SIGNATURE

MEMBER	INDIVIDUAL STAKE (to be paid IN ADVANCE of each Match Day by the agreed deadline)	DATE JOINED SYNDICATE	MANAGER'S SIGNATURE	MEMBER'S SIGNATURE	DATE LEFT SYNDICATE	MANAGER'S SIGNATURE

Agreed deadline for payment of Individual Stakes: Time: _____

Day: _____ days before each Match Day

(Syndicate Rules on next page)

Pools Syndicate Agreement Rules

1. Definitions

'**Coupon**' means an appropriate coupon or coupons for the agreed pools competition;

'**Individual Stake**' means the stake payable by each Member as set out in this Agreement and received by the Manager in advance of each Match Day before the agreed deadline;

'**Manager**' means the Manager of the Syndicate, who shall be appointed and may be replaced at any time without notice by a majority of the Members;

'**Match Day**' means a day or days of scheduled football matches for which a Coupon may be submitted under the agreed pools competition;

'**Members**' means all those persons who have joined and not left the Syndicate;

'**Syndicate Stake**' means the total of the Members' Individual Stakes in respect of any Match Day.

2. Manager's Responsibilities

2.1 The Manager will:

(**a**) establish a procedure for agreeing the match selections to be entered by the Syndicate for each Match Day;

(**b**) complete and enter a Coupon bearing the agreed match selections for the amount of the Syndicate Stake for each Match Day. However, if the Syndicate Stake is not sufficient to buy a Coupon bearing all agreed match selections for any Match Day, the Manager shall have absolute discretion as to which of the match selections to enter;

(**c**) collect any prize money and account to the Members for it in proportion to their Individual Stakes, holding it in trust for the Members in the meantime.

2.2 If any Member fails to pay his or her Individual Stake to the Manager in advance of any Match Day by the agreed deadline, the Manager may (but shall not be obliged to) pay that Individual Stake on the Member's behalf and, if the Manager does so, the Member will reimburse the Manager forthwith upon demand.

2.3 The Manager shall not be liable to any Member for any loss or damage arising out of any failing of the Manager under this Agreement, provided that the Manager has acted honestly.

3. Member's Responsibilities

The Members will each pay their Individual Stake to the Manager in advance of each Match Day by the agreed deadline.

4. Ceasing to be a Member

A Member shall be removed from the Group:

4.1 if the Member wishes to leave; or

4.2 at the discretion of the Manager, if the Member fails to pay his or her Individual Stake in accordance with Rule 3 in respect of any 3 weeks (whether consecutive or non-consecutive); or

4.3 at the discretion of the Manager, if the Member fails to reimburse the Manager in accordance with Rule 2.2.

5. This Agreement

5.1 It shall be the responsibility of the Manager to update and amend this Agreement. Any such amendment, other than the removal of a Member in accordance with Rule 4, must have been authorised by majority vote of the Members.

5.2 The list of Members in this Agreement shall be conclusive as to the membership of the Syndicate at any point in time, provided that a person whose application for membership has been accepted by the Manager and who has duly paid an agreed Individual Stake shall not be excluded from a share of prize money under Rule 2.1(c) merely because the Agreement has not been updated to record that person as a Member.

5.3 The appointment or replacement of the Manager shall take effect whether or not this Agreement has been amended to that effect.

PREMARITAL AGREEMENT

THIS AGREEMENT IS MADE the _____ day of _____ 19 _____

BETWEEN:

(1) _____ of _____ (the "First Party"); and

(2) _____ of _____ (the "Second Party").

WHEREAS:

The parties contemplate legal marriage under the law, and it is their mutual desire to enter into this agreement so that they will continue to own and control their own property, and are getting married because of their love for each other but do not desire that their present respective financial interests be changed by their marriage.

NOW IT IS HEREBY AGREED as follows:

1. All property which belongs to each of the above parties shall be, and shall forever remain, their personal estate, including all interest, rents, and profits which may accrue from said property, and said property shall remain forever free of claim by the other.

2. The parties shall have at all times the full right and authority, in all respects as if the parties had not married, to use, sell, enjoy, manage, give and convey all property as may presently belong to him or her.

3. In the event of a separation or divorce, the parties shall have no right against each other by way of claims for support, alimony, maintenance, compensation or division of property existing as of this date.

4. In the event of separation or divorce, marital property acquired after marriage shall nevertheless remain subject to division, either by agreement or judicial determination.

5. This agreement shall be binding upon and inure to the benefit of the parties, their successors and assigns.

IN WITNESS OF WHICH the parties have signed this agreement the day and year first above written

_____   _____

Signed by or on behalf of the First Party   Signed by or on behalf of the Second Party

_____   _____

in the presence of (witness)   in the presence of (witness)

Name _____   Name _____

Address _____   Address _____

_____   _____

Occupation _____   Occupation _____

PRODUCT DEFECT NOTICE

Date _____

Ref _____

To _____

_____

_____

Dear _____

Recently I purchased a product manufactured, distributed or sold by you and described as:

_____

This is to inform you that the product is defective; details as follows:

1. Date of purchase _____

2. Nature of defect _____

_____

3. Injuries or damage _____

4. Item purchased from _____

This information is provided to give you the earliest possible notice of the claim. Please inform me as to what course of action you intend to take to repair or replace the product.

Yours sincerely

_____

Name _____

Address _____

_____

_____

Tel _____

PROMISSORY NOTE

Principal Amount £ _____   Date _____

I, the undersigned, hereby promise to pay on demand to the order of _____

_____ the sum of _____pounds (£ _____)

together with interest thereon from the date hereof until paid at the rate of ___% per annum.

_____
Signed

_____
Name

_____
Witness

PROMISSORY NOTE WITH GUARANTEE

THIS DEED IS MADE the _____ day of _____ 19 _____

BETWEEN:

(1) _____ of _____ (the "Borrower");

(2) _____ of _____ (the "Lender"); and

(3) _____ of _____ (the "Guarantor").

NOW THIS DEED WITNESSES as follows:

1.   The Borrower hereby promises to pay to the order of the Lender the sum of _____ _____Pounds (£ _____), with interest thereon at the rate of _____ % per annum on the unpaid balance in the following manner:

2.   All payments shall be first applied to interest and the balance to principal.

3.   The Borrower shall have the right to prepay without penalty. In the event any payment due hereunder is not made when due, the entire unpaid balance shall, at the option of the Lender, become immediately due and payable.

4.   In the event of default, the Borrower agrees to pay all reasonable solicitors fees and costs of collection.

5.   In consideration for the sum of £_____, receipt of which from the Borrower the Guarantor hereby acknowledges, the Guarantor hereby guarantees to the Lender payment of this note and agrees to remain fully bound until full payment is made.

IN WITNESS OF WHICH the parties have signed this deed the day and year first above written

---

Signed by or on behalf of the Borrower   Signed by or on behalf of the Guarantor

---

in the presence of (witness)   in the presence of (witness)

Name _____   Name _____

Address _____   Address _____

Occupation _____   Occupation _____

Signed by or on behalf of the Lender

---

in the presence of (witness)

Name _____

Address _____

Occupation _____

PROPERTY INVENTORY

OF

_____ (NAME)

ITEM	ESTIMATED VALUE	LOCATION
_____	_____	_____
_____	_____	_____
_____	_____	_____
_____	_____	_____
_____	_____	_____
_____	_____	_____
_____	_____	_____
_____	_____	_____
_____	_____	_____
_____	_____	_____
_____	_____	_____
_____	_____	_____
_____	_____	_____
_____	_____	_____
_____	_____	_____
_____	_____	_____
_____	_____	_____
_____	_____	_____
_____	_____	_____

PURCHASE ORDER

_____ Ltd

Order to:		Order date:
		Order no.:
Deliver to:		Our ref no.:
		Account no.:

Product no	Description	Quantity	Unit price	Net

	Total Goods	
	Total VAT	
	Total £	

Please quote our order number on all correspondence.
Conditions of Purchase available on request.

Signed _____

For & on behalf of _____ Limited

QUOTATION

_____ Ltd

To: _____   ' Date: _____

_____   Contact: _____

We have pleasure in providing our quotation as follows:

Your Ref.	Spec No.	Description	Quantity	Unit cost £
			VAT	
			Total	

Delivery time from order:
Payment terms:
Samples available:
CONDITIONS OF SALE AVAILABLE ON REQUEST

RECEIPT

Date _____

Ref _____

To _____

_____

_____

BE IT KNOWN, that the undersigned hereby acknowledges receipt of the sum of £ _____
paid by _____which payment constitutes _____
payment of the below described debt:

_____

_____

_____

_____

If this is in partial payment of said obligation the remaining unpaid balance on this date is

£ _____.

Signed this _____ day of _____ 19 _____.

_____

RECEIPT FOR COMPANY PROPERTY

Employee: _____

Identification No:_____

Department/Section: _____

I hereby acknowledge receipt of the company property listed below. I agree to keep the property in good condition and to return it when I leave the company, or earlier on request. I agree to report immediately any loss or damage to the property. In addition, I agree to use the property only for work-related purposes.

1. Item_____ Received From_____ Date _____

Serial No_____ Returned To _____ Date _____

2. Item_____ Received From_____ Date _____

Serial No_____ Returned To _____ Date _____

3. Item_____ Received From_____ Date _____

Serial No_____ Returned To _____ Date _____

4. Item_____ Received From_____ Date _____

Serial No_____ Returned To _____ Date _____

5. Item_____ Received From_____ Date _____

Serial No_____ Returned To _____ Date _____

6. Item_____ Received From_____ Date _____

Serial No_____ Returned To _____ Date _____

_____
Employee

_____
Date

RECEIPT IN FULL

Date _____

Ref _____

To _____

_____

_____

Received from _____, the

amount of _____ Pounds (£ _____), in full payment

of all demands.

_____
Signed

RECEIPT ON ACCOUNT

Date _____

Ref _____

To _____

_____

_____

The undersigned acknowledges receipt of the sum of £ _____ paid by _____ _____. This payment will be applied and credited to the following account:

_____

_____

_____

_____
Signed

RECEIPT TO ACCOMPANY SHARE CERTIFICATE

of

_____

On this date, _____ has purchased _____ shares of common stock in this company, represented by share certificate number _____.
The shareholder has transferred to the company the following assets, with a fair market value of £ _____, in consideration for the receipt of the shares:

_____

_____

_____

Payment in full has been received for these shares and the share certificate representing the shares has been issued by the company to the shareholder. Record of this transaction has been recorded in the share transfer book of this company.

Date _____

_____
Secretary of the company

_____
Shareholder

REDUNDANCY WITH EX GRATIA PAYMENT

Date _____

To _____

_____

_____

Dear _____

I regret that you will be made redundant with effect from _____ , due to:

_____

_____

We have made every effort to find alternative employment for you but I regret that there are no suitable positions available at present.

The redundancy benefits that you are entitled to are:

1. Statutory redundancy pay   £ _____

2. Pay in lieu of notice
    (if less than the full notice is given)   £ _____

3. Other _____   £ _____

4. TOTAL   £ _____

In addition, in recognition of your years of good service to the company, you will be paid an ex gratia sum of £ _____. We will be writing to you separately about your pension entitlement.

Thank you for your past efforts on behalf of the company and I hope that you will soon find other suitable employment. You may submit our name as a reference in the confidence that the reference will be favourable.

If you wish to discuss any aspect of this letter, please do not hesitate to contact me.

Yours sincerely

_____

REFERENCE LETTER ON EMPLOYEE

Date _____

Ref _____

To _____

_____

_____

Dear _____

Re _____

In reply to your request for a reference for the above job application, I report to you as follows:

_____

_____

_____

I confirm that the individual was employed by this firm between the dates of
_____ 19 _____ and _____ 19 _____ in the capacity of
_____. My additional comments are as follows:

_____

_____

_____

This reference is given to be of help to you and in fairness to your proposed employee. It is given on the basis that we accept no legal liability and that you must rely upon your own judgment whether or not to proceed with your proposed employment of this individual. We trust you shall hold this reference in strict confidence.

Yours sincerely

_____

REJECTED GOODS NOTICE

Date _____

Ref _____

To _____

_____

_____

Dear _____

Please note that on _____ 19____, we received goods from you under our

order or contract dated _____ 19____.

We hereby notify you of our intent to reject and return the goods for the reason(s) indicated
below:

_____   Goods were not delivered within the time specified.

_____   Goods were defective or damaged as described overleaf.

_____   Goods did not conform to sample, advertisement, specifications, or price, as
stated overleaf.

_____   An order acknowledgment has not been received, and we therefore ordered
these goods from other sources.

_____   Goods represent only a partial shipment.

Please credit our account or issue a refund if prepaid, and provide instructions for the return
of these goods at your expense. Return of these goods however shall not be a waiver of any
legal claim we may have.

Yours sincerely

_____

REMINDER OF UNPAID ACCOUNT

Date _____

Ref _____

To _____

_____

_____

Dear _____

Re: Date   Invoice No.   Invoice Amount

_____19 _____   _____   £ _____

Our records indicate that the above account remains outstanding. We would be grateful for an early remittance.

If you have paid the amount within the past seven days, please ignore this letter.

Yours sincerely

_____

REMITTANCE ADVICE

Date _____

Ref _____

To _____

_____

_____

Dear _____

We enclose our cheque no._____ in the amount of £ _____. This cheque is only to be credited to the following charges/invoices/orders:

Invoice	Amount
_____	£_____
_____	£_____
_____	£_____
_____	£_____
_____	£_____

Please note that this payment shall only be applied to the items listed and shall not be applied, in whole or in part, to any other, charge, order or invoice that may be outstanding.

Yours sincerely

_____

RENT REVIEW MEMORANDUM

The PROPERTY _____

Name(s) of
LANDLORD(S) _____

_____

Name(s) of
TENANT(S) _____

_____

DATE OF
TENANCY _____

RENT REVIEW
DATE _____

NEW RENT _____

The Landlord(s) and the Tenant(s) hereby record their agreement that with effect from the rent review date stated above (and subject to any provisions in the tenancy for any further review in the future) the rent payable under the tenancy shall be the figure stated as the new rent above.

SIGNED _____   _____

_____   _____

(The Landlord(s))   (The Tenant(s))

RENT STATEMENT

Property _____

Name of Landlord/Owner _____

Address of Landlord/Owner _____

_____

Name of Tenant/Sharer _____

_____

Date Due	Amount Due	Date of Payment	Amount Paid	Cumulative Arrears	Signature of Landlord/Owner

IMPORTANT NOTICE:

This Rent Statement, or a Rent Book, must be supplied to the Tenant/Sharer if the rent/payment is paid weekly.

continued on next page

1. Address of premises _____

_____

_____

(1) These entries must be kept up-to-date

2. (1) Name and address of Landlord _____

_____

_____

3. (1) Name and address of agent (if any) _____

_____

_____

(2) Cross out whichever does not apply

4. (1) The rent payable   (2) including/excluding council tax) is

£ _____ per week.

5. Details of accommodation (if any) which the occupier has the

right to share with other persons _____

_____

_____

6. The other terms and conditions of the tenancy are _____

_____

_____

_____

_____

_____

_____

_____

_____

7. If you have an Assured Tenancy or an Assured Agricultural Occupancy you have certain rights under the Housing Act 1988. These include the right not to be evicted from your home unless your Landlord gets a possession order from the courts. Unless the property is let under an Assured *Shorthold* Tenancy, the courts can only grant an order on a limited number of grounds. Further details regarding Assured Tenancies are set out in the Department of the Environment and Welsh Office booklets "Assured Tenancies" No. 19 in the series of the housing booklets. These booklets are available from the rent officers, council offices and housing aid centres, some of which also give advice.

8. You may be entitled to get help to pay your rent through the housing benefit scheme. Apply to your local council for details.

9. It is a criminal offence for your Landlord to evict you without an order from the court or to harass you or interfere with your possessions or use of facilities in order to force you to leave.

10. If you are in any doubt about your legal rights or obligations, particularly if your Landlord has asked you to leave, you should go to a Citizens Advice Bureau, housing aid centre, law centre or solicitor. Help with all or part of the cost of legal advice from a solicitor may be available under the Legal Aid Scheme.

THE HOUSING ACT 1985

Summary of Part X of the Housing Act 1985, to be inserted in a Rent Book or similar document.

1. An occupier who causes or permits his dwelling to be overcrowded is liable to prosecution for an offence under the Housing Act 1985, and, if convicted, to a fine of up to level 2 of the standard scale, and a further fine of up to one-tenth of that level in respect of every day on which the offence continues after conviction. Any part of a house which is occupied by a separate household is a "dwelling".

2. A dwelling is overcrowded if the number of persons sleeping in it is more than the "permitted number", or is such that two or more of those persons, being ten years old or over, of opposite sexes (not being persons living together as husband and wife), must sleep in the same room.

3. The "permitted number" for the dwelling to which this Rent Statement relates is _____ persons. In counting the number of persons each child under ten counts as half a person, and a child of less than a year is not counted at all.

305

RENTAL AGREEMENT
(For a Furnished House or Flat on an Assured Shorthold Tenancy)

The PROPERTY _____

_____

The LANDLORD _____

of _____

_____

The TENANT _____

_____

_____

_____

_____

The Term _____ months beginning on _____

The RENT £ _____ per week/month* payable in advance on the _____ of each week/month*

The Deposit £ _____

The Inventory means the list of the Landlord's possessions at the Property which has been signed by the Landlord and the Tenant

DATED _____

SIGNED _____   _____

_____   _____

(The Landlord)   _____

(The Tenant)

THIS RENTAL AGREEMENT comprises the particulars detailed above and the terms and conditions printed overleaf whereby the Property is hereby let by the Landlord and taken by the Tenant for the Term at the Rent.

(* delete as appropriate)

IMPORTANT NOTICE TO LANDLORDS:
(1) The details of 'The LANDLORD' near the top of this Agreement must include an address for the Landlord in England or Wales as well as his/her name.
(2) Always remember to give the written Notice to Terminate to the Tenant two clear months before the end of the Term.

IMPORTANT NOTICE TO TENANTS:
(1) In general, if you currently occupy this Property under a protected or statutory tenancy and you give it up to take a new tenancy of the same or other accommodation owned by the same Landlord, that tenancy cannot be an Assured Shorthold Tenancy and this Agreement is not appropriate.
(2) If you currently occupy this Property under an Assured Tenancy which is not an Assured Shorthold Tenancy your Landlord is not permitted to grant you an Assured Shorthold Tenancy of this Property or of alternative property.

Terms and Conditions on next page

306

Terms and Conditions

1. This Agreement is intended to create an assured shorthold tenancy as defined in Section 19A Housing Act 1988 and the provisions for the recovery of possession by the Landlord in Section 21 thereof apply accordingly

2. The Tenant will:

2.1 pay the Rent at the times and in the manner aforesaid without any deduction abatement or set-off whatsoever

2.2 pay all charges in respect of any electric, gas, water and telephonic or televisual services used at or supplied to the Property and Council Tax or any similar tax that might be charged in addition to or replacement of it during the Term

2.3 keep the interior of the Property in a good, clean and tenantable state and condition and not damage or injure the Property

2.4 yield up the Property at the end of the Term in the same clean state and condition it was in at the beginning of the Term and if any item listed on the Inventory requires repair, replacing, cleaning or laundering pay for the same (reasonable wear and tear and damage by insured risks excepted)

2.5 not make any alteration or addition to the Property nor without the Landlord's prior written consent do any redecoration or painting of the Property

2.6 not do or omit to do anything on or at the Property which may be or become a nuisance or annoyance to the Landlord or owners or occupiers of adjoining or nearby premises or which may in any way prejudice the insurance of the Property or cause an increase in the premium payable therefor

2.7 not without the Landlord's prior consent allow or keep any pet or any kind of animal at the Property

2.8 not use or occupy the Property in any way whatsoever other than as a private residence

2.9 not assign, sublet, charge or part with or share possession or occupation of the Property

2.10 permit the Landlord or anyone authorised by the Landlord at reasonable hours in the daytime and upon reasonable prior notice (except in emergency) to enter and view the Property for any proper purpose (including the checking of compliance with the Tenant's obligations under this Agreement and during the last month of the Term the showing of the Property to prospective new tenants)

2.11 pay interest at the rate of 4% above the Base Lending Rate for the time being of the Landlord's bankers upon any Rent or other money due from the Tenant under this Agreement which is more than 3 days in arrear in respect of the period from when it became due to the date of payment

3. The Landlord will:

3.1 Subject to the Tenant paying the rent and performing his/her obligations under this Agreement allow the Tenant peaceably to hold and enjoy the Property during the term without lawful interruption from the Landlord or any person rightfully claiming under or in trust for the Landlord

3.2 insure the Property and the items listed on the Inventory

3.3 keep in repair the structure and exterior of the Property (including drains gutters and external pipes)

keep in repair and proper working order the installations at the Property for the supply of water, gas and electricity and for sanitation (including basins, sinks, baths and sanitary conveniences)

keep in repair and proper working order the installation at the Property for space heating and heating water

But the Landlord will not be required to:

carry our works for which the Tenant is responsible by virtue of his/her duty to use the Property in a tenant-like manner

rebuild or reinstate the Property in the case of destruction or damage by fire or by tempest flood or other inevitable accident

4. In the event of the Rent being unpaid for more than 10 days after it is due (whether demanded or not) or there being a breach of any other of the Tenant's obligations under this Agreement then the Landlord may re-enter the Property (subject to any statutory restrictions on his power to do so) and this Rental Agreement shall thereupon determine absolutely but without prejudice to any of the Landlord's other rights and remedies in respect of any outstanding obligations on the part of the Tenant

5. The Deposit has been paid by the Tenant and is held by the Landlord to secure compliance with the Tenant's obligations under this Agreement (without prejudice to the Landlord's other rights and remedies) and if, at any time during the Term, the Landlord is obliged to draw upon it to satisfy any outstanding breaches of such obligations then the Tenant shall forthwith make such additional payment as is necessary to restore the full amount of the Deposit held by the Landlord. As soon as reasonably practicable following termination of this Agreement the Landlord shall return to the Tenant the Deposit or the balance thereof after any deductions properly made

6. The Landlord hereby notifies the Tenant under Section 48 of the Landlord & Tenant Act 1987 that any notices (including notices in proceedings) should be served upon the Landlord at the address stated with the name of the Landlord overleaf

7. In the event of damage to or destruction of the Property by any of the risks insured against by the Landlord the Tenant shall be relieved from payment of the Rent to the extent that the Tenant's use and enjoyment of the Property is thereby prevented and from performance of its obligations as to the state and condition of the Property to the extent of and so long as there prevails such damage or destruction (except to the extent that the insurance is prejudiced by any act or default of the Tenant) the amount in case of dispute to be settled by arbitration

8. Where the context so admits:

8.1 The "Landlord" includes the persons for the time being entitled to the reversion expectant upon this Tenancy

8.2 The "Tenant" includes any persons deriving title under the Tenant

8.3 The "Property" includes any part or parts of the Property and all of the Landlord's fixtures and fittings at or upon the Property

8.4 The "Term" shall mean the period stated in the particulars overleaf or any shorter or longer period in the event of an earlier termination or an extension or holding over respectively

9. All references to the singular shall include the plural and vice versa and any obligations or liabilities of more than one person shall be joint and several and an obligation on the part of a party shall include an obligation not to allow or permit the breach of that obligation

RENTAL AGREEMENT
(For an Unfurnished House or Flat on an Assured Shorthold Tenancy)

The PROPERTY   _____

_____

The LANDLORD   _____

of   _____

_____

The TENANT   _____

_____

_____

_____

_____

The TERM   _____ months beginning on _____

The RENT   £ _____ per week/month* payable in advance on the _____ of each week/month*

The DEPOSIT   £ _____

DATED   _____

SIGNED   _____   _____

_____   _____

(The Landlord)   _____

(The Tenant)

THIS RENTAL AGREEMENT comprises the particulars detailed above and the terms and conditions printed overleaf whereby the Property is hereby let by the Landlord and taken by the Tenant for the Term at the Rent.

IMPORTANT NOTICE TO LANDLORDS:
(1)   The details of 'The LANDLORD' near the top of this Agreement must include an address for the Landlord in England or Wales as well as his/her name.
(2)   Always remember to give the written Notice to Terminate to the Tenant two clear months before the end of the Term.

IMPORTANT NOTICE TO TENANTS:
(1)   In general, if you currently occupy this Property under a protected or statutory tenancy and you give it up to take a new tenancy of the same or other accommodation owned by the same Landlord that tenancy cannot be an Assured Shorthold Tenancy and this Agreement is not appropriate.
(2)   If you currently occupy this Property under an Assured Tenancy which is not an Assured Shorthold Tenancy your Landlord is not permitted to grant to you an Assured Shorthold Tenancy of this Property or of alternative property.

Terms and Conditions on next page

Terms and Conditions

1. This Agreement is intended to create an assured shorthold tenancy as defined in Section 19A Housing Act 1988 and the provisions for the recovery of possession by the Landlord in Section 21 thereof apply accordingly

2. The Tenant will:

2.1   pay the Rent at the times and in the manner aforesaid without any deduction abatement or set-off whatsoever

2.2   pay all charges in respect of any electric, gas, water and telephonic or televisual services used at or supplied to the Property and Council Tax or any similar tax that might be charged in addition to or replacement of it during the Term

2.3   keep the interior of the Property in a good, clean and tenantable state and condition and not damage or injure the Property

2.4   yield up the Property at the end of the Term in the same clean state and condition it was in at the beginning of the Term (reasonable wear and tear and damage by insured risks excepted)

2.5   not make any alteration or addition to the Property nor without the Landlord's prior written consent do any redecoration or painting of the Property

2.6   not do or omit to do anything on or at the Property which may be or become a nuisance or annoyance to the Landlord or owners or occupiers of adjoining or nearby premises or which may in any way prejudice the insurance of the Property or cause an increase in the premium payable therefor

2.7   not without the Landlord's prior consent allow or keep any pet or any kind of animal at the Property

2.8   not use or occupy the Property in any way whatsoever other than as a private residence

2.9   not assign, sublet, charge or part with or share possession occupation of the Property

2.10   permit the Landlord or anyone authorised by the Landlord at reasonable hours in the daytime and upon reasonable prior notice (except in emergency) to enter and view the Property for any proper purpose (including the checking of compliance with the Tenant's obligations under this Agreement and during the last month of the Term the showing of the Property to prospective new tenants)

2.11   pay interest at the rate of 4% above the Base Lending Rate for the time being of the Landlord's bankers upon any Rent or other money due from the Tenant under this Agreement which is more than 3 days in arrear in respect of the period from when it became due to the date of payment

3. The Landlord will:

3.1   Subject to the Tenant paying the rent and performing his/her obligations under this Agreement allow the Tenant peaceably to hold and enjoy the Property during the term without lawful interruption from the Landlord or any person rightfully claiming under or in trust for the Landlord

3.2   insure the Property

3.3   keep in repair the structure and exterior of the Property (including drains gutters and external pipes)

keep in repair and proper working order the installations

at the Property for the supply of water, gas and electricity and for sanitation (including basins, sinks, baths and sanitary conveniences)

keep in repair and proper working order the installation at the Property for space heating and heating water

But the Landlord will not be required to:

carry our works for which the Tenant is responsible by virtue of his/her duty to use the Property in a tenant-like manner

rebuild or reinstate the Property in the case of destruction or damage by fire or by tempest flood or other inevitable accident

4. In the event of the Rent being unpaid for more than 10 days after it is due (whether demanded or not) or there being a breach of any other of the Tenant's obligations under this Agreement then the Landlord may re-enter the Property (subject to any statutory restrictions on his power to do so) and this Rental Agreement shall thereupon determine absolutely but without prejudice to any of the Landlord's other rights and remedies in respect of any outstanding obligations on the part of the Tenant

5. The Deposit has been paid by the Tenant and is held by the Landlord to secure compliance with the Tenant's obligations under this Agreement (without prejudice to the Landlord's other rights and remedies) and if, at any time during the Term, the Landlord is obliged to draw upon it to satisfy any outstanding breaches of such obligations then the Tenant shall forthwith make such additional payment as is necessary to restore the full amount of the Deposit held by the Landlord. As soon as reasonably practicable following termination of this Agreement the Landlord shall return to the Tenant the Deposit or the balance thereof after any deductions properly made

6. The Landlord hereby notifies the Tenant under Section 48 of the Landlord & Tenant Act 1987 that any notices (including notices in proceedings) should be served upon the Landlord at the address stated with the name of the Landlord overleaf

7. In the event of damage to or destruction of the Property by any of the risks insured against by the Landlord the Tenant shall be relieved from payment of the Rent to the extent that the Tenant's use and enjoyment of the Property is thereby prevented and from performance of its obligations as to the state and condition of the Property to the extent of and so long as there prevails such damage or destruction (except to the extent that the insurance is prejudiced by any act or default of the Tenant) the amount in case of dispute to be settled by arbitration

8. Where the context so admits:

8.1   The "Landlord" includes the persons for the time being entitled to the reversion expectant upon this Tenancy

8.2   The "Tenant" includes any persons deriving title under the Tenant

8.3   The "Property" includes any part or parts of the Property and all of the Landlord's fixtures and fittings at or upon the Property

8.4   The "Term" shall mean the period stated in the particulars overleaf or any shorter or longer period in the event of an earlier termination or an extension or holding over respectively

9. All references to the singular shall include the plural and vice versa and any obligations or liabilities of more than one person shall be joint and several and an obligation on the part of a party shall include an obligation not to allow or permit the breach of that obligation

REPLY TO CREDIT CLAIM

Date _____

Ref _____

To _____

_____

_____

Dear _____

We have investigated your claim that we should credit your account for the following ticked reason(s):

_____ Prices are above the agreed amount.

_____ Non-credited payments in the amount of £_____.

_____ Goods invoiced for have not been received.

_____ Goods were not ordered.

_____ Goods were defective or wrongly delivered.

_____ Goods are available for return.

_____ Other: _____.

We regret we must reject your claim for a credit for the following reason:

_____

_____

We now request payment in the amount of £ _____ without further delay. Please contact us if you have any further questions.

Yours sincerely

_____

REQUEST FOR ADVANCE PAYMENT

Date _____

Ref _____

To _____

_____

_____

Dear _____

Upon reviewing your past credit record with us, we are compelled to say that we cannot continue to offer credit terms to you. Consequently, future orders can only be delivered with payment in advance.

We regret any inconvenience this may cause, but remind you that this arrangement will allow you to take advantage of the discounts we offer for early payment.

We hope this will be only a temporary arrangement, and that in the near future we can again extend credit terms to you.

Yours sincerely

_____

REQUEST FOR BANK CREDIT REFERENCE

Date _____

Ref _____

To _____

_____

_____

Dear _____

Re _____

The above account holder has requested the we obtain a banking reference from you. In order that we may evaluate trade terms for this account, we would appreciate the following information:

1. How long has the account holder had an account with you?

2. What is the average balance on the account?

3. Is the account routinely overdrawn?

4. Is the account a borrowing or non-borrowing account?

5. If the account holder borrows, please advise:

   i) present balance on loans;

   ii) terms of repayment;

   iii) is repayment satisfactory;

6. Is the overall banking relationship satisfactory?

Any additional comments or information you provide would be greatly appreciated and, of course, we would equally appreciate any future information involving a change in the account holder's financial situation or their banking relationship with you. We accept your reference without liability on your part.

All information will be held in the strictest confidence.

Yours sincerely

_____

REQUEST FOR CREDIT REFERENCE

Date _____

Ref _____

To _____

_____

_____

Dear _____

Re _____

The above named has recently applied to us for credit terms and has cited you as a credit reference. We would be grateful if you could provide us with the following information:

i) Credit limit.

ii) Terms.

iii) How long the credit account has been open.

iv) Present amount owed.

v) Payment history.

Any other information you believe to be helpful is welcome. All information will be held in the strictest confidence. We accept your reference without liability on your part.

A pre-paid envelope is enclosed for your convenience. Thank you for your help.

Yours sincerely

_____

REQUEST FOR GUARANTEE

Date _____

To _____

_____

_____

Dear _____

We often find that we do not have sufficient credit information to allow us to offer trade credit to newly established businesses applying for credit.

However, we are happy to offer you our normal trade credit if you provide us with the personal guarantee of the directors of your company, and we find their credit satisfactory. Accordingly, we enclose our standard guarantee and guarantor's credit application.

Thank you for your interest in our firm, and we sincerely hope you will accept our suggestion in order that we may both enjoy a mutually beneficial business relationship.

Yours sincerely

_____

REQUEST FOR INFORMATION ON DISPUTED CHARGE

Date _____

Ref _____

To _____

_____

_____

Dear _____

We have received your correspondence disputing your account balance.

To help us resolve this matter, we ask you to provide us with the following.

_____   Copies of endorsed cheques issued for payment.

_____   Copies of returned goods authorisations.

_____   Credit notes outstanding.

_____   List of goods claimed as not received.

_____   List of goods claimed to be damaged.

_____   List of goods claimed to be non-conforming.

_____   Other: _____.

Upon receipt of the above information, we shall consider your claim at the earliest opportunity and attempt to resolve the issue.

Thank you for your prompt attention to this matter.

Yours sincerely

_____

REQUEST FOR QUOTATION

Date _____

Ref _____

To _____

_____

_____

Dear Sirs

Re: Request for Quotation

We are interested in purchasing the following goods:

_____

_____

_____

Please provide us with a firm quotation of your standard price for these goods. Please also provide us with your discount structure for volume purchases and the following information:

i)   Standard terms of payment.

ii) Availability of an open credit account with your firm. If available, please provide us with the appropriate credit application form.

iii) Delivery costs for orders.

iv) VAT applicability.

v)   Delivery time for orders from the date of your receipt of a purchase order to our receipt of the goods.

vi) Length of the validity of the quotation.

Yours faithfully

_____

REQUEST FOR REPLACEMENT SHARE CERTIFICATE

To: The Secretary

_____ Limited (the "Company").

_____

_____

_____

I, _____ do hereby request that the Company (or its registrars) issue to me a duplicate certificate no _____ for _____ shares in the capital of the Company, the original certificate having been mislaid, destroyed or lost, and in consideration of the Company so doing, I hereby indemnify the Company against all claims and demands, monies, losses, damages, costs and expense which may be brought against or be paid, incurred or sustained by the Company by reason or in consequence of the issuing to me of the duplicate certificate, or otherwise howsoever in relation thereto. I further undertake and agree, if the original certificate shall hereafter be found, forthwith to deliver up the same or cause the same to be delivered up to the Company, its registrars or their successors and assigns without cost, fee or reward.

Dated this _____ day of _____ 199 ___

_____
Member's signature

RESIGNATION

Date _____

Ref _____

To _____

_____

_____

Dear _____

This is to inform you that I hereby tender my resignation with immediate effect. Please acknowledge receipt and acceptance of this resignation by signing below and returning to me a copy of this letter.

Thank you for your co-operation.

Yours sincerely

Name _____

Address _____

_____

_____

The foregoing resignation is hereby accepted and is effective as of this _____ day of _____ _____ 19 _____.

Name _____

Company _____

RESIGNATION OF DIRECTOR RELINQUISHING ALL CLAIMS

Date _____

To: Board of Directors

_____Limited

Dear Sirs

I hereby resign my office of director of the company with immediate effect and confirm that I have no outstanding claims whatsoever against the company.

Yours faithfully

_____

RESOLUTION TO PAY INTERIM DIVIDEND

_____ **LIMITED**

RESOLUTION PURSUANT TO REGULATION 93 OF TABLE A

We, the directors entitled to receive notice of meetings of the directors of _____

_____ Limited, do resolve:

"That an interim dividend for the year ended _____ 19 _____ of

£ _____ on the ordinary shares of the company be paid/declared payable on

_____ 19 _____ to all members whose name appears on the register of

members on _____ 19 _____."

_____
Director's signature

_____
Director's signature

_____
Director's signature

RESPONSE TO EMPLOYEE'S COMPLAINT

Date _____

Ref _____

To _____

_____

_____

Dear _____

We acknowledge receipt of your letter dated _____ 19 ____ regarding your complaint about:

_____

_____

_____

_____

As you are aware, the company follows a standard complaints procedure in these circumstances. I would be grateful if you could complete the attached form and return it to the Personnel Manager as quickly as possible so that we may follow that procedure. An investigation will then be made into the matter.

Yours sincerely

_____

REVOCATION OF POWER OF ATTORNEY

THIS DEED OF REVOCATION is made on the _____ day of _____, 199___

by me _____ of _____

WITNESSES as follows:

1.   I revoke the instrument dated _____, 199___ (the "Instrument") in which

I appointed _____ of _____

to be my attorney for the purpose of the Power of Attorney Act 1971 (Section 10).

2.   I declare that all power and authority conferred by the Instrument is now revoked and

withdrawn by me.

3.   I verify everything done by my attorney under the Instrument.

4.   This deed of resolution is a deed and has been executed by me as a deed.

IS WITNESS OF WHICH the said _____ has executed

this deed the day and year first above written.

_____

Signature

_____

Signed by Witness

Name _____

Address _____

_____

_____

Occupation _____

SALE AGREEMENT SUBJECT TO DEBT

THIS AGREEMENT is made the _____ day of _____ 19_____

BETWEEN:

(1) _____ (the "Buyer"); and

(2) _____ (the "Seller").

NOW IT IS HEREBY AGREED as follows:

1.   In consideration for the sum of £ _____, receipt of which the Seller hereby acknowledges, the Seller hereby transfers and sells the following property to the Buyer (the "Property"):

_____

_____

2.   The Seller warrants that he/she owns the Property and that he/she has the authority to sell the Property to the Buyer. The Seller also states that the Property is sold subject to the following debt:

_____

_____

3.   The Buyer buys the Property subject to the above debt and agrees to pay the debt. The Buyer also agrees to indemnify and hold the Seller harmless from any claim arising from any failure by the Buyer to pay off this debt.

4.   The Seller also warrants that the Property is in good working condition as of this date.

IN WITNESS OF WHICH the parties have signed this agreement the day and year first above written

_____   _____
Signed by or on behalf of the Buyer   Signed by or on behalf of the Seller

_____   _____
in the presence of (witness)   in the presence of (witness)

Name _____   Name _____

Address _____   Address _____

Occupation _____   Occupation _____

SALES REPRESENTATIVE AGREEMENT

THIS AGREEMENT is made the _____ day of _____ 199__

BETWEEN:

(1)   _____ of _____ (the "Principal"); and

(2)   _____ of _____ (the "Representative").

PARTICULARS

This appointment commences on the _____ day of _____ 199__

Sales Territory:_____

Products/Services: _____

Commission Rates: (a)   (subject to (c) below), _____ per cent of the price charged to the customer on all prepaid sales, net of freight, insurance and duties;

(b)   (subject to (c) below), _____ per cent of the price charged to the customer on all credit sales, net of freight, insurance and duties;

(c)   a commission percentage to be negotiated between the Principal and the Representative in advance of sale on all orders on which the Principal allows a quantity discount or other trade concession.

Run Off Period: _____ months from the termination of this Agreement.

NOW IT IS HEREBY AGREED as follows:

1. The Representative hereby agrees:

1.1 To represent and sell the Principal's Products/Services in the Sales Territory.

1.2 To represent and state accurately the Principal's policies to all potential and present customers and to make or give no other representations or warranties other than those contained in any standard terms of the Principal.

1.3 To notify promptly all contacts and orders within the Sales Territory, and all enquiries and leads from outside the Sales Territory, to the Principal.

1.4 To inform the Principal or the Principal's sales manager of any problems concerning customers of the Principal within the Sales Territory.

1.5 To inform the Principal or the Principal's sales manager if the Representative is representing, or plans to represent, any other business firm. In no event shall the Representative be involved directly or indirectly with a competing company or product line either within or outside the Sales Territory.

1.6 To provide the Principal upon request with sales reports detailing sales progress within the Sales Territory.

1.7 To return promptly at its expense all materials and samples provided by the Principal to the Representative, if either party terminates this Agreement.

1.8 To indemnify the Principal against any and all loss suffered by the Principal resulting from any breach of this Agreement by the Representative.

2. The Principal agrees:.

2.1 Not later than the last day of the month following the quarter in which the Principal receives payment, to provide the Representative with a statement of commission due, and to pay commission to the Representative at the appropriate Commission Rate on all sales concluded prior to the end of the Run Off Period as a result of, or mainly attributable to, the actions or efforts of the Representative during the appointment.

2.2 To provide the Representative with reasonable quantities of business cards, brochures, catalogues, and product samples required for sales purposes.

3. It is further agreed that:

3.1 Should refunds be made to any customer of the Principal, commission already paid to the Representative on that transaction shall be deducted from future commissions to be paid to the Representative by the Principal.

3.2 Either Party may terminate this Agreement by giving written notice to the other Party. If the Agreement has run for one year or less when notice is served, one month's notice must be given. If it has run for between one and two years, two months' notice must be given. Otherwise, three months' notice must be given unless one Party has committed a material breach in which case the other can terminate without notice.

3.3 The Representative shall have the right to be indemnified as provided in the Commercial Agents (Council Directive) Regulations 1993, but the Representative shall have no right to compensation under those Regulations.

3.4 This constitutes the entire Agreement.

3.5 This Agreement shall be binding upon the Parties and their successors and assigns.

3.6 The Parties are not partners or joint venturers, nor is the Representative able to act as the agent of the Principal except as authorised by this Agreement.

3.7 This Agreement is governed by and shall be construed in accordance with English law.

IN WITNESS OF WHICH the Parties have signed this Agreement the day and year above written

_____   _____

Signed by the Representative   Signed for and on behalf of the Principal

SAMPLES AND DOCUMENTS RECEIPT

_____ Ltd

I, _____, employed in the position of

_____, confirm that I have received from

the company the following samples:

No. Rec'd	Serial No.	Description	Value Each	Total Value
_____	_____	_____	_____	_____
_____	_____	_____	_____	_____
_____	_____	_____	_____	_____
_____	_____	_____	_____	_____
_____	_____	_____	_____	_____
_____	_____	_____	_____	_____

In addition I confirm that I have received the following documents:

_____

_____

_____

_____

_____

_____

I accept responsibility to safeguard these materials, prevent the disclosure of confidential material and return these (except those authorised for and delivered to customers) to the company on demand and, in any event, upon termination of employment

_____

Employee

Date _____

SECOND NOTICE OF OVERDUE ACCOUNT

Date _____

Ref _____

To _____

_____

_____

Dear _____

Payment of your account is now unacceptably overdue. Your account balance currently stands as follows.

PAST DUE DATE

Over 30 days	£_____
Over 60 days	£_____
Over 90 days	£_____
Total	£_____

May we please now have your immediate payment without further delay.

Yours sincerely

_____

SECOND WARNING FOR LATENESS

Date _____

To _____

_____

_____

Dear _____

You have been warned about your bad timekeeping. Since there was no improvement, you have been given a formal written warning.

Despite these verbal and written warnings, you continue to be late for work, in breach of your employment terms. Your hours of work are stated in the Statement of Terms and Conditions of Employment previously given to you. A further copy of the terms and conditions is enclosed.

Since you have ignored the previous warnings, we have no alternative but to issue this second formal warning. If you fail to improve your timekeeping, we may have no option but to consider your dismissal.

This second written warning is being recorded on your personnel file.

Yours sincerely

_____

SECURITY AGREEMENT

THIS DEED IS MADE the _____ day of _____ 19 _____

BETWEEN:

(1) _____ of _____ (the "Debtor"); and

(2) _____ of _____ (the "Secured Party").

WHEREAS:

(A) The Debtor is indebted to the Secured Party in the Sum of £ _____ (the "Debt").

(B) The Secured Party wishes to obtain from the Debtor security for the Debt.

NOW THIS DEED WITNESSES as follows:

1.   The Debtor grants to Secured Party of and its successors and assigns a security interest in the following property (the "Security"), which shall include all after-acquired property of a like nature and description and proceeds and products thereof:

_____

_____

2.   This Security is granted to secure payment and performance on the following obligations as well as the Debt and all other debts now or hereinafter owed to the Secured Party by the Debtor:

_____

_____

3.   The Debtor hereby acknowledges to the Secured Party that the collateral shall be kept at the Debtor's above address and not moved or relocated without written consent.

4.   The Debtor warrants that the Debtor owns the Security and it is free from any other lien, encumbrance and security interest or adverse interest and the Debtor has full authority to grant this security interest.

5.   The Debtor agrees to execute such financing statements as are reasonably required by the Secured Party to perfect this security agreement.

6.   Upon default in payment or performance of any obligation for which this security interest is granted, or breach of any term of this security agreement, then in such instance the Secured Party may declare all obligations immediately due and payable and shall have all remedies of a secured party under the law, which rights shall be in addition to any other rights or remedies that may be available to it.

7.   The Debtor agrees to maintain such insurance coverage on the Security as the Secured Party may from time to time reasonably require and the Secured Party shall be named the beneficiary of any insurance policy taken out for such purpose.

8.   This security agreement shall further be in default upon the death, insolvency or bankruptcy of the Secured Party or upon any material decrease in the value of the Security or adverse change in the financial condition of the Debtor.

9.   Upon default the Debtor shall pay all reasonable solicitors' fees and costs of collection necessary to enforce this agreement.

IN WITNESS WHEREOF the parties have signed this deed the day and year first above written

_____   _____
Signed by or on behalf of the Debtor   Signed by or on behalf of the Secured Party

_____   _____
in the presence of (witness)   in the presence of (witness)

Name _____   Name _____

Address _____   Address _____

_____   _____
Occupation   Occupation

SETTLEMENT STATEMENT

NOTE: This statement complies with the Consumer Credit (Settlement Information) Regulations 1983 (S.I. 1983 No. 1564).

To _____

_____

_____

_____

(Name and address of customer)

From: _____

_____

_____

_____

(Name and address of hirer)

This statement is given in respect of an agreement dated _____ 19 _____

which was made between you and _____ in

respect of the hire purchase (credit sale) of _____

_____ and has the reference number _____.

Settlement date _____ 19 _____ calculated in accordance with regulation 3 of the Consumer Credit (Settlement Information) Regulations 1983.

Amount required to settle the agreement early without any rebate due: £ _____

[**Note:** Include one of the three alternatives below as appropriate; NB: if the customer is entitled to a rebate, the rebate must be the higher of (a) the customer's entitlement under the agreement, (b) the customer's entitlement under section 95 of the Consumer Credit Act 1974]

1. The customer is not entitled to any rebate for settlement of the outstanding amount before the settlement date.

2. Rebate calculation made in regard to the Consumer Credit (Rebate on Early Settlement) Regulations 1983.

3. Rebate made in accordance with the agreement.

[Include the following if a rebate is due]

Amount due under agreement	£ _____
Less: rebate	_____
Amount required to settle:	£ _____

(General information about the operation of the Consumer Credit Act and Regulations made under it is made available by the Office of Fair Trading, Field House, Bream's Buildings, London EC4 1PR, and advice may be obtained by contacting the local Trading Standards Department or nearest Citizens' Advice Bureau).

Certificate No. ——————

Number of Shares ——————

LIMITED

This is to Certify that ——————

of ——————

—————— shares of £ —————— each —————— paid

is/are the Registered holder(s) of

in the above-named Company, subject to the Memorandum and Articles of Association of the Company.

* This document is hereby executed by the Company /

The Common Seal of the Company was hereto affixed in the presence of:

——————
—————— Directors
——————

—————— Secretary

—————— 19 ——————

* Delete as appropriate

SHARE SUBSCRIPTION/APPLICATION

I/We offer to acquire _____ ordinary shares of_____

_____ (company) at the offer price of £_____

per share.

I/We attach a cheque or bankers draft for the amount of £_____.

Applicant's name   _____

Applicant's full address _____

_____

Applicant's signature   _____

Additional joint applications:

Second Applicant's name _____.

Address _____

_____.

Signature _____

Third Applicant's name _____.

Address _____

_____.

Signature _____

SPECIAL NOTICE FOR THE REMOVAL OF A DIRECTOR

Date _____

Ref _____

To The Directors

_____ Limited

_____

_____

_____

Dear Sirs

I/We hereby give notice pursuant to s.303 and s.379 of the Companies Act 1985 of my/our intention to propose the following ordinary resolution at the next Annual General Meeting of the Company.

Resolution

"That _____ be and is hereby removed from his office as a Director of the company with immediate effect."

Yours faithfully

_____

(To be sent to the company at least 28 days before the date of the Annual General Meeting)

SPECIAL NOTICE FOR THE REMOVAL OF AUDITORS

Date _____

Ref _____

To The Directors

_____ Limited

_____

_____

_____

Dear Sirs

I hereby give notice pursuant to s.379 and s.391A of the Companies Act 1985 of my intention to propose the following ordinary resolution at the next Annual General Meeting of the company.

Resolution

"That _____ be and are hereby removed from office as auditors of the company and that _____ be appointed as auditors of the company in their place to hold office until the conclusion of the next General Meeting at which accounts are laid before the company at a remuneration to be fixed by the directors."

Dated this _____ day of _____ 199___.

Yours faithfully

_____

(To be sent to the company at least 28 days before the date of the Annual General Meeting)

STANDARD BOARD MINUTES

LIMITED

MINUTES of Meeting of the Board of Directors held at_____
on_____,19_____ at_____ a.m./p.m.

PRESENT: _____ (in the chair)

_____

_____

_____

IN ATTENDANCE: _____

_____

_____

1.   The Chairman confirmed that notice of the meeting had been given to all the directors of the Company and that a quorum of the board of directors was present at the meeting.

2.   _____

_____

_____

_____

_____

[ ]   There being no further business the meeting then ended.

_____ Chairman

SUMMARY OF EMPLOYMENT TERMS

Date _____

To _____

_____

_____

Dear _____

We are pleased you have accepted a position with our company, and want to take this opportunity to summarise your initial terms and conditions of employment.

1. Commencement date of employment _____

2. Position/title _____

3. Starting salary: _____

4. Weeks holiday per year: _____

5. Eligible for holiday starting: _____

6. Health insurance: _____

_____

7. Pension/profit-sharing: _____

_____

8. Other benefits: _____

_____

9. Other terms/conditions: _____

_____

If this is not in accordance with your understanding, please let me know immediately. We look forward to you joining us.

Yours sincerely

_____

SUPPLIER QUESTIONNAIRE

_____ Ltd

We are introducing a supplier rating system to meet the requirements of BS5750/ISO9000. We would be grateful if you could complete this questionnaire and return it to us.

Company name   _____   Tel _____

Reg. Number   _____   Fax _____

Address   _____

                _____

                _____ Post Code _____

Products/Services Provided _____

1) Is your firm registered as a firm of assessed capability
   to BS5750/ISO9000?   Yes ☐ No ☐

2) Does your firm hold any other nationally or internationally
   recognised approvals?   Yes ☐ No ☐

3) Has your firm been approved by an accredited assessing body? Yes ☐ No ☐

   Please give your certificate number and expiry date _____

   If you answered Yes to question 1) and 3) please move to question 7).

4) Does your firm intend to apply for registration to BS5750/ISO9000? Yes ☐ No ☐

   If Yes please state when you expect this _____

5) Does your firm have a quality or procedures manual?   Yes ☐ No ☐

6) Does your firm have a documented system to control the following?

   a) recording of changes to customers orders/contracts   Yes ☐ No ☐

   b) receipt and checking of purchased products/services   Yes ☐ No ☐

   c) identification of products during manufacture, storage & delivery Yes ☐ No ☐

d) calibration and maintenance of measuring and testing equipment   Yes ☐   No ☐

e) inspection of products at each stage of manufacturing process   Yes ☐   No ☐

f) identification, segregation and disposal of
   non-conforming products   Yes ☐   No ☐

g) investigating and taking action against the cause of
   non-conforming products   Yes ☐   No ☐

h) personnel training   Yes ☐   No ☐

7) Does your firm implement internal quality audits?   Yes ☐   No ☐

8) Does your firm provide Certificates of Conformity
   for your products?   Yes ☐   No ☐

9) Does your firm have a Quality Control Officer or nominated
   quality representative?   Yes ☐   No ☐

   Name _____   Position _____

10) Would your firm object to a representative of our company
    visiting you and reviewing your quality system?   Yes ☐   No ☐

11) Additional supplier comments: _____

    _____

    _____

Questionnaire completed by

Name _____   Signature _____

Position _____   Date _____

TENANT'S BANK STANDING ORDER MANDATE

TO _____ (Tenant's bank name & address)

_____

PLEASE PAY _____ (Landlord's bank name & address)

_____

_____

_____ □□—□□—□□ (& sort code)

TO THE
CREDIT OF _____ (Landlord's account name & account number)

_____

THE SUM OF _____ (Amount in figures & words)

_____

COMMENCING _____ (Date of first payment)

AND THEREAFTER
EVERY _____ (Due date & frequency e.g. "13th monthly")

UNTIL _____ (Date of last payment, you may write "until further notice")

QUOTING THE _____ (The address of the Property being let)
REFERENCE
_____

ACCOUNT NAME _____ (Tenant's name)
TO BE DEBITED

ACCOUNT No. _____ (Tenant's A/C No.)
TO BE DEBITED

SIGNED _____ **DATED** _____

_____

(Tenant(s))

UNSOLICITED IDEA ACKNOWLEDGEMENT

Date _____

Ref _____

To _____

_____

_____

Dear _____

We appreciate your interest in submitting for our consideration an idea or proposal relating to:

_____

_____

_____

_____

_____

Our company receives many commercial ideas, suggestions and proposals, and we also have many of our own projects under development or consideration. It is possible, therefore, that the idea or proposal you plan to submit to us has been considered and/or may already be in the planning or development stages.

Therefore, we would be pleased to accept your idea or proposal for consideration provided you acknowledge:

1.   Samples or other submissions will be returned only if a stamped addressed envelope is enclosed or carriage is prepaid.

2.   The company accepts no responsibility for damage or loss to samples or other submitted material in our possession.

3.   The company accepts no responsibility for holding any submitted information in confidence, but shall use its best efforts to do so.

4. The company shall pay compensation only in the event it (a) accepts the submitted idea, (b) has received the idea only from you, and (c) reaches agreement with you as to terms and conditions for the use of the idea.

5. The company agrees not to exploit your idea, directly or indirectly, without first entering into an agreement that is acceptable to you.

6. Nothing in this agreement shall be deemed to give the company any rights in the materials submitted.

7. The company shall have no obligation to you in the event this idea or material is presently under consideration by the company.

If these terms are acceptable to you, please sign where indicated below and return this letter with your idea or proposal. Please keep the copy for your records.

Yours sincerely

_____

_____
Company

The foregoing terms and conditions are understood and acknowledged this _____

day of _____ 19 _____ .

_____
Signature

VARIATION OF CONTRACT

THIS DEED is made the_____ day of _____ 19 _____

BETWEEN

(1) _____ of _____ (the "First Party");and

(2) _____ of _____ (the "Second Party").

WHEREAS:

(A) The two parties above have entered into an agreement dated_____19 ___
    (the "Agreement")

(B) The two parties above now wish to vary the terms of the Agreement.

NOW THIS DEED WITNESSES as follows:

1.   The two parties agree that the following additions and amendments to the Agreement
shall apply _____

_____

_____

2.   All other terms and conditions of the Agreement shall remain in full force and effect.

IN WITNESS OF WHICH the parties have executed this deed the day and year first above written

(Individual)

_____
Signed by the First Party

_____
in the presence of (witness)

Name
_____
Address
_____

_____
Occupation

_____
Signed by the Second Party

_____
in the presence of (witness)

Name
_____
Address
_____

_____
Occupation

(Company)

Signed for and on behalf of

_____ Ltd

_____
Director

_____
Director/Secretary

Signed for and on behalf of:

_____ Ltd

_____
Director

_____
Director/Secretary

VARIATION OF EMPLOYMENT AGREEMENT

THIS DEED is made the_____ day of _____ 19 _____

BETWEEN

(1) _____ of _____ (the "Employer");and

(2) _____ of _____ (the "Employee").

WHEREAS:

(A) The Employer and the Employee have entered into an agreement dated _____ 19 _____ (the "Agreement") by which the Employer employs the Employee under the terms therein.

(B) The Employer and the Employee wish to vary the terms of the Agreement.

NOW THIS DEED WITNESSES as follows:

1. The Employer and the Employee agree to vary the Agreement by making the following changes and/or additions:

_____

_____

_____

2. All other terms and provisions of the Agreement shall remain in full force and effect.

IN WITNESS OF WHICH the parties have executed this deed the day and year first above written

(Company)   (Individual Employer)

Signed for and on behalf of

_____ Ltd   _____
                                    Signed by the Employer

_____   in the presence of (witness)
Director
                                    Name _____
_____   Address _____
Director/Secretary

(Employee)   _____
                                    Occupation _____

_____
Signed by the Employee

in the presence of (witness)

Name _____

Address _____

_____
Occupation

WAIVER OF LIABILITY AND ASSUMPTION OF RISK

I, the undersigned, _____ (the "Customer"), voluntarily make and grant this Waiver of Liability and Assumption of Risk in favour of _____ _____ (the "Seller") as partial consideration (in addition to monies paid to the Seller) for the opportunity to use the facilities, equipment, materials and/or other assets of the Seller; and/or to receive assistance, training, guidance and/or instruction from the personnel of the Seller; and/or to engage in the activities, events, sports, festivities and/or gatherings sponsored by the Seller; I hereby waive and release any and all claims whether in contract or for personal injury, property damage, damages, losses and/or death that may arise from my aforementioned use or receipt, as I understand and recognise that there are certain risks, dangers and perils connected with such use and/or receipt, which I hereby acknowledge to have been fully explained to me and which I fully understand, and which I nevertheless accept, assume and undertake after inquiry and investigation as to the nature and extent of such risks has shown those risks to be wholly satisfactory and acceptable to me. I further agree to use my best judgment in undertaking these activities, use and/or receipt and to strictly adhere to all safety instructions and recommendations, whether oral or written. I hereby certify that I am a competent adult assuming these risks of my own free will, being under no compulsion or duress. This Waiver of Liability and Assumption of Risk is effective from_____ 19 ____, to _____ 19 ____, inclusive, and may not be revoked or amended without the prior written consent of the Seller.

_____
Customers signature

Name _____

Address _____

_____

_____

Date _____

Age _____

WARRANTY INCREASING STATUTORY RIGHTS

1.   This warranty is given in addition to your statutory rights and does not affect your statutory rights in any way.

2.   We warrant that, in the event that any fault or defect is discovered in the goods within one year of the date of sale, we will, unless the fault or defect has been caused by a misuse of the goods by the purchaser or by the goods being used for a purpose for which they have not been designed, either repair or, at our option, replace the goods free of charge to the purchaser.

WITHHELD DELIVERY NOTICE

Date _____

Ref _____

To _____

_____

_____

Dear _____

Reference is made to your order no._____ dated _____ 19 _____.

We are withholding delivery of the goods for the reason(s) ticked:

_____   Overdue balance of £_____ must first be paid.

_____   Required payment of £_____ has not been made.

_____   You previously cancelled the order.

_____   You have not provided us with delivery instructions.

_____   Certain goods are back ordered and delivery will be made in a single lot.

_____   Other:_____

Please respond to this notice so we may fulfil your order without further delay or inconvenience.

Yours sincerely

_____

GLOSSARY OF CONTENTS

A

Accident Claim Notice— Notice to an insurance company of claim following an accident.

Acknowledgement and Acceptance of Order— Notice that a purchase order has been received and accepted.

Acknowledgement of Alteration of Terms to Order— Letter confirming an amendment to a purchase order.

Acknowledgement of Temporary Employment— A statement by a temporary employee who agrees to abide by the limitations placed on temporary employment.

Affidavit— A sworn statement of fact to be used as evidence in court.

Anti-Gazumping Agreement — An exclusivity contract between the buyer and seller of property, protecting the buyer against being gazumped.

Affidavit of Power of Attorney— A sworn statement by an attorney that the power of attorney under which he was appointed remains in effect and has not been revoked.

Affidavit of Title— A sworn statement by a seller of goods that he has the right to transfer title to those goods.

Agency Agreement with Retention of Title— An agreement by which a principal delivers goods to its sales agent for sale while retaining title to the goods.

Agreement— An all-purpose contract between two parties.

Agreement for Sale of Goods— A general agreement between a seller and a buyer of goods.

Agreement for the Sale of a Vehicle— An agreement to record the private sale of a motor vehicle.

Agreement to Accept Night Work— An agreement by which an employee agrees to work a night shift if required.

Agreement to Assume Debt— An agreement by which a debtor agrees to be responsible for the debt of a customer to a creditor in return for transfer of the customer's goods.

Agreement to Compromise Debt— An agreement by which a creditor agrees to reduce a customer's debt on certain terms.

Agreement to Extend Debt Payment— An agreement by which a creditor agrees to extend the terms under which a customer must repay his debt.

Agreement to Extend Performance Date— An agreement by which two parties agree to extend the time for the completion of an existing contract.

Agreement to Sell Personal Property— A simple agreement to record the sale of private property other than land.

Applicant's Request for a Reference— A letter requesting an employment reference from a previous employer.

Application to Open a Credit Account– A form issued by a company to a potential customer wanting to open a credit account.

Assignment of Accounts Receivable with Non-Recourse— An Agreement by which a creditor sells his interest in a debt to a third party. This form must be used in conjunction with the Notice of Assignment which the assignor should send to the debtor.

Assignment of Contract— An assignment by one party to an existing contract of its rights and obligations under the contract to an outside party.

Assignment of Insurance Policy— An assignment by an insurance policy holder of the benefit of the policy to a third party.

Assignment of Money Due— An assignment by a creditor of the benefit of a debt owed to him to a third party in return for a payment.

Assignment of Option— An assignment by an option holder of the benefit of an option to a third party in return for a payment.

Assignment of Option to Purchase Land— An assignment by an option holder of the benefit of an option to purchase land to a third party in return for payment.

Authorisation to Release Confidential Information— A letter giving authority to a company or individual to release confidential information.

Authorisation to Release Employment Information— A letter giving authority to a company to release employment information.

Authorisation to Release Medical Information— A letter giving a doctor or hospital authority to release medical information.

Authorisation to Return Goods— A letter authorising a buyer of goods to return those goods on certain conditions.

B

Breach of Contract Notice— A notice sent to a party of a contract specifying the terms violated.

C

Cancellation of an Order to Stop a Cheque— A letter instructing a bank to honour a cheque which has previously been stopped.

Certificate of Product Conformity— A certificate from a supplier certifying product conformity.

Change in Pay or Grading Following Job Evaluation— A letter notifying an employee of a pay rise following change of job title.

Change in Sales Representative Agreement— A letter agreement between a company and its sales representative recording a change in the terms of engagement.

Change of Address Notice— Letter notifying a change of address.

Change to Employment Contract— A letter agreement between an employer and an employee recording a change in the terms of employment.

Child Guardianship Consent Form— A form appointing of a guardian with specified powers.

Cohabitation Agreement— An agreement by which two people agree on the terms under which they will live together without marrying.

Company Let— A rental agreement to let residential property to a company for the temporary use of its employees, officers, or visitors.

Concession Note– A request for non-conformity to product standards to be accepted.

Confidentiality Agreement— An agreement between a company and an employee that the employee will keep proprietary information secret.

Confirmation of Agreement to Pay— A letter reminding a debtor of his agreement to pay.

Confirmation of Verbal Order— A letter from a buyer confirming the placement of a verbal order with a seller.

Conflict of Interest Declaration— A declaration by an employee that his personal affairs do not conflict with his duty to his employer.

Consent to Drug/Alcohol Screening— A written form of consent by a potential employee to drug/alcohol screening results to be released to an employer.

Consent to Release of Information— A request for permission from an employee for his employer to release information regarding the employee form a third party.

Consent to Short Notice of an Annual General Meeting— Shareholder's written consent to an annual general meeting being held at short notice.

Consent to Short Notice of Extraordinary General Meeting— Shareholder's written consent to an extraordinary general meeting being held at short notice.

Consultant Non-Disclosure Agreement— An agreement by which a consultant agrees not to disclose his client's confidential information.

Contract for Sale of Goods by Collection— A simple commercial contract for the sale of goods collected by the buyer.

Contract for Sale of Goods by Delivery— A simple commercial contract for the sale of goods delivered to the buyer under certain terms.

Contractor/Subcontractor Agreement— A works contract between a building contractor and his subcontractor.

Disciplinary Rules and Procedures— A document which sets out an employer's disciplinary rules and procedures policy.

Credit Information— A response to a request for credit information from another company.

Credit Information Request— A supplier's request for credit information from a potential customer.

Credit Reference— A response to a request for a credit reference.

D

Damaged Goods Acceptance— A letter from a buyer to a seller accepting damaged goods subject to a price reduction.

Debt Acknowledgement— A statement by a debtor admitting indebtedness to creditor.

Defect Report Memorandum— An in-house memo for recording product/service non-conformity and corrective action.

Defective Goods Notice— A letter for a buyer to a seller rejecting defective goods and requesting a credit note.

Demand for Delivery— A letter from a buyer to a seller demanding delivery of goods ordered and paid for.

Demand for Explanation of Rejected Goods— A letter from a seller to a buyer requesting an explanation for the buyer's rejection of goods delivered.

Demand for Payment— A demand for payment from a creditor to a debtor.

Demand to Acknowledge Delivery Dates— A letter from a buyer requesting a seller to confirm delivery arrangements.

Demand to Guarantor for Payment— A creditor's demand for payment from the guarantor of a debt upon default by the debtor.

Demand to Pay Promissory Note— A demand from a creditor on a debtor to repay a loan in full on default in instalments.

Director's Resignation Without Prejudice— A letter from a director to his board announcing his resignation and maintaining his right to bring proceedings against the company.

Directors' Resolution Calling Annual General Meeting— A written resolution by the directors of a company to call an annual general meeting of the company.

Disciplinary Rules and Procedures— A document which sets out an employer's disciplinary rules and procedures policy.

Directors' Resolution Calling Extraordinary General Meeting— A written resolution by the directors of a company to call an extraordinary general meeting of the company in order to pass one or more special resolutions.

Dishonoured Cheque Notice— A notice to a customer/debtor that a cheque has bounced.

Dismissed Letter for Intoxication on the Job— A letter of summary dismissal on the grounds of drunkenness to an employee.

Disputed Account Settlement— An agreement by which a debtor and a creditor agree to resolve a disputed account.

Dormant Company Accounts— A declaration by a director that a company has been dormant since its incorporation.

Dormant Company Resolution— A written resolution by the directors of a dormant company to call an extraordinary general meeting of the company in order to pass a resolution under s.250 of the Companies Act 1985.

E

Employee Agreement on Inventions and Patents— An agreement between a company and an employee that the employee keeps proprietary information confidential and waives rights to any inventions.

Employee Disciplinary Report— A company report on an employee's breach of discipline.

Employee Dismissal for Lateness— A notice to an employee of dismissal after verbal and written warnings.

Employee File— A simple résumé of an employee's details and employment history.

Employee Let— A rental agreement to let residential property to an employee.

Employee Non-Competition Agreement— An agreement between a company and an employee that the employee will not compete with the employer's business during or after his employment.

Employee Non-Disclosure Agreement— An agreement between a company and an employee that the employee will not disclose confidential information during or after his employment.

Employee Suspension Notice— A notice to an employee of suspension without pay due to unsatisfactory conduct.

Employee Warning— A notice to an employee of unsatisfactory work performance.

Employee's Covenants— An employee's combined promises of non-competition and non-disclosure in return for employment or continued employment.

Employer's Request for Reference— A letter from an employer asking for a reference on a potential employee.

Employment Agreement— A basic employment contract between an employer and an employee.

Employment Confirmation— A letter confirming a position of employment.

Enduring Power of Attorney— A statutory form to create a power of attorney that continues in the event that the donor becomes mentally incapable (to be used with forms EP1 & EP2 below).

Enduring Power of Attorney - Application for Registration EP2— A statutory form for registering an enduring power of attorney under the Enduring Powers of Attorney Act 1985.

Enduring Power of Attorney - General Form of Application EP3— A statutory form for the application for a court order under the Enduring Power of Attorney Act 1985.

Enduring Power of Attorney - Notice of Intention to Apply for Registration EP1— A statutory notice of intention to register an enduring power of attorney under the Enduring Powers of Attorney Act 1985.

Enquiry on Overdue Account— A letter requesting explanation for an overdue account.

Exercise of Option— A letter from an option holder giving notice of the exercise of the option.

Expenses Record— An employee's business expenses record form for claiming reimbursement.

Extension of Option to Purchase Property— The owner of property grants an option holder further time in which to exercise his option.

F

Family Tree— A record of family relationships.

Final Notice Before Legal Proceedings— A final demand from a creditor to a debtor with the threat of legal proceedings.

Final Warning Before Dismissal— A letter to an employee giving final written warning on conduct before dismissal.

Final Warning for Lateness— A letter to an employee giving final written warning on lateness before dismissal.

First Warning for Lateness— A letter to an employee giving first written warning.

Form of Letter to Executor— A letter to notify an individual of their appointment as an executor to a Last Will & Testament.

Form of Resolution for Submission to Companies House— Written notice of a resolution passed by company shareholders for filing at Companies House.

Funeral Wishes— Funeral instructions of the deceased.

G

General Assignment— A basic agreement in which one party transfers its rights or title to a specific item or contract to another.

General Proxy— A notice to appoint another to vote on your behalf at a shareholders' meeting.

General Release— An agreement by which one party releases another from any claims or demands it may have against the other.

General Subordination— An agreement by which one creditor agrees that another creditor's debt will take precedence over his own.

Grievance Procedure— An employer's procedure for settling disputes and grievances of its employees.

Guarantee— An agreement by which a guarantor guarantees payment of a customer's debts to induce the creditor to extend credit to that customer.

H

Holiday Letting Agreement— A rental agreement for letting a furnished property as a holiday let only.

House/Flat Share Agreement - Non-Resident Owner— A tenancy agreement for letting part of a shared house or flat with the owner being non-resident.

House/Flat Share Agreement - Resident Owner— A tenancy agreement for letting a room in a furnished house or flat with a resident owner.

House Rules— A suggested list of rules for use in short-term bed & breakfast accommodation.

Household Inventory— A record of the contents of a property to accompany a rental agreement.

I

Indemnity Agreement— An agreement by which one party agrees to repay to another party that other party's costs.

Independent Contractor Agreement— An agreement between a property owner and a building contractor for the performance of works to the property.

Insurance Claim Notice— A letter to insurance company giving details of an insurance claim.

Internal Customer Complaint Memorandum— A customer services memo detailing a customer's complaint and the corrective action taken.

J

Joint Venture Agreement— An agreement between partners to form a business joint venture.

L

Landlord's Reference Requirements— Details what references a landlord requires from a potential tenant.

Last Will & Testament (Residue Direct to Children)— A form of Will that leaves the residue of your estate to one of more children.

Last Will & Testament (Residue to Adult)— A form of Will that Leaves the residue of your estate to one or more adults.

Last Will & Testament (Residue to Adult but if He/She Dies to Children)— A form of Will that leaves the residue of your estate to an adult but, if that adult dies, to children.

Letter Accepting Liability— A letter to a customer from a supplier accepting liability for faulty goods.

Letter Accepting Return of Goods— A letter from a seller to a buyer accepting the return of goods.

Letter Accompanying Unsolicited Goods— A letter from a supplier introducing samples to a prospective buyer.

Letter Acknowledging Complaint— A general letter acknowledging complaint and offering to investigate.

Letter Acknowledging Request for Trade Credit— A letter to a prospective customer requesting a credit reference.

Letter Agreeing Appointment of an Estate Agent— A letter from a property owner to an estate agent stating the terms of appointment.

Letter Agreeing to Trade Terms— A letter from a seller to a buyer agreeing to grant credit.

Letter Alleging Passing Off— A letter demanding that a competitor stops using a similar product name and threatening legal action.

Letter Confirming Appointment of Independent Consultant— A letter from a company to a consultant setting out the terms under which the consultant is engaged.

Letter Confirming Reason for Instant Dismissal— A letter from a company to an employee explaining the reasons for a dismissal.

Letter Denying Liability on Complaint— A general letter denying fault and suggesting arbitration.

Letter Expelling Partner from Continuing Partnership— A letter from remaining partners explaining the terms of one partner's dismissal from a partnership.

Letter from Employee Intending to Resume Work Before End of Maternity Leave— A letter from an employee to an employer giving at least seven days' notice of her intention to return to work before the end of her statutory maternity leave.

Letter of Claim Addressed to a Carrier— A letter from a supplier to his carrier for reimbursement of the cost of goods damaged while in the carrier's possession.

Letter of Redundancy— A letter from an employer to an employee giving notice of dismissal by way of redundancy.

Letter Offering to Purchase Property— A letter to a property owner setting out the terms of an offer for the property.

Letter re Agent's Authority— A letter from a landlord to a tenant regarding the appointment of an agent to act on the landlord's behalf.

Letter re Bills— A letter from a landlord to an utility company or authority regarding a new tenant's responsibility for paying bills.

Letter re Breach of Tenant's Covenants— A letter from a landlord detailing breaches of a tenant's obligations and asking that they be rectified.

Letter Refusing Return of Goods— A letter from a seller to a buyer refusing the buyer's return of goods delivered without good reason.

Letter Refusing Trade or Financial References— A letter refusing a request for a reference.

Letter Refusing Trade Terms— A letter from a seller to a prospective buyer refusing a request for credit.

Letter Rejecting Conditions of Order, and Reimposing Conditions of Sale— A letter from a seller to a buyer rejecting an order on the buyer's terms and notifying supply on the seller's terms.

Letter Rejecting Incorrect Goods— A letter from a buyer to a seller rejecting incorrect delivery of goods.

Letter Requesting that Company be Treated as Defunct— A letter from a company to Companies House requesting removal from the Register of Companies.

Letter Requesting Trade Terms of Payment— A letter from a prospective buyer to a seller requesting credit and offering a bank reference.

Letter Rescinding Contract— A notice from a seller to a buyer in receivership that a supply contract is terminated and payment is due.

Letter Sending Copy of an Agreement Regulated under the Consumer Credit Act 1974 — A statutory letter from a supplier to a customer informing the customer of his right to cancel a hire purchase agreement.

Letter Taking Up Bank Reference— A letter from a supplier to a bank taking up the bank reference of a prospective customer.

Letter Taking Up Trade Reference— A letter from a supplier to a company taking up the trade reference of a prospective customer.

Letter to a Solicitor to Collect a Debt— A letter from a creditor to a solicitor requesting that a debt be collected.

Letter to Credit Reference Agency for Report— A letter from a supplier requesting a credit report on a potential customer.

Letter to Credit Reference Agency Requesting Registered Personal Data— A letter to a credit reference agency requesting personal data under the Data Protection Act 1984.

Letter to Customer who has Exceeded their Credit Limit— A letter from a supplier to a customer stating that credit is no longer available.

Letter to Employee Concerning Salary Rise— A letter from an employer to an employee informing of increase in salary.

Letter to Employee on Maternity Leave Intending to Take Maternity Absence— A letter from an employer to an employee asking about her intentions to return to work after maternity absence.

Letter to Employee, Absent Believed Sick— A letter from an employer to an employee asking for reasons for absence.

Letter to Employee by a Mother Taking Maternity Absence— A letter from a mother on maternity absence who intends to return to work.

Letter to Former Employee who is Using Confidential Information— A letter from an employer to a former employee threatening legal action unless use of confidential information ceases.

Letter to Receiver or Liquidator Reclaiming Goods— A letter from a supplier to a receiver or liquidator of a customer demanding payment for or return of goods delivered.

Letter to Shareholders and Auditors with Resolution to be Passed— A letter from a company to shareholders enclosing a written resolution for the signature of shareholders, together with a letter to the company's accountants.

Letter to Unsuccessful Candidate— A letter to an unsuccessful job applicant.

Letter Treating Breach of Contract as Repudiation and Claiming Damages— A letter from one party to a contract to another cancelling the contract, claiming that the other party has not performed their obligation.

Licence for Use of a Car Parking Space— A licence granted by a car-park owner to a car owner.

Licence to Use Copyright Material— An agreement by which a copyright owner licences use of his copyright work to another.

Limited Guarantee— An agreement by which a guarantor guarantees payment of a customer's debts up to a certain limit to induce the customer to extend credit to that customer.

Limited Proxy— A notice to appoint another to vote as specified on your behalf at a shareholders' meeting.

Living Will— A statement of request regarding the medical treatment you want in the event that you are unable to communicate the information yourself through incapacity.

Loan Agreement— An agreement between a lender and a borrower setting out the terms of a loan (to be accompanied by a **Loan Note**)

Loan Note (Long Form)— An agreement by which a borrower agrees to repay money borrowed.

Loan Note (Short Form)— An agreement by which a borrower agrees to repay money borrowed (for a longer Form see above).

Loan Payment Record— A creditor's record of payments made on a loan by a debtor.

Location of Important Documents and Summary of Personal Information— A record of information that an executor will need in the event of a testator's death.

Lodger/Bed & Breakfast Licence— A residential rental agreement for letting a room to a lodger or bed & breakfast guest.

Lost Credit Card Notice— A letter from a cardholder to a credit card company confirming loss of a credit card.

M

Magazine Article Royalty Contract— An agreement between an author and a publisher for the submission of a work to be published.

Mailing List Name Removal Request— A letter to company requesting removal of your name from their mailing list.

Mileage Reimbursement Report—A record of business-related mileage.

Minutes of Annual General Meeting— Minutes of any annual general meeting.

Minutes of Directors' Meeting Changing Objects of Company— Minutes of a meeting of directors at which it is resolved to update the company's memorandum.

Minutes of Extraordinary General Meeting— Minutes of an extraordinary general meeting of a company.

Minutes of Extraordinary General Meeting Changing Objects of Company— Minutes of an extraordinary general meeting at which it is resolved to update the company's memorandum.

Model Release— Permission granted by a model to a publisher for use of photographs of him/her.

Mutual Cancellation of Contract— An agreement by which two parties agree to cancel an existing contract between them.

Mutual Releases— An agreement by which two parties agree to discharge one another from any claims they might have in respect of a particular contract or event.

N

National Lottery Syndicate Agreement— An agreement for a group playing the National Lottery.

Nomination of a Replacement Room (House/ Flat Share Agreement)— A letter from a landlord to a tenant asking the tenant to move from one room in a property to another in accordance with the terms of the tenancy agreement.

Nominee Shareholder's Declaration of Trust— Shareholder transfers shares in trust to another party.

Notice for Regulated Hire Purchase or Credit Sale Agreements— A statutory form informing a customer of his right to cancel a consumer credit agreement.

Notice of Acceptance of Order— A letter from customer to a supplier acknowledging receipt of a purchase order.

Notice of an Assured Shorthold Tenancy— A notice to be given by a landlord to a tenant prior to an assured shorthold tenancy being entered into.

Notice of Annual General Meeting— A notice from a company to shareholders of a forthcoming annual general meeting of the company.

Notice of Assignment— A letter from one party to contract to a debtor that that party has assigned his interest in the contract to another.

Notice of Cancellation of Purchase Order— A letter from a buyer to a seller cancelling an order for undelivered goods and requesting a refund.

Notice of Claim for Indemnity from Joint-Venturer— A notice from one party to another of his right to an indemnity from the other in respect of the claim that has been made against them.

Notice of Conditional Acceptance of Faulty Goods— A letter from a buyer to a seller accepting faulty goods subject to the seller offering a credit note.

Notice of Conditional Acceptance of Non-Conforming Goods— A letter from a buyer to a seller accepting incorrect goods subject to the seller offering a credit note.

Notice of Default in Payment— A notice by one party to a contract to the other that his payment under the contract is in default.

Notice of Demand for Delivery of Goods— A letter from a buyer to a seller demanding delivery of undelivered goods or requesting a refund.

Notice of Dismissal Letter (Capability)— An employer's letter to an employee setting out the grounds for dismissal based upon the employee's sub-standard performance.

Notice of Dismissal Letter (Sickness)— An employer's letter to an employee setting out the grounds for dismissal based upon the employee's poor health.

Notice of Disputed Account— A letter from a customer to a supplier explaining why an account is disputed.

Notice of Dormant Company— A notice to Companies House that a company has been dormant since its formation and it be exempt from appointing auditors.

Notice of Election under s.113 of the Income and Corporation Taxes Act 1988— A request from a partnership to HM Inspector of Taxes that the partnership be treated as continuing after the admission/departure of a partner.

Notice of Extraordinary General Meeting— A notice from a company to shareholders of a forthcoming extraordinary general meeting of the company.

Notice of Extraordinary General Meeting to Change Objects of Company— A notice from a company to shareholders of a forthcoming extraordinary general meeting of the company called to update the memorandum.

Notice of Goods Sold on Approval— A letter from a supplier accompanying goods sent on approval.

Notice of Intention to Recover Payment in Default— A letter from a finance company to a customer requesting payment of overdue amounts under a consumer credit agreement.

Notice of Rejection of Non-Conforming Goods— A letter from a buyer to a seller rejecting delivery of incorrect goods and requesting a refund.

Notice of Rejection of Order— A letter from a buyer to a seller rejecting delivery of goods for reasons stated and requesting a refund.

Notice of Replacement of Rejected Goods— A letter from a seller to a buyer accepting the buyer's rejection of goods and giving notice of replacement.

Notice of Result of Grievance Investigation— A letter from a company to an employee replying to the employee's complaint.

Notice of Return of Goods Sold on Approval— A letter from a customer to a supplier rejecting goods sent on approval.

Notice of Special Resolution— A written notice of a resolution passed by company shareholders for filing at Companies House.

Notice of Trade Term Violations— A letter from a supplier to a customer warning the customer that they have breached their credit terms.

Notice of Withheld Delivery— A letter from a seller to a buyer requesting payment of unpaid invoices before delivery.

Notice of Wrongful Refusal to Accept Delivery— A letter from a seller to a buyer giving notice that the seller regards the buyer's rejection of goods to be in breach of contract.

Notice to Cancel Delayed Goods— A letter from a buyer to a seller cancelling order for undelivered goods.

Notice to Dissolve a Two-Party Partnership— A notice from one partner to another that their partnership is dissolved.

Notice to Employer of Intention to Take Maternity Leave— A letter from an employee to an employer giving notice of her intention to take her entitled maternity leave.

Notice to Employer of Intention to Take Maternity Leave and Maternity Absence— A letter from an employee entitled to take maternity leave and maternity absence until the 28th week after the week of childbirth.

Notice to End Employment— A letter from an employer to an employee giving notice of the termination of his employment.

Notice to Revoke an Election under s.113 of the Income and Corporation Taxes Act 1988— A request from a partnership to H M Inspector of Taxes that an election for the partnership to continue is revoked.

Notice to Stop Goods in Transit— A letter requesting shipper to return goods to the seller.

Notice to Terminate - Given by Sharers— A notice from house or flat sharer that they wish to terminate a rental agreement with the owner.

Notice to Terminate-Given by Landlords/ Owners— A notice from a landlord or owner to the tenant or sharer that they require possession of a property.

Notification of Business Transfer-No Redundancy— A notification to an employee that his employment continues although the company has a new owner.

O

Offer of Employment to Avoid Redundancy— A letter from a company to an employee offering alternative employment instead of redundancy.

Offer to Settle by Arbitration— A letter from one party to another offering to settle a dispute by arbitration.

Option to Buy Land Agreement— An agreement by which a seller gives a potential buyer an option to purchase land.

Option to Purchase— An agreement by which a seller gives a potential buyer an option to purchase goods.

Order to Stop a Cheque— Request to a bank to stop a cheque.

Ordinary Power of Attorney— A document by which one person gives another person the power to act on his behalf (usually in the event of absence).

Organ Donation— A document in which an organ donor specifies his wishes.

Overdue Account Reminder— A simple letter reminding a debtor that a payment is overdue.

P

Partial Delivery Request— A letter from a seller to a buyer suggesting partial delivery of order within the terms of the buyer's credit limit.

Partnership Agreement— An agreement between individuals wanting to establish a business partnership.

Pay Advice— A form advising employee of salary and deductions.

Permission to Use Photograph— Permission given by a photographer for another to use his work.

Permission to Use Quotation or Personal Statement— Permission given by one party to another for the use and publication of spoken words and other material.

Personal Property Rental Agreement— An agreement between an owner and a renter for the use of personal property, for example, a boat.

Pools Syndicate Agreement— An agreement for a group playing the football pools.

Premarital Agreement— An agreement between a couple intending to marry as to the ownership of property during the marriage and in the event of divorce.

Product Defect Notice— A letter from a customer advising manufacturer, distributor or seller of a defective product.

Promissory Note— A promise by a borrower to repay a loan on demand.

Promissory Note with Guarantee— An agreement by which a borrower agrees to repay money borrowed and a guarantor guarantees the repayment.

Property Inventory— List of property owned.

Purchase Order— A company's record of an order for goods bought in.

Q

Quotation— A suppliers written statement of prices for specific goods.

R

Receipt— General receipt for payment or part payment.

Receipt for Company Property— Itemises company property issued to an employee.

Receipt in Full— Basic receipt recording full payment.

Receipt on Account— Basic receipt for money paid on account.

Receipt to Accompany Share Certificate— A document to record the receipt by a company of property in return for the issue of shares.

Redundancy with Ex Gratia Payment— A letter from an employer notifying an employee of his redundancy and redundancy pay.

Reference Letter on Employee— A letter in response to a request for a reference for an ex-employee.

Rejected Goods Notice— A letter from a buyer giving notice and reasons for the rejection of goods.

Reminder of Unpaid Account— A letter from a seller to a buyer requesting payment of an outstanding invoice.

Remittance Advice— A letter from a buyer to a seller requesting that payment be set against certain invoices.

Rent Review Memorandum— A record of an agreement between a landlord and a tenant on a new rent payable subsequent to a rent review.

Rent Statement— A record of rent payment receipts kept by a tenant or sharer.

Rental Agreement for a Furnished House or Flat on an Assured Shorthold Tenancy— A tenancy agreement for a letting of at least six months ensuring the landlord can regain possession (see Notice of an Assured Shorthold Tenancy).

Rental Agreement for an Unfurnished House or Flat on an Assured Shorthold Tenancy— As above, but for an unfurnished house or flat.

Reply to Credit Claim— A letter from a seller to a buyer refusing request for a credit and giving reasons for refusal.

Request for Advance Payment— A letter from a seller to buyer requesting money on account.

Request for Bank Credit Reference— A letter requesting a reference from a bank.

Request for Credit Reference— A letter requesting a credit reference from another supplier.

Request for Guarantee— A letter from a seller to a buyer requesting a personal guarantee from the directors of the buyer's company.

Request for Information on Disputed Charge— A letter from a seller to a buyer requesting justification for a disputed account.

Request for Quotation— A letter from a potential customer to a supplier seeking a price quotation.

Request for Replacement Share Certificate— A notice to a company secretary of the loss of a share certificate and the request for a replacement.

Resignation— A general form of resignation from an office or job.

Resignation of Director Relinquishing All Claims— A letter from a director to his board announcing his resignation without claim.

Resolution to Pay Interim Dividend— A director's written resolution that a company pays an interim dividend.

Response to Employee's Complaint— A letter from an employer requesting that an employee follows a formal complaints procedure.

Revocation of Power of Attorney— A document by which a donor revokes a power of attorney previously granted by him.

S

Sale Agreement Subject to Debt— An agreement by which a buyer agrees to buy property on which a debt is payable and agrees to pay the debt.

Sales Representative Agreement— An agreement between a company and its sales representative setting out the terms of engagement.

Samples and Documents Receipt— An employee's receipt for samples and company documents.

Second Notice of Overdue Account— A letter from a seller to a buyer making a second request for payment of an overdue account.

Second Warning for Lateness— An employer's second written warning to an employee for being late for work.

Security Agreement— An agreement between a creditor and a debtor by which the debtor offers property as a security for the debt.

Settlement Statement— A statutory statement sent by a supplier to a customer who wishes to repay early a consumer credit agreement.

Share Certificate— A document to record the ownership of shares in a company.

Share Subscription/Application— An application by a prospective shareholder for shares in a company.

Special Notice for the Removal of a Director— A proposal for a company's annual general meeting for the removal of a director from the board.

Special Notice for the Removal of Auditors— A proposal for a company's annual general meeting for the removal and replacement of auditors.

Standard Board Minutes— A standard format for recording the minutes of a company's board meeting.

Summary of Employment Terms— A potted terms and conditions of employment.

Supplier Questionnaire— A questionnaire to a supplier issued by a company meeting the requirements of BS5750/ISO9000.

T

Tenant's Bank Standing Order Mandate— A form for setting up a tenant's standing order payable to his landlord.

U

Unsolicited Idea Acknowledgement— A letter from a company acknowledging receipt of an unsolicited idea on certain terms.

V

Variation of Contract— An agreement by which two parties agree to vary the terms of an existing contract.

Variation of Employment Agreement — An agreement by which an employer and employee agree to vary the term of an existing contract.

W

Waiver of Liability and Assumption of Risk— A document by which a customer agrees not to hold a supplier liable for any loss, damage or injury suffered by the customer.

Warranty Increasing Statutory Rights— A supplier's promise to replace faulty goods in addition to the customer's basic statutory rights.

Withheld Delivery Notice— A letter from a seller to a buyer giving reasons for the non-delivery of goods.